CONTE

D0779101

Introduction

The Rough Guide Hindi & Urdu phrasebook is a highly practical introduction to the major languages of India. Laid out in clear A-Z style, it uses key-word referencing to lead you straight to the words and phrases you want – so if you need to book a room, just look up 'room'. The Rough Guide gets straight to the point in every situation, in bars and shops, on trains and buses, and in hotels and banks.

The main part of the Rough Guide is a double dictionary: English-Hindi/Urdu then Hindi/Urdu-English. Before that, there's a section called The Basics, which sets out the fundamental rules of the language and its pronunciation, with plenty of practical examples. You'll also find here other essentials like numbers, dates, telling the time and basic phrases.

Forming the heart of the guide, the English-Hindi/Urdu section gives easy-to-use transliterations of the Hindi/Urdu words, and to get you involved quickly in two-way communication, the Rough Guide includes dialogues featuring typical responses on key topics – such as asking directions. Feature boxes fill you in on cultural pitfalls as well as the simple mechanics of how to make a phone call, what to do in an emergency, where to change money and more. Throughout this section, cross-references enable you to pinpoint key facts and phrases, while asterisked words indicate where further information can be found in The Basics.

The Hindi/Urdu-English section is in two parts: a dictionary, arranged phonetically, of all the words and phrases you're likely to hear (starting with a selection of slang and colloquialisms); then two compilations (Hindi then Urdu), arranged by subject, of all the signs, labels, instructions and other basic words you might come across in print or in public places.

Finally the Rough Guide rounds off with an extensive Menu Reader. Consisting of food and drink sections (each starting with a list of essential terms), it's indispensable whether you're eating out, stopping for a quick drink or browsing through a local food market.

yātrā sukhad rahe! (H)
have a good trip!

KhAriyat se jāye!
have a good trip!

Basics

Pronunciation

Throughout this book, Hindi and Urdu words have been transliterated into romanized form so that they can be read as though they were English, bearing in mind the notes on pronunciation given below. A number of Hindi/Urdu sounds have no exact equivalent in English: ask someone to say them for you.

Vowels

a	as in about, like unstressed English **a**
ā	**a** as in f**a**r
A	**a** as in m**a**t
ai	as in Th**ai**
aw	as in **aw**e
e	long **e** sound somewhere between the bold characters in **ai**r or m**ay**, similar to the **a** in c**a**ble
i	as in b**i**t
ī	**ee** as in n**ee**d
ō	like the **oa** in m**oa**n
u	as in p**u**t
ū	**oo** as in f**oo**l

Nasal Vowels

Hindi and Urdu vowels are sometimes nasalized, that is they are pronounced as if followed by a slight **ng** sound, similar to the nasal sound as at the end of the French pronunciation of restaurant. In this book nasal vowels are shown in bold type.

Consonants

Unless listed below, consonants are pronounced more or less as in English:

d	similar to the **th** in **th**e (**d** pronounced with the tongue against the teeth
D	similar to **d** as in **d**one (**d** pronounced with the

	tongue back against the roof of the mouth)
h	**h** as in English or can be part of ch or sh as in English; elsewhere it indicates a breathy sound
k	short **k** sound as in s**k**in
kh	**k** as above but with a breathy sound
K	similar to **ch** as in the Scottish word lo**ch** (like k but pronounced further back in the throat)
Kh	**K** as above but with a breathy sound
r	similar to English **r** but rolled slightly
R	**r** pronounced with the tongue back against the roof of the mouth with a flap of the tongue
Rh	**R** as above but with a breathy sound
t	**t** pronounced with the tongue against the teeth
T	**t** pronounced with the tongue back against the roof of the mouth

In the English-Hindi/Urdu section, English words used in Hindi/Urdu, but pronounced as in English are shown in quotes, for example 'TV' and 'inch'.

Abbreviations

adj	adjective	masc	masculine
fam	familiar	pl	plural
fem	feminine	pol	polite
lit	literally	sing	singular

Notes

India has fifteen main languages and around seven hundred minor languages and dialects. Hindi is widely spoken and understood everywhere, except in the far south. Urdu (the official language of Pakistan) is also widely spoken in India. Spoken Hindi and Urdu are generally very similar – the main difference between them is that Hindi is written in

Devanagri script and Urdu is written in the Perso-Arabic script (which is read from right to left). Most of the words and phrases in this book will be understood by both Hindi and Urdu speakers; however, (H) in the text means the word is Hindi only and (U) means the word is Urdu only.

An asterisk next to a word in the English-Hindi/Urdu section means that you should refer to the Basics section for further information.

In the Hindi/Urdu-English section of this book, alphabetical order is as follows:

a, ā, A, b, ch, d, D, e, f, g, h, i, ī, j, k, K, l, m, n, ō, p, r, R, s, t, T, u, ū, v, y, z

Word order

The word order of a basic sentence in Hindi and Urdu is:

subject – object – verb

Any negatives are positioned just before the verb at the end:

mA chiTThī likhūgā	**mA chiTThī nahī likhūgā**
I'll write a letter	I won't write a letter
lit: I letter will write	lit: I letter will not write

Articles

There are no definite or indefinite articles in Hindi or Urdu. Context determines whether, for example,

hāthī means 'an elephant' or 'the elephant'.

Nouns

Genders

Nouns in Hindi and Urdu have one of two genders, masculine or feminine.

There are two types of masculine noun:

type 1   nouns ending in -ā
type 2   nouns not ending in -ā

beTā	**bhāi**
son	brother

There are also two types of feminine noun:

type 1   nouns ending in -ī
type 2   nouns not ending in -ī

beTī	**bahan**
daughter	sister

Natural gender dictates the grammatical gender.

Plurals

The plural of type 1 masculine nouns is formed by changing the final -ā to -e:

beTā	**beTe**
son	sons

The plural of type 2 masculine nouns is the same as the singular:

bhāi	**bhāi**
brother	brothers

The plural of type 1 feminine nouns is formed by changing the final -ī to -iyā:

beTī	**beTiyā**
daughter	daughters

The plural of type 2 feminine nouns is formed by adding -e:

bahan	**bahane**
sister	sisters

Cases

There are two cases in Hindi and Urdu. These are the direct and the oblique. The oblique form is used when there is a word like **kā** (of) or **kō** (to) (see page 17) after the noun:

mere beTe kā	**merī beTī kō**
of my son	to my daughter

The endings for these forms are:

masculine type 1

	sing	pl			sing	pl
direct	**beTā**	**beTe**	oblique	**beTe**	**beTō**
	son	sons		son	sons

masculine type 2

	sing	pl		sing	pl
direct	**bhāi**	**bhāi**	oblique	**bhāi**	**bhāiyō**
	brother	brothers		brother	brothers

feminine type 1

	sing	pl		sing	pl
direct	**beTī**	**beTiyā**	oblique	**beTī**	**beTiyōō**
	daughter	daughters		daughter	daughters

feminine type 2

	sing	pl		sing	pl
direct	**bahan**	**bahane**	oblique	**bahan**	**bahanō**
	sister	sisters		sister	sisters

Adjectives

Adjectives can be divided into two categories: those that change forms with the nouns they qualify and those that do not change form at all. When adjectives do change form, the ending **-ā** becomes **-ī** or **-e** according to the number, gender and case of the noun.

acchā (good) is an adjective that changes:

	sing	pl
masc	**acchā kamrā**	**acchhe kamre**
	good room	good rooms
fem	**acchhī gāRī**	**acchhī gāRīā**
	good train	good trains

mashhūr (famous) is an adjective that does not change:

	sing	pl
masc	**mashhūr hōtal**	**mashhūr hōtal**
	famous hotel	famous hotels
fem	**mashhūr gāRī**	**mashhūr gāRīyā**
	famous train	famous trains

Note that, for adjectives which change, the feminine form stays the same in the singular and the plural.

Comparatives

In Hindi and Urdu there are no special separate forms like 'better' or 'best' in English:

ravi ashōk se chhōTā hA
Ravi is smaller than Ashok
lit: Ravi Ashok than small is

ashōk ravi se chhōTā hA
Ashok is smaller than Ravi

is se sastā dikhāiye
can you show me some cheaper ones?

You can use **zyādā** (more, much) or **kam** (less) where no direct comparison is made:

ye zyadā mahangā hA
this is more expensive

For the superlative **sabse** (above all) precedes the adjective:

ye sabse acchā hA
this is the best

Demonstratives

Demonstrative adjectives and pronouns are the same:

sing		pl	
this	**ye**	these	**ye**
that	**vō**	those	**ve**

ye kyā hA?	**ye kamrā**
what's this?	this room

When used with oblique case nouns, demonstratives take the oblique case form of third person pronouns:

sing		pl	
this	**is**	these	**in**
that	**us**	those	**un**

15

is kamre kā kirāyā kyā hA?
what is the rent for this room?

merā dōst us hōTal me hA
my friend is in that hotel

Possessives

There is no distinction between possessive pronouns and possessive adjectives, between, for example, 'my/mine', 'your/yours':

merā	my/mine	**uskā** (far)	his, her/hers
tumhārā	your/yours (fam)	**hāmārā**	our/ours
āpkā	your/yours (pol)	**inkā** (near)	their/theirs
iskā (near)	his, her/hers	**unkā** (far)	their/theirs

Possessives follow the same rules for agreement as adjectives ending in **-ā**:

ye āpkā kamrā hA
this is your room

ye āpkī chābī hA
this is your key

āpke kamre me
in your room

Reflexive Form

The form **apnā** refers to the person who is the subject of the verb. It is used when the person referred to is the same as the subject of the main verb:

apnā pāspōrT dikhāiye
show me your passport please

Although **āp** (you) is not given in this sentence, it is implied. It differs from:

āpkā pāspōrT kahā hA?
where is your passport?

Postpositions

English prepositions (in, on, with etc) are placed before nouns and pronouns. In Hindi and Urdu they are placed after nouns and pronouns and are called 'postpositions'. They may be simple, one-word postpositions or compound postpositions, made up of more than one word. Examples are:

simple		compound	
kō	to	**ke pās**	at
kā	of	**ke sāth**	with
me	in	**ke liye**	for
par	at	**ke bāhar**	outside
se	from, by	**ke andar**	inside
ne	'agent marker'		
tak	until, up to		

Nouns and pronouns take the oblique case when they are followed by a postposition:

uske kamre me
in his/her room

saRak par
on the road

gāRī se
by train

dōst ke sāth
with a friend

jApur ke liye
for Jaipur

The word **kō** is used to mark times of the day and days of the week, where English uses 'on' or 'at':

āp shām kō kyā kar rahe hA?
what are you doing in the evening?

āp itvār kō kitne baje jāyegi?
at what time will you be leaving on Sunday?

Pronouns

I	**mA**	we	**ham**
you (fam)	**tum**	they (near)	**ye**
you (pol)	**āp**	(far)	**ve, vō**
he/she/it (near)	**ye**		
(far)	**vō**		

mA bhūl jātā hū
I forget

kyā vō ārahā hA?
is he coming?

There is no distinction of gender in Hindi or Urdu pronouns. So, for example, **vō** can mean either 'he' or 'she'. It is the verb that indicates masculinity or femininity:

vō kahā rahtā hA?
where does he live?

vō kahā rahtī hA?
where does she live?

The third person pronouns (he/she/it and they) have two forms. Which is used depends on the distance of the person referred to from the person speaking. The **ye** form is used when the person or object being referred to is physically near to the speaker. The **vō/ve** form is used if the person or object is not physically near or present. If you use the wrong form, if, say, you use the 'far' form to refer to someone who is standing close by, it is considered rude. In the English-Hindi/Urdu section we have generally given the 'nearby' form (unless the phrase obviously relates to someone further away or not present).

These forms are also used as emphatic pronouns in the following type of expression:

kawn? – ye
who? – them

mA?
me?

Pronouns, like nouns, have different forms for the oblique case:

18

me		mujhkō, mujhe
you (fam)		tumkō, tumhe
you (pol)		āpkō
him/her/it	(near)	iskō, ise
	(far)	uskō, use
us		hamkō, hame
them	(near)	inkō, inhe
	(far)	unkō, unhe

In each of the above, the second form is a shortened form of the first and is more usual in conversation.

mA uskō/use jāntā hū
I know him

āp mujhkō/mujhe sun sakte hA?
can you hear me?

mA use le āūgā
I'll fetch him

The following forms are used in combination with many postpositions:

me		mujh	us		ham
you (fam)		tum	them	(near)	in
you (pol)		āp		(far)	un
him/her/it	(near)	is			
	(far)	us			

ye uske liye hA
this is for him

mujh se
from me

unke sāth
with them

Although sometimes Hindi uses a form of the possessive pronoun where English uses a pronoun:

ye mere liye hA
that's for me

The second person pronoun also has a **tū** form. Use of this **tū** form shows either intimacy or disrespect and is best avoided by non-native speakers.

The **tum** form is used in familiar relationships among people who are equal in age and status. To avoid embarrassment it is safer to use the **āp** form in all situations, unless you are sure of the reciprocity of the relationship. This book uses the **āp** form in all the dialogues.

Polite forms

To show respect when using the third person, plural forms are used:

ye Indirā h**A**	inkā nām Indirā h**A**
this is Indira	her name is Indira
(plural form h**A**)	

In the last example respect is shown by the use of **inkā** (a plural form) as against **iskā** (the singular form).

Verbs

The infinitive form of a Hindi or Urdu verb is, for example:

uThnā   to get up
hōnā   to be

The suffix **nā** corresponds to the English 'to'. The stem of a verb is derived by dropping the **nā** suffix:

infinitive	stem
uThnā	uTh
hōnā	hō

Simple Present

For the simple present tense, which is used to denote habitual actions, the verb consists of three parts:

(uThnā to get up)

verb stem +	imperfect suffix +	tense marker
uTh	-tā, -tī, -te	hū, hA, hA

The second part of the verb agrees in number and gender with the subject of the verb. The third part of the verb agrees in person and number with the subject of the verb.

first person

	I	we
masc	m**A** u**T**htā h**ū**	ham u**T**hte h**A**
fem	m**A** u**T**htī h**ū**	ham u**T**htī h**A**

second person   sing & pl

	you	
masc	āp u**T**hte h**A**	
fem	āp u**T**htī h**A**	

third person

	he	they
masc	ye/vō u**T**htā h**A**	ye/ve u**T**hte h**A**
	she	they
fem	ye/vō u**T**htī h**A**	ye/ve u**T**htī h**A**

vō sāt baje uT**htā h**A****   **vō sāt baje u**T**htī h**A****
he gets up at 7 o'clock   she gets up at 7 o'clock

ve sāt baje uT**hte h**A****   **ve sāt baje u**T**htī h**A****
they get up at 7 o'clock (**masc**)   they get up at 7 o'clock (**fem**)

Present Continuous

The verb in the present continuous tense consists of three parts:

verb stem +
perfect of auxiliary **rahnā** +
simple present of **hōnā** (**hū, hA, hA**).

The second part, the perfect of the auxiliary verb **rahnā**, is inflected for number and gender. It gives the sense of the English '-ing'.

The third part, the simple present of the verb **hōnā** (to be), is inflected for number and person.

(**uThnā** to get up)

first person

	I	we
masc	**mA uTh rahā hū**	**ham uTh rahe hA**
fem	**mA uTh rahī hū**	**ham uTh rahī hA**

second person sing & pl

	you
masc	**āp uTh rahe hA**
fem	**āp uTh rahī hA**

third person

	he	they
masc	**ye/vō uTh rahā hA**	**ye/ve uTh rahe hA**
	she	they
fem	**ye/vō uTh rahī hA**	**ye/ve uTh rahī hA**

vō ab uTh rahā hA	**vō ab uTh rahī hA**
he is getting up now	she is getting up now

Past Imperfect

The past imperfect tense, which denotes the sense of 'used to', is formed in the same way as the present simple except for the third part, where the past tense of **hōnā** is used:

verb stem +	imperfect suffix +	tense marker
uTh	-tā, -tī, -te	thā, thī, the, thī

The third part is inflected for gender and number:

vō sāt baje uThtā thā
he used to get up at 7 o'clock

vō sāt baje uThtī thī
she used to get up at 7 o'clock

ve sāt baje uThte the
they used to get up at 7 o'clock (masc)

ve sāt baje uThtī thī
they used to get up at 7 o'clock (fem)

Past Perfect (Intransitive)

The past perfect of intransitive verbs is formed with two parts:

verb stem +	suffixes
uTh	-ā, -ī, -e

The suffixes agree in gender and number with the subject of the verb:

vō sāt baje uThā
he got up at 7 o'clock

vō sāt baje uThī
she got up at 7 o'clock

ve sāt baje uThe
they got up at 7 o'clock (masc)

ve sāt baje uThī
they got up at 7 o'clock (fem)

This tense is used for completed actions in the past.

Past Perfect (Transitive)

Transitive verbs in the past perfect take the postposition **ne** after the subject. In this tense the verb agrees not with the subject but with the object. So for example, with the subject **usne** (he/she) and the verb **khānā** (stem **khā**):

usne āTh baje nāshtā khāyā
he/she ate breakfast at 8 o'clock

Note that when the stem ends in **-ā**, a **y** is inserted before any endings.

Present Perfect

The present perfect is similar in structure to the past perfect except that a third part is added. This is the present tense of **hōnā**:

The verb agrees with its subject in number and gender:

mA abhī uThā hū̃
I have just got up

vō abhī uThā hA
he has just got up

vō abhī uThī hA
she has just got up

ve abhī uThe hA
they have just got up (masc)

ve abhī uThī hA
they have just got up (fem)

As with the past perfect, the verb does not agree with its subject in transitive uses:

usne nāshtā khāyā hA
he/she has eaten breakfast

Past Continuous

The first two parts are the same as in the present continuous. A third part is added which is the past tense of **hōnā**, ie **thā, thī, the**:

vō uTh rahā thā
he was getting up

vō uTh rahī thī
she was getting up

ham uTh rahe the
we were getting up

Future

The future tense consists of three parts:

verb stem +   suffix **-ū, -e, e** or **-ō** +   **-gā, -ge, -gī**

The second part agrees with the subject in number and person.

The third part agrees with the subject in gender and number:

(**uThnā** to get up)
first person

	I	we
masc	**mA uThūgā**	**ham uThege**
fem	**mA uThūgī**	**ham uThegī**

second person	sing & pl polite	
	you	
masc	**āp uThege**	
fem	**āp uThegī**	

second person	sing & pl familiar	
	you	
masc	**tum uThōge**	
fem	**tum uThōgī**	

third person		
	he	they
masc	**ye/vō uThegā**	**ye/ve uThege**
	she	they
fem	**ye/vō uThegī**	**ye/ve uThegī**

mA uThūgā	**ham uThege**
I'll get up	we'll get up

Subjunctive

The subjunctive is commonly used in Hindi and Urdu to express a wish, request, uncertainty or a possibility. By dropping the ending **-gā**, **-ge** or **-gī** from the future tense you are left with the subjunctive form:

mA uThū?
should I get up?

Infinitive

The infinitive can be used to express commands, intentions or obligation:

(**lenā** to take)
davā dō bār lenā
take the medicine twice a day

(**jānā** to go)
mujhe manālī jānā hA
I want to go to Manali

(**milnā** to see)
mujhe das baje dākTar se milnā hA
I have to see the doctor at 10 o'clock

25

The infinitive followed by the verb **chāhiye** gives the sense of 'ought' or 'should':

> **mujhe ab ghar jānā chāhiye**
> I should go home now

■ Imperatives

Polite requests and commands, when English uses 'please', can be expressed in Hindi and Urdu by adding **-iye** to the verb stem:

> (**ānā** to come)
> **andar āiye**
> please come in

The familiar imperative is formed by adding **-ō** to the verb stem:

> (**ruknā** to stop)   (**jānā** to go)
> **yahā rukō!**   **jāō!**
> stop here!   go away!

Negatives

To make a verb negative the word **nahī** is placed before the verb. In negative sentences in the simple present and the present continuous the third part of the auxiliary **hōnā** is often omitted:

> **mA yahā nahī rahtā (hū)**   **mujhe ye mālūm nahī (hA)**
> I don't live here   I didn't know that

> **vō abhī tak nahī uThī**
> she hasn't got up yet

In imperatives **nahī** is replaced by **na**:

> **itnī jaldī na bōliye**
> please don't speak so fast

A stronger negative imperative can be expressed by **mat**:

merā intzār mat karō
don't wait for me

'To Be'

The verb **hōnā** (to be) is used in Hindi and in Urdu both as a main verb and as an auxiliary. It differs from other verbs in its pattern:

present

I am		**mA hū**
you are	(fam)	**tum hō**
	(pol)	**āp hA**
he/she/it is		**ye/vō hA**
we are		**ham hA**
they are		**ye/ve hA**

past

I was	(masc)	**mA thā**
	(fem)	**mA thī**
you were	(fam, masc)	**tum the**
	(fam, fem)	**tum thī**
	(pol, masc)	**āp the**
	(pol, fem)	**āp thī**
he/she/it was	(masc)	**ye/vō thā**
	(fem)	**ye/vō thī**
we were	(masc)	**ham the**
	(fem)	**ham thī**
they were	(masc)	**ye/ve the**
	(fem)	**ye/ve thī**

future

I will be	(masc)	mA hūgā
	(fem)	mA hūgī
you will be	(fam, masc)	tum hõge
	(fam, fem)	tum hõgī
	(pol, masc)	āp hõge
	(pol, fem)	āp hõgī
he will be		ye/võ hõgā
she will be		ye/võ hõgī
we will be	(masc)	ham hõge
	(fem)	ham hõgī
they will be	(masc)	ye/ve hõge
	(fem)	ye/ve hõgī

'To Have'

Hindi and Urdu have no exact equivalent to the English verb 'to have':

mere dō bhāi hA
I have two brothers
lit: my two brothers are

This structure is used when the objects of 'to have' are persons or non-movable possessions (like houses, parts of the body).

With movable objects, if ownership is not implied, **ke pās** is used:

āpke pās pAnsil hA?
have you got a pencil?
lit: your near pencil is?

mere pās pAnsil nahī
I haven't got a pencil
lit: my near pencil is not

Possession of something abstract is expressed as follows:

mere sir me dard hA
I have a headache
lit: my head in ache is

mujhe zukām hA
I have a cold
lit: to me cold is

'To Be Able To'

The equivalents of the English verb 'to be able to, can' are formed by placing **saknā** after the verb stem; **saknā** itself conjugates:

võ hindī samajh saktā/saktī hA
he/she can understand Hindi
lit: he/she Hindi understand can is

mA hindī nahī bōl sakta/saktī
I can't speak Hindi
lit: I Hindi not speak can

saknā is a 'helping word' and cannot be used on its own.

Interrogatives

kyā?	what?	**kyõ?**	why?
kahā?	where?	**kab?**	when?
kAsā?	how?	**kitnā?**	how much?

When a question is being asked for information, the question word is usually placed before the verb:

āp kahā rahte hA?
where do you live?
lit: you where live are

āp kyā kām karte hA?
what do you do?
lit: you what work do are

If **kyā** is placed at the beginning of the sentence, it becomes a yes/no question:

kyā āp kām karte hA?
do you work?

The word **kyā** is used when a question contains no other interrogative word. But it can be omitted if the question can be expressed by tone of voice:

(kyā) āp nayī dillī me rahte hA?
do you live in New Delhi?

Dates

For the first and second days of the month either cardinal or ordinal numbers can be used:

pahlī mārch or **ek mārch**
1st March

From the third onwards, cardinals (3, 4, 5) generally are used rather than ordinals (third, fourth, fifth). See Numbers pages 32–33.

Days

Monday sōmvār (H), pīr (U)
Tuesday mangalvār
Wednesday budhvār
Thursday brihaspat vār (H), jumme rāt (U)
Friday shukrvār (H), zummā (U)
Saturday shanīchar, hafta (U)
Sunday itvār

Months

January janvarī
February farvarī
March mārch
April aprAl
May mayī
June jūn

July julāi
August agast
September sitambar
October akTūbar
November navambar
December disambar

Time

what time is it? kitne baje hA?
1 o'clock ek bajā
2 o'clock dō baje

3 o'clock tīn baje
4 o'clock chār baje
5 o'clock pāch baje
6 o'clock chhA baje

7 o'clock sāt baje
8 o'clock āTh baje
9 o'clock naw baje
10 o'clock das baje
11 o'clock giārā baje
12 o'clock bārā baje
it's one o'clock ek bajā hA
it's two/three/four o'clock
 dō/tīn/chār baje hA
it's five o'clock pāch baje hA
five past one ek bajkar pāch
 minaT
ten past two dō bajkar das
 minaT
quarter past one savā baje
quarter past two savā dō
 baje
half past one deRh baje

half past ten sāRhe das baje
twenty to ten das bajne me
 bīs minaT
quarter to two pawne dō
 baje
quarter to ten pawne das
 baje
at one o'clock ek baje
at two/three/four o'clock
 dō/tīn/chār baje
at five o'clock pāch baje
at half past four sāRhe chār
 baje
14.00 din ke dō baje
17.30 shām ke sāRhe pāch
 baje
noon dōpahar
midnight ādhī rāt

Note that **subah** (morning) refers roughly to the period
from daybreak to about 10am, while **din** (day) is used for the
period between about 10am and about 4pm; **dōpahar** is also
used for the time between noon and 2pm. **Sham** (evening)
extends from approximately 4pm to 8pm and **rāt** (night)
from 8pm to daybreak.

5am subah ke pāch baje
5pm shām ke pāch baje
2am rāt ke dō baje
2pm din ke dō baje, dōpahar ke dō baje
hour ghanTā
minute minaT
second sekanD
quarter of an hour chawthāi ghanTā
half an hour ādhā ghanTā
three quarters of an hour tīn chawthāi ghanTā

Numbers

0	sifar, shūny (H)	33	tetīs
1	ek	34	chawtīs
2	dō	35	pAtīs
3	tīn	36	chhattīs
4	chār	37	sAtīs
5	pāch	38	aRtīs
6	chhA	39	untālīs
7	sāt	40	chālīs
8	āTh	41	iktālīs
9	naw	42	bayālīs
10	das	43	tAtālīs
11	giārā	44	chavālīs
12	bārā	45	pAtālīs
13	terā	46	chhiālīs
14	chawdā	47	sAtālīs
15	pandrā	48	aRtālīs
16	sōlā	49	unanchās
17	satrā	50	pachās
18	aTThārā	51	ikyāvan
19	unnīs	52	bāvan
20	bīs	53	trepan
21	ikkis	54	chavvan
22	bā-īs	55	pachpan
23	teis	56	chhappan
24	chawbīs	57	sattāvan
25	pachchīs	58	aTThāvan
26	chhabbīs	59	unsaTh
27	sattā-īs	60	sāTh
28	aTThā-īs	61	iksaTh
29	unattīs	62	bāsaTh
30	tīs	63	tresaTh
31	ikattīs	64	chawsaTh
32	battīs	65	pasaTh

66	chhiāsaTh	200	dō saw
67	saRsaTh	300	tīn saw (etc)
68	aRsaTh	1000	ek hazār
69	unhattar	2000	dō hazār (etc)
70	sattar	100,000	ek lākh
71	ikhattar	200,000	dō lākh (etc)
72	bahattar	1,000,000	das lākh
73	tihattar		
74	chawhattar		
75	pichhattar		

Ordinals

first	pahlā
second	dūsrā
third	tīsrā
fourth	chawthā
fifth	pāchvā
sixth	chhaTā
seventh	sātvā
eighth	āthvā
ninth	nawvā
tenth	dasvā

76	chhihattar
77	sathattar
78	aThattar
79	unāsī
80	assī
81	ikyāsī
82	bayāsī
83	tirāsī
84	chawrāsī
85	pachāsī
86	chhiāsī
87	satāsī
88	aTThāsī
89	navāsī
90	navve
91	ikyānave
92	bānve
93	tirānve
94	chawrānve
95	pachānve
96	chhiānve
97	sattānve
98	aTThānve
99	ninyānave
100	saw

Basic Phrases

yes
hā

no
nahī

OK
Thīk

hello
namaste (H), salām (U)
(on phone)
halō

good morning
namaste (H), assalam
  ālekam (U)

good evening
namaste (H), assalam
  ālekam (U)

good night
namaste (H), Khudā hāfiz (U)

goodbye
namaste (H), Khudā hāfiz (U)

hi!
halō

cheerio!
phir milege!

see you!
phir milege!

please
meharbānī karke, kripayā (H)

yes, please
jī hā

thank you
shukriyā, dhanyvād (H)

thanks
shukriyā

no, thanks
jī nahī

thank you very much
bahut shukriyā

don't mention it
kōī bāt nahī

how do you do?
kyā hāl hA?

how are you? (to man/woman)
āp kAse/kAsī hA?

I'm fine thanks
Thīk hū, shukriyā

nice to meet you
āp se milkar baRī Khushī
  huī

excuse me (to get past, to say
  sorry)
māf kījiye
(to get attention)
suniye

sorry: (I'm) sorry
māf kījiye

sorry? (didn't understand)
kyā kahā?

what?
kyā?

what did you say?
āpne kyā kahā?

I see (I understand)
mA samjhā

I don't understand
mA nahī samjhā

do you speak English? (to
  man/woman)
āp angrezī bōlte/boltī hA?

I don't speak ... (said by
  man/woman)
mA ... nahī bōltā/boltī

**could you speak more
  slowly?**
dhīre dhīre boliye

could you repeat that?
phir kahiye

could you write it down?
ise likh de

I'd like a ...
mujhe ... chāhiye

I'd like to ... (said by
  man/woman)
mA ... chāhtā/chāhtī hū

can I have a ...? (said by
  man/woman)
kyā mA ... le saktā/saktī hū?

do you have ...?
āpke pās ... hA?

how much is it?
is kī kīmat kyā hA?

cheers! (toast)
chīyars!

it is ...
ye ... hA

where is it?
ye kahā hA?

where is ...?
... kahā hA?

is it far from here?
kyā yahā se dūr hA?

what's the time?
kyā vakt hA?, kitne baje hA?

Conversion tables

1 centimetre = 0.39 inches   1 inch = 2.54 cm

1 metre = 39.37 inches = 1.09 yards   1 foot = 30.48 cm

1 kilometre = 0.62 miles = 5/8 mile   1 yard = 0.91 m

1 mile = 1.61 km

km	1	2	3	4	5	10	20	30	40	50	100
miles	0.6	1.2	1.9	2.5	3.1	6.2	12.4	18.6	24.8	31.0	62.1

miles	1	2	3	4	5	10	20	30	40	50	100
km	1.6	3.2	4.8	6.4	8.0	16.1	32.2	48.3	64.4	80.5	161

1 gram = 0.035 ounces   1 kilo = 1000 g = 2.2 pounds

1 oz = 28.35 g

g	100	250	500
oz	3.5	8.75	17.5

1 lb = 0.45 kg

kg	0.5	1	2	3	4	5	6	7	8	9	10
lb	1.1	2.2	4.4	6.6	8.8	11.0	13.2	15.4	17.6	19.8	22.0

kg	20	30	40	50	60	70	80	90	100
lb	44	66	88	110	132	154	176	198	220

lb	0.5	1	2	3	4	5	6	7	8	9	10	20
kg	0.2	0.5	0.9	1.4	1.8	2.3	2.7	3.2	3.6	4.1	4.5	9.0

1 litre = 1.75 UK pints / 2.13 US pints

1 UK pint = 0.57 l   1 UK gallon = 4.55 l

1 US pint = 0.47 l   1 US gallon = 3.79 l

centigrade / Celsius   °C = (°F - 32) x 5/9

°C	-5	0	5	10	15	18	20	25	30	36.8	38
°F	23	32	41	50	59	64	68	77	86	98.4	100.4

Fahrenheit   °F = (°C x 9/5) + 32

°F	23	32	40	50	60	65	70	80	85	98.4	101
°C	-5	0	4	10	16	18	21	27	29	36.8	38.3

English

→

Hindi/Urdu

a, an* ek
about: about 20 Karīb bīs, lagbhag bīs (H)
 it's about 5 o'clock pāch baje ke Karīb
 a film about India bharat ke bāre me 'film'
above ūpar
abroad pardesh
absolutely (I agree) bilkul
absorbent cotton ruī
accelerator AkselareTar
accept Kabūl karnā
accident durghaTnā (H), hādasā (U)
 (collision) Takkar
 there's been an accident ek durghaTnā hōgAi
accommodation Thaharne kī jagah
 see room and hotel
accurate sahī
ache dard
 my back aches merī pīTh me dard hA
across: across the road saRak ke pār
adapter aDApTar
address patā
 what's your address? āpkā patā kyā hA?

You'll invariably need to ask directions when looking for a particular address in India, as urban development is fairly haphazard. The place you're looking for might be located at the back of the building identified by the address, or be in a smaller road adjacent to the one in the address. Roads are often known by their old and new names – for example, the old colonial name of Dalhousie Square in Calcutta is still commonly used along with the new official name of BBD Bagh. Similarly the word 'road' is still used but **mārg** and other variations such as **rāstā** (path) are increasingly common. Initials and acronyms are often used: thus Mahatma Gandhi Road may also be referred to as MG Marg.
Addresses are written as follows (M.P. refers to the state):
 Shri Rajkumar Sharma
 B 5/7, Subhash Nagar
 Govindpura
 Bhopal (M.P.) 47 65 75

address book pate kī kitāb
admission charge dāKhilā, pravesh shulk (H)
adult bālig, vayask (H)
advance: in advance peshgī, agrim (H)
aeroplane havāi jahāz
Afghanistan afgānistān
Africa afrīkā
African afrīkī
after (ke) bād
 after you pahle āp
 after lunch dōpahar ke khāne ke bād

afternoon dōpahar
 in the afternoon dōpahar me
 this afternoon āj dōpahar
aftershave āftarshev
aftersun cream dhūp sekne
 ke bād lagāne vālī krīm
afterwards bād me
again phir
against ke Khilāf,
 viruddh (H)
age umar, āyu (H)
ago: a week ago ek hafte
 pahle
 an hour ago ek ghanTe
 pahle
agree: I agree (said by man/
 woman) mA māntā/māntī hū
AIDS eDS bīmārī
air havā
 by air havāi jahāz se
air-conditioned eyar
 kanDīshan, vātānukūlit (H)
air-conditioned room eyar
 kanDīshan kamrā
air-conditioning eyar
 kanDīshan karnā

Air-conditioning is not
necessarily the
advantage you might
expect – in some hotels you can find
yourself paying double for a system
that is so dust-choked, wheezy and
noisy as to preclude any possibility
of sleep – but providing it is what
seems to entitle a hotel to consider
itself mid-range. Some also offer a
halfway-house option known as 'air-
cooled'.

airmail: by airmail havāi Dāk
 se
airmail envelope havāi lifāfā,
 havāi patr (H)
airplane havāi jahāz
airport havāi aDDā
 to the airport, please havāi
 aDDe chaliye
airport bus havāi aDDe kī bas
aisle seat galiyāre kī sīT
alarm clock alāram (ghanTī
 vālī) ghaRī
alcohol sharāb

Although alcohol is
officially banned in a
handful of Indian states
such as Gujarat and Tamil Nadu, it is
widely available elsewhere in India.
A large and increasing selection
includes beer, blended Scotch
bottled in India, local whiskies and
brandies, gin, vodka, rum and
liqueurs. Although bars in five-star
hotels are similar to those in the
West, with similar prices, other bars
tend to be male-dominated drinking
dens that women may find
oppressive. Instigated by Hindu
fundamentalist politics, Delhi has
numerous 'dry' days when alcohol is
not served in public places; dry days
are also common once a week,
usually Thursdays, in other parts of
the country.

alcoholic nashīlā, mādak (H)
all sab
 all of it sārā

all of them sāre

that's all, thanks bas, shukriyā

allergic: I'm allergic to ... mujhe ... se Alarjī hA

allowed: is it allowed? (kyā) is kī ijāzat hA?

all right Thīk

I'm all right mA Thīk hū

are you all right? āp Thīk hA?

almond bādām

almost lagbhag (H), TaKriban(U)

alone akelā

already pahle se hī

also bhī

although hālāki, yadyapi (H)

altogether kul milākar

always hameshā

am*: I am mA hū

am: at seven am subah sāt baje

amazing (surprising) āshcharyajanak (H), hAratangez (U)

(very good) tājjub kā

ambulance AmbulAns

call an ambulance! AmbulAns bulāō!

America amrīkā

American amrīkī

I'm American mA amrīkī hū

among me

amount tādād

(money) raKam, rāshī (H)

amp: a 13-amp fuse terah Ampiyar kā fyūz

and awr

angry nārāz

animal jānvar

ankle Takhnā

anniversary (wedding) shādī ki sālgirah

annoy: this man's annoying me ye ādmī mujhe pareshān kar rahā hA

annoying pareshānī bharā

another dūsrā

can we have an another room? kyā āp hame dūsrā kamrā dege?

another beer, please ek awr bīyar dījiye

antibiotics AnTibāyōTik davā

antifreeze jamne se rōkne vālī chīz

antihistamine AnTihisTāmin

antique: is it an antique? kyā ye purāne zamāne kī chīz hA?

antique shop purāne zamāne ke chīzō kī dukān

antiseptic AnTisApTic

any: have you got any bread/tomatoes? āpke pās Dabal rōTī/TamāTar hA?

do you have any ...? kyā āpke pās ... hA?

sorry, I don't have any jī nahī, nahī hA

anybody kōī

does anybody speak English? kōī angrezī bōltā hA?

there wasn't anybody there vahā kōī nahī thā

anything kuchh

dialogues

anything else? awr kuchh?
nothing else, thanks awr kuchh nahī, shukriyā

would you like anything to drink? (to man/woman) āp kuchh pīyege/pīyegī?
I don't want anything, thanks jī nahī, mujhe kuchh nahī chāhiye, shukriyā

apart from ke alāvā
apartment flAT
apartment block bilding
aperitif apariTīf
apology māfī, kshamā (H)
appendicitis apanDisāTis
appetizer pahlā dawr
apple seb
appointment mulākāt

dialogue

can I help you? bōliye
I'd like to make an appointment with ... mujhe ... se milnā hA
what time would you like? (to man/woman) āp kis vakt milnā chāhte/chāhtī hA?
three o'clock tīn baje
I'm afraid that's not possible, is four o'clock all right? māf kījiye, ye tō mumkin nahī hA, kyā

chār baje Thīk rahegā?
yes, that will be fine jī hā, Thīk hA
the name was ...? āpkā nām ...?

apricot khūbānī
April aprAl
are*: we are ham hA
  you are āp hA
  (fam) tum hō
  they are ve hA
area ilāKā
area code ilāKe kā kōD
arm bāh
arrange: will you arrange it for us? kyā āp hamāre liye is kā intzām kar dege?
arrival pahuch
arrive pahuchnā
  when do we arrive? ham kab pahuchege?
  has my fax arrived yet? kyā merā fAks āgayā?
  we arrived today ham āj pahuche
art kalā (H), fan (U)
art gallery chitr-shālā (H), tasvīr khānā (U)
artist kalākār (H), fankār (U)
as: as good as itnā hī acchhā
  as big as itnā hī baRā
  as soon as possible jitnī jaldī hōsake
ashtray rākhdānī
ask pūchhnā
  ask for māgnā
  I didn't ask for this mAne ye nahī māgā

could you ask him to ...? in se kahiye ki ...?

asleep: she's asleep vō sōī huī hA

aspirin Aspirin

asthma damā

astonishing tājjub kā

at*: at the hotel hōTal me

  at the station sTeshan par

  at six o'clock chhA baje

  at Sunil's sunil ke yahā

attractive khūbsūrat

aubergine bAgan

August agast

aunt (paternal) chāchī

  (maternal) māsī, khālā (U)

Australia āsTreliyā

Australian āsTreliyan

  I'm Australian mA āsTreliyan hū

automatic (adj) āTomATik

  (car) apne āp chalne vālī kār

automatic teller naKdī kī mashīn

autumn patjhaR (H), Khizā (U)

  in the autumn patjhaR me

avenue chawRī saRak

average (not good) māmūlī

  on average awsatan

awake: is he awake? kyā vō jāgā huā hA?

away: go away! jāō!

  is it far away? kyā vō bahut dūr hA?

awful bahut burā

axle dhurī

B

baby (male/female) bacchā/bacchī

baby food bacche kā khānā

baby's bottle bacche kī bōtal

baby-sitter bebī siTar

back (of body) pīTh

  (back part) pichhlā hissā

  at the back pīche

  can I have my money back? merā pAsā vāpas kar dījiye

  to come/go back anā/vāpas jānā

backache pīTh dard

bacon sūar kā mās

bad burā

  a bad headache tez sirdard

badly burī tarah (se)

bag ThAlā

  (handbag) hAnDbAg

  (suitcase) sūTkes, baksā

baggage sāmān, asbāb (U)

baggage checkroom chhuTe sāmān kā daftar

baggage claim sāmān kī māg (H), asbāb kī māg (U)

bakery Dabal rōTī kī dukān

balcony chhajjā

  a room with a balcony chhajje vālā kamrā

bald ganjā

ball ged

ballpoint pen bālpōint pAn

bamboo bās

banana kelā

band (musical) bAnD

bandage paTTī

Bandaid® palastar
Bangladesh banglādesh
Bangladeshi banglādeshī
bank (money) bAnk

Banking hours are roughly Mon–Fri 10am–2pm, plus Sat 10am–noon. Most branches of the State Bank of India, ANZ Grindlays, Bank of Baroda and Allahabad Bank offer exchange facilities, as do a few branches of the Central Bank of India. Several overseas banks, American Express, Thomas Cook and a handful of authorized foreign exchange dealers can be found in the cities. International airports have exchange facilities and so do the more upmarket tourist hotels. Traveller's cheques are the safest method of carrying money around although you should change money whenever you have the opportunity, as there are few exchange facilities away from the main tourist routes. ATM machines are becoming increasingly common in the cities but although they advertise the leading credit cards, few are able to handle foreign accounts.

bank account khāta
bar sharāb-Khānā, baar
  a bar of chocolate chākleT kī DanDī
barber's nāi kī dukān, hajjām (U)

bargaining
Good-natured bargaining or haggling is standard procedure in markets and with most street vendors. After being told the cost, initiate the negotiations with a gentle 'It's a bit expensive' and see how far the vendor is willing to drop the price. When looking for souvenirs, textiles, carpets or curios – especially in tourist centres such as Agra and Jaipur – you may be up against unscrupulous tradesmen. Shop around, bargain, and do not be pressed into a sale. Central Cottage Industries, a government-sponsored handicraft chain with shops in major Indian cities, have a fixed price policy and offer handicrafts of guaranteed quality at a reasonable price.

dialogue

how much is this? is kī kyā kīmat hA?
200 rupees dō saw rupaye
that's too expensive ye tō bahut mahangā hA
how about 100 rupees? ek saw rupaye me kAsā rahegā?
I'll let you have it for 150 rupees āp ke liye sirf DeDh saw rupaye
can you reduce it a bit more? jarā awr kam kare?
OK, it's a deal acchhā, ye pakkā rahā

basket chhawRī
  (in shop) Tōkrī
bath snān (H), gusal (U)
  can I have a bath? (said by
  man/woman) kyā mʌ nahā
  saktā/saktī hū̃?
  see **hotel**
bathroom gusalKhānā
  with a private bathroom nijī
  gusalKhānā
bath towel nahāne kā tawliyā
bathtub nahāne kā Tab
battery bATarī
bay khāRī
be* hōnā
beach samandar kā kinārā
  on the beach samandar ke
  kināre par
  see **dress**
beach mat bīch kī chaTāi
beach umbrella bīch kā chātā
beans sem (phalī)
  French beans chhōTī sem
  broad beans baRī sem
beard dāRhī
beautiful sundar
because kyō̃ki
  because of ... ... kī vajah se
bed bistar
  I'm going to bed now (said by
  man/woman) mʌ ab sōne jā
  rahā/rahī hū̃
bed and breakfast rāt kī
  rihāish awr nāshtā
  see **hotel**
bedroom sōne kā kamrā
beer bīyar
  two beers, please dō bīyar,
  dījiye

Beer is widely available, if
rather expensive by local
standards. **Kingfisher** is
the leading brand, but there are
plenty of others. All lagers, they tend
to contain chemical additives, but
are usually pretty palatable if you
can get them cold. In certain places,
notably unlicensed restaurants in
Tamil Nadu, beer comes in the form
of 'special tea' – a teapot of beer,
which you pour into and drink from
a teacup to disguise what it really is.
A cheaper, and often delicious,
alternative to beer in Kerala and one
or two other places is **toddy** (palm
wine). In Bengal a similar wine,
found in rural areas and made from
the date palm, is known as **tad**. In
the morning it's a mild and pleasant
juice; by the evening, strong
fermentation leaves it smelling like
essence of old socks.

before pahle
beggar bhikhārī
begin shuru hōnā
  (doing something) shuru karnā
  when does it begin? kab
  shuru hōtā hʌ?
beginner (man/woman) sīkhne
  vālā/vālī
beginning: at the beginning
  shuru me
behind pīchhe
  behind me mere pīchhe
Belgian beljiyan
Belgium beljiyam
believe yaKīn karnā, vishvās

karnā (H)
below nīche
belt peTī
bend (in road) mōR
Bengali bangālī
berth (on ship) barth
beside: beside the ... ... ke pās
best sab se acchhā
betel nut supārī
better behtar
 are you feeling better? (kyā)
āpkī tabiyat behtar hA?
between bīch me
beyond ke pare
bicycle sāikil

In many ways a bicycle is the ideal form of transport, offering total independence without loss of contact with local people. You can camp out, though there are cheap lodgings in almost every village – take the bike into your room with you – and, if you get tired of pedalling, you can put it on top of a bus as luggage or transport it by train (it goes in the luggage van: get a form and pay a small fee at the station luggage office).

Bringing a bike from abroad requires no special paperwork, but spare parts and accessories may be of different sizes and standards in India, and you may have to improvise. Bring basic spares and tools, and a pump.

Buying a bike in India presents no great difficulty; most towns have cycle shops and even cycle markets. The advantages of a local bike are that spare parts are easy to get, locally produced tools and parts will fit, and your bike will not draw a crowd every time you park it. Disadvantages are that Indian bikes are heavier and less state-of-the-art than ones from abroad (bikes with gears, let alone mountain bikes, are unheard of). Selling should be quite easy: you won't get a tremendously good deal at a cycle market, but you may well be able to sell privately, or even to a rental shop.

Bicycles can be rented in most towns. 10–20 rupees per day is the going rate, usually more in tourist centres, and you may have to leave a deposit or even your passport as security. Most bicycle-rental firms rent bikes for in-town use only; they won't take too kindly to you disappearing round the country on them. If you want to do that, buying would be a much better option.

bicycle pump sāikil pamp
big baRā
 too big bahut baRā
 it's not big enough ye kam
 baRā hA
bike sāikil
 (motorbike) mōTar sāikil
bikini bikinī
bill bil
 (US: from bank) nōT
 could I have the bill? bil
 lāiye?

see **tipping**
bin kūRedān
bird chiRiyā
birthday sāl girah, janmdin
(H)
  happy birthday! sālgirah
  mubāraK!, shubh
  janmdin! (H)
biscuit biskuT
bit: a little bit zarā ThōRā
  a big bit ThōRā baRā
  a bit of ... ThōRā sā ...
  a bit expensive zarā
  mahangā
bite (noun) KāT
  (verb) kāTnā

Mosquitoes and other
biting insects may be a
problem. The obvious
ones are bed bugs – look for signs
of squashed ones around cheap
hotel beds. An infested mattress can
be left in the hot sun all day to get
rid of them, but they often live in the
frame or even in walls or floors.
Head and body lice can also be a
nuisance but medicated soap and
shampoo (preferably brought from
home) usually see them off. Do not
scratch bites as this can lead to
infection. Bites from ticks and lice
can spread typhus, characterized by
fever, muscle aches, headaches and
eventually red eyes and a measles-
like rash. If you think you have it,
seek treatment.
Worms may enter your body through
your skin (especially the soles of

your feet) or food. They are easy to
treat; if you suspect you have them,
get some worming tablets from any
pharmacy.
Snakes are unlikely to bite unless
disturbed, and most are harmless in
any case. If you do get bitten,
remember what the snake looked
like (kill it if you can), try not to
move the affected part, and seek
medical help: anti-venoms are
available in most hospitals. A few
spiders have poisonous bites too.
Remove leeches, which are a hazard
in jungle areas, with salt or a lit
cigarette rather than just pulling
them off.

bitter (taste etc) kaRvā
black kālā
black market kālā bāzār
blanket kambal
bleach (for toilet) blīch
bless you! bhagvān āpkā
  bhalā kare! (H), allāh kā
  shukr hA! (U)
blind andhā
blinds jhilmilī pardā
blister chhālā
blocked (road, sink etc) band
blond (adj: man/woman) chiTTe
  bālō vālā/vālī
blood Khūn
  high blood pressure Khūn kā
  dabāv, raktchāp (H)
blouse blāwz, chōlī
blow-dry sukhāna-savārnā
  I'd like a cut and blow-dry
  mujhe bāl banvāne hA

blue nīlā
  blue eyes nīlī ākhe
blusher lālī singār
boarding house rahne awr
  khāne kī jagah
boarding pass borDing pās
boat kishtī, nāv (H)
  (for passengers) pānī kā jahāz
body sharīr (H), jism (U)
boiled egg ublā anDā
boiled water ublā pānī
bone haDDī
bonnet (of car) bāneT
book (noun) kitāb
  (verb) buk karānā
  can I book a seat? (said by
  man/woman) kyā mA sīT buk
  karā saktā/saktī hū?

dialogue

> **I'd like to book a table for
> two** dō lōgō ke liye mez
> buk kar dege?
> **what time would you like it
> booked for?** kitne baje ke
> liye buk karū?
> **half past seven** sāRhe sāt
> baje
> **that's fine** Thīk hA
> **and your name?** awr apkā
> nām?

bookshop, bookstore kitābō
  kī dukān
boot (footwear) būT
  (of car) sāmān rakhne kī peTī
border (of country) sarhad,
  sīmā (H)

bored: I'm bored (said by man/
  woman) mA ūb gayā/gayī hū
boring boring
**born: I was born in
  Manchester** (said by
  man/woman) mA mAnchesTar
  me pAdā huā thā/thī
  I was born in 1960 (said by
  man/woman) mA unnis saw
  sāTh me pAdā huā thā/thī
borrow mãgnā
  (money) udhār lenā
  may I borrow ...? (said by
  man/woman) kyā mA ... mãg
  saktā/saktī hū?
both dōnō
bother: sorry to bother you
  taklīf dene ke liye māf
  kījiye
bottle bōTal
bottle-opener bōTal khōlne
  kī chābī
bottom (of person) kūlhā
  at the bottom of ... (hill) ... ke
  nīche
  (street) ... ke āKhir me
box baks
box office TikaT ghar
boy laRkā
boyfriend bawy frenD
bra chōlī, brā
bracelet kangan
brake brek
brandy brānDī
brass pītal
bread Dabal rōTī
  white bread safed Dabal rōTī
  brown bread bhūrī Dabal
  rōTī

wholemeal bread chōkar vālī Dabal rōTī

break: I've broken the ... mujh se ... TūT gayā

I think I've broken my wrist lagtā hA merī kalāi TūT gayī

break down bigaRnā

I've broken down merī gāRī bigaR gayī

breakdown Kharāb

breakfast nāshtā

Getting a Western-style breakfast is likely to be a problem. **Chanā pūrī** (chick peas with deep-fried bread) is an option in the north, if a little spicy for some, and **ālū parāthā** with **dahī** (potato-filled bread with yoghurt) is another traditional start to the day. **Iddlī sāmbar** (steamed rice cake with lentil and vegetable curry) and **masālā dosa** (crispy rice pancake with spicy filling) is the most common equivalent in the south, where members of the India Coffee House chain can usually be depended on for some decent coffee and toast.

In those towns which have established a reputation as hang-outs for 'travellers', budget hotels and restaurants serve up the usual hippy fare – banana pancakes, muesli etc – as well as omelettes, toast, porridge (not always oatmeal), cornflakes, and even bacon and eggs.

break-in: I've had a break-in mere yahā chōrī hōgayī

breast chhātī

breathe sās lenā

breeze havā

bridge (over river) pul

brief chhōtā

briefcase brīf kes

bright (light etc) Tez

bright red chaTkīlā lāl

brilliant (idea) bahut baRhiyā (person) kamāl kā

bring lānā

I'll bring it back later (said by man/woman) mA ye bād me vāpas lāūgā/lāūgī

Britain bartāniyā, briTen

British bartānvī, briTish

brochure pustikā (H), risālā (U)

broken TūTī huī (leg etc) TūTī

it's broken ye TūT gayā hA

bronze kāsā

brooch jaRāū pin

broom jhāRū

brother bhāi

brother-in-law (wife's brother) sālā (husband's older brother) jeThh (husband's younger brother) devar (sister's husband) bahnōī

brown bhūrā

brown hair bhūre bāl

brown eyes bhūrī ākhe

bruise chōT

brush (for hair) burush (artist's) kūchī (for cleaning) jhāRū

bucket bālTī
Buddhist (adj) bawddh
buffet car khāne-pīne kā Dibbā
buggy (for child) bacchā gāRī
building makān
bulb (light bulb) bijlī kā balb
bumper bampar
bunk taKhtā
bureau de change sikke badalne kā daftar
see **bank**
burglary chōrī
Burma barmā
Burmese barmī
burn (noun) jale kā dāh
(verb) jalnā
burnt: this is burnt ye jalā huā hA
burst: a burst pipe phaTā nal
bus bas
 what number bus is it to ...? ... ke liye kawnse nambar kī bas hA?
 when is the next bus to ...? ... ke liye aglī bas kab hA?
 what time is the last bus? āKhirī bas kis vaKt hA?

 Travelling by long-distance bus is unavoidable on certain routes, especially in the mountains. The experience is rarely relaxing: road conditions, the poor state of vehicles and the almost anarchic traffic will transform most journeys into epic voyages. Buses can be unbearably overcrowded and often

the roof provides additional seating space. There is usually a choice between basic government-run buses and slightly more comfortable private buses; '2x2' means there are two seats on either side of the aisle, while 'express' can mean anything from a fast non-stop service to a fairly swift stopping service. Air-conditioned buses are occasionally available on main routes.

dialogue

 does this bus go to ...?
 kyā ye bas ... jātī hA?
 no, you need a number ...
 jī nahī, āp ... nambar kī bas le

business kārōbār, vyāpār (H)
bus station bas kā aDDā, bas sTeshan
bus stop bas sTāp
bust chhāTī
busy (restaurant etc) kām me lage hue, vyast (H)
 I'm busy tomorrow ma kal vyast hū (H), ma kal masrūf hū (U)
but lekin
butcher's kasāi kī dukān
butter makkhan
button baTan
buy Kharīdnā
 where can I buy ...? (said by man/woman) ma ... kahā Kharīd saktā/saktī hū

by*: by bus/car bas/kār se
  written by ... ... ne likhā
  by the window khiRkī ke
  pās
  by the sea samundar ke
  kināre
  by Thursday brihaspativār
  tak (H), jumme rāt tak (U)
bye namaste (H), Khudā
  hāfiz (U)

C

cabbage pattā gōbhī
cabin (on ship) kAbin
cable car tār par chalne vālī
  gāRī
café chāy-pānī kī dukān
cake kek
call (verb) bulānā
  (to phone) phōn karnā
  what's it called? is kō kyā
  kahte hA?
  he is called ... inkā nām ...
  hA
  please call the doctor
  DākTar kō bulāiye
  **please give me a call at 7.30
  am tomorrow** (kripayā)
  sāRhe sāt baje mujhe phōn
  kījiye
  please ask him to call me
  kripayā unkō kahiye ki
  mujhe phōn kare
  call back: I'll call back later
  (said by man/woman) mA phir
  vāpas āūgā/āūgī
  (phone back) mA phir phōn

karūgā/karūgī
**call round: I'll call round
  tomorrow** (said by man/woman)
  mA kal phir āūgā/āūgī
camcorder kAm karDar
camera kAmrā
camera shop kAmre kī
  dukān
camp (verb) kAmp lagānā
  can we camp here? kyā ham
  yahā kAmp lagā sakte hA?

 In most of the country it's
hard to see why you'd
want to be cooped up in a
tent overnight when you could be
sleeping on a cool **charpāī** (a sort of
basic bed) on a roof terrace for a
handful of rupees – let alone why
you'd choose to carry a tent around
India in the first place. Except
possibly on treks, it's not usual to
pitch a tent in the countryside, but
many hotels allow camping in their
grounds. The YMCA run a few sites,
as do the state governments
(Maharashtra in particular), and the
scouts and guides.

camping gas kAmp kī gAs
campsite kAmp kī jagah
can (tin) Dibbā
  a can of beer bīyar kā kAn
can*: can you ...? (to
  man/woman) kyā āp ... sakte/
  saktī hA?
  can I have ...? (said by
  man/woman) kyā mA ... le
  saktā/saktī hū?

I can't ... (said by man/woman)
mA nahī ... saktā/saktī
Canada kanāDā
Canadian kanāDiyan
I'm Canadian mA kanāDiyan
hū
canal nahar
cancel radd karnā
candle mōmbattī
candy miThāī
can-opener Tin khōlne kī
chābī
cap (hat) Tōpī
(of bottle) Dhakkan
car kār, mōTar
by car kar se
caravan kārvā
caravan site kārvā kī jagah
card (birthday etc) karD
here's my (business) card ye
merā bijnes karD hA
cardigan ūnī jākeT
cardphone phōn kā karD
careful hōshiyār, sāvdhān (H)
be careful! hōshiyār rahe!
caretaker (man/woman)
rakhvālā/rakhvālī
car ferry kār le jāne vālā
jahāz
carnival melā
car park kār Pārk
carpet galīchā
car rental kirāye kī kar
carriage (of train) Dibbā
carrier bag Kharīdārī rakhne
kā ThAlā
carrot gājar
carry le jānā
carry-cot bacche kī

bichhawnī
carton Dibbā
case (suitcase) sūTkes, baksā
cash (noun) nakdī
(verb) bhunānā
will you cash this for me? is
kō bhunā dege?
cash desk nakDī kā kāunTar
cash dispenser naKdī kī
mashīn
cashier (cash desk) kAsh
kāunTar
cashew kājū
cassette kasAT
cassette recorder kasAT
rikārDar
castle Kilā
casualty department
durghaTnā vibhāg (H),
hādse ka mahakmā (U)
cat billī
catch (verb) pakaRnā
**where do we catch the bus
to ...?** ... ke liye ham bas
kahā pakRe?
cathedral khās girjā
Catholic (adj) kAThōlik (īsāi)
cauliflower gōbhī
cave gufā
ceiling chhat
celery selerī (DanThal)
cemetery kabristān
centigrade senTigreD
centimetre senTimīTar
central bīch kā, kendrīy (H)
centre bīch, kendra (H)
**how do we get to the city
centre?** ham shahar ke
bīchō–bīch kAse jāe?

cereal nāshte kā anāj
certainly zarūr
 certainly not bilkul nahī
chair kursī
champagne shAmpen
change (noun: small change)
 rezgārī
 (money back) bākī pAse
 (verb) badalnā
 can I change this for ...? kyā
 is kō mA ... me badal sakte
 hA?
 I don't have any change
 mere pās kōī rezgārī nahī
 hA
 **can you give me change of a
 10-rupee note?** āp das
 rupaye kī rezgārī de sakte
 hA?

dialogue

 **do we have to change
 (trains)?** kyā hame gāRī
 badalnī paRegī?
 **yes, change at Kanpur/no
 it's a direct train** jī hā, āp
 kānpur me gāRī badle/jī
 nahī ye sīdhī gāRī hA

changed: to get changed
 kapRe badalnā
charge (noun: fee, cost) kīmat
 (verb) pAse lagnā
charge card chārj kārD
 see **credit card**
cheap sastā
 **do you have anything
 cheaper?** āpke pās is se

 kuchh sastā hA?
check (verb) dekhnā
 could you check it? ise jarā
 dekh lege?
check (US) chAk
 (US: in restaurant etc) bil
 could I have the check? bil
 lāiye?
check in darj karānā
 **where do we have to check
 in?** hame kahā darj karānā
 hōgā?
check-in chAk in
cheek (on face) gāl
cheerio! phir milege!
cheers! (toast) chīyars!
cheese panīr
chemist's davāKhānā
 see **pharmacy**
cheque chAk
 see **traveller's cheque** and
 bank
chess shatranj
chest chhātī
chewing gum chuing gam
chicken (meat) murgī
chickenpox chhōTī mātā
child (male/female)
 bacchā/bacchī
 children bacche

 Travelling with children
can be a challenge, given
the general difficulties of
transport and the lack of amenities.
But Indians are very receptive to
children, familiar or strange, and this
can help in breaking the ice.

child minder bacche kī dekhbhāl karne vālā
children's pool bacchõ ke nahāne kā pūl
children's portion bacchõ ke liye
chilli mirch
  green chilli harī mirch
  red chilli lāl mirch
  with chillies mirch vālā
  without chillies binā mirch kā
chin ThōDī
China chīn
Chinese chīnī
chips tale ālū ke katle (US) krisp
chocolate chākleT
  milk chocolate dūdhvālī chākleT
  plain chocolate sādī chākleT (binā dūdh kī)
  a hot chocolate garam chākleT
choose chunnā
Christmas baRā din, krismas
  Christmas Eve krismas se pahlā din
  merry Christmas! baRā din mubārak!
church girjā
cider seb kī sharāb
cigar churuT
cigarette sigreT

Various brands of cigarette, including imported makes such as Rothmans and Benson and Hedges, are available in India, most of them tolerable to foreign smokers. One of the great smells of India is the **birī**, the cheapest smoke, made of a low-grade tobacco leaf.

cigarette lighter lāiTar
cinema sinemā

India's film industry is the largest in the world. Bombay produces an enormous number of action-packed Hindi films that also offer lots of singing, dancing and romance. These are popular throughout India and to see a Hindi film is to see part of India. In large cities there will be at least one cinema showing English language films only.

circle gōlā
  (in theatre) bālkanī
city shahar
city centre shahar kā bīch
clean (adj) sāf
  can you clean these for me? mere liye sāf kar dege?
cleaning solution (for contact lenses) sāf karne kā ghōl
cleansing lotion safā karne kā lōshan
clear sāf
  (obvious) spashT (H), zāhir (U)
clever hōshiyār
cliff ūchī chaTTān
climbing chaRhnā
cling film chipchipī parat
clinic klinik

cloakroom kōT rakhne kā
kamrā
clock ghaRī
close (verb: shop, suitcase etc)
band karnā
(of shop etc) band hōnā

dialogue

what time do you close?
āp kis vakt band karte
hA?
we close at 8pm on
weekdays and 6pm on
Saturdays sōm se
shukrvār tak āTh baje
shām kō awr shanīchar
kō chhA baje band karte
hA
do you close for lunch? āp
dōpahar ke khāne ke liye
band karte hA?
yes, between 1 and
3.30pm jī hā, ek awr
sāRhe tīn baje ke bīch

closed band
cloth (fabric) kapRā
(for cleaning etc) sāf karne kā
kapRā
clothes kapRe
clothes line kapRe phAlāne
kī rassī
clothes peg kapRe Tāngne kī
chimTī
cloud bādal
cloudy dhudhlā
clutch klach
coach (bus) bas

(on train) Dibbā
coach station bas kā aDDā
coach trip bas kī sAr
coast samandar kā kinārā,
samudra taT (H)
on the coast samandar ke
kināre par
coat (overcoat) kōT
(jacket) jākeT
coathanger kōT Tāngne kī
khūTī
cobbler mōchī
cobra phaniyar sāp, nāg (H)
cockroach tilchaTTā
cocoa kōkō
coconut nāriyal
code (for phoning) kōD
nambar
what's the (dialling) code for
Kanpur? kānpur kō Dāyal
karne kā kōD kyā hA?
coffee kahvā, kāfī
two coffees, please dō kāfī
dījiye

In the south, coffee is
more common than tea,
and far better than it is in
the north. One of the best places to
get it is in outlets of the India Coffee
House chain, found in every
southern town, and apparently
creeping ever northwards. A whole
ritual is attached to the drinking of
milky Keralan coffee in particular,
which is poured in flamboyant
sweeping motions between tall
glasses to cool it down.

CO

coin sikkā
Coke® kōkā kōlā®
cold (adj) ThanDā
  I'm cold mujhe ThanD lag
  rahī hA
  I have a cold mujhe zukām
  hA
collapse: he/she has
  collapsed vō behōsh
  hōgayā/hōgayī
collar kālar
collect lenā
  I've come to collect ... (said by
  man/woman) mA ... lene
  āyā/āyī hū
collect call rivars chārj kawl
college kālej
colour rang
  do you have this in other
  colours? āpke pās ye dūsre
  rang me hA?
colour film rangīn 'film'
comb (noun) kanghī
come ānā

dialogue

  where do you come from?
  āp kahā se hA?
  I come from Edinburgh mA
  eDinbarā se hū

come back vāpas ānā
  I'll come back tomorrow (said
  by man/woman) mA kal vāpas
  āūgā/āūgī
come in andar āiye
comfortable ārām deh
compact disc kāmpecT Disk

company (business) kampanī
compartment (on train) Dibbā
compass kampās
complain shikāyat karnā
complaint shikāyat
  I have a complaint mujhe ek
  shikāyat hA
completely pūrī tarah se
computer kampūTar
concert sangīt sammelan
concussion chōT
conditioner (for hair)
  kanDīshanar
condom kanDōm
conference kānfrens,
  sammelan (H)
confirm pakkā karnā
congratulations!
  mubārakbād!, badhāi! (H)
connecting flight milānevālī
  flāit
connection (in travelling) mel
conscious hōsh me hA
constipation kabz
consulate up-dūtāvās (H),
  sifārat Khānā (U)
contact (verb) sampark karnā
contact lenses kōnTacT lAns
contraceptive garbh
  nirodhak golī
convenient suvidhā janak (H),
  māKul (U)
  that's not convenient ye
  suvidhā janak nahī hA

  conversation
  As a traveller in India, you
  will constantly come
across Indian people who want to

strike up a conversation. English not being their first language, they may not be familiar with the conventional ways of doing this, and thus their opening line may seem abrupt if at the same time very formal. 'Excuse me good gentleman, what is your mother country?' is a typical one. Some of the questions may baffle at first, some may be enquiries about the ways of the West or the purpose of your trip, but mostly they will be about your family and your job. You may find this intrusive, but these are subjects which are considered to be polite conversation between strangers in India, and help people place each other in terms of social position. Moreover, your family, job and even your income, are not considered 'personal' subjects in India, and it is quite normal to ask people about them. Asking the same questions back will not be taken amiss – far from it.

Things that Indian people are likely to find strange about you are lack of religion, travelling alone, leaving your family to come to India, being an unmarried couple (letting people think you're married can make life easier), and travelling second class or staying in cheap hotels when, as a tourist, you are obviously rich. You will probably end up having to explain the same things many times to many different people; on the other hand, you can ask questions too, so you could take it as an opportunity to ask things you want to know about India.

cook (verb) pakānā
  not cooked (underdone) adhpakā
cooker kukar
cookie biskuT
cooking utensils pakāne ke bartan
cool ThanDā
cork DāT
corkscrew kāgpech
corner: on the corner kōne par
  in the corner kōne me
cornflakes kārn flex
correct (right) Thīk
corridor galiyārā
cosmetics sāj-singār kī chīze
cost (verb) kīmat lagnā
  how much does it cost? is kī kīmat kyā hA?, kitne pAse lagege?
cot khaTiyā
cotton sūt
cotton wool ruī
couch (sofa) sōfā
couchette barth, shāyikā (H)
cough (noun) khāsī
cough medicine khāsī ki davā
could: could you ...? (to man/woman) kyā āp ... sakte/saktī hA?
  could I have ...? (said by man/woman) kyā mA ... le saktā/saktī hū?
  I couldn't ... (said by man/woman) mA nahī ...

sakā/sakī
country (nation) mulk, desh (H)
(countryside) dehāt
countryside dehāt
couple (two people) jōRā
a couple of ... dō ...
courier harkārā
course (main course etc) dawr
of course beshak
of course not bilkul nahī̃
cousin (male/female) chacherā bhāī/chacherī bahan
cow gāy
cracker taRtaRā biskuT
craft shop dastkārī kī dukān
crash (noun) Takkar
I've had a crash merī Takkar hōgayī
crazy pāgal
cream (in cake) krīm
(lotion) marham
(colour) krīm ke rang kā
creche krAch, shishu grih (H)
credit card kredit kārD
do you take credit cards? kyā āp kredit kārD lete hA?

Credit cards such as American Express, Visa, Access/Mastercard and Diners Club are accepted in mid-range and upmarket hotels and restaurants in the cities and major tourist centres. You will find that tourist shops generally accept cards, but be aware of credit card fraud. Never let your card be taken away into a backroom for confirmation.

Make sure all the forms are completed in full with no room for unauthorized additions. Be discreet at the same time so as not to offend – not all merchants are fraudsters.

dialogue

can I pay by credit card?
kyā āp kredit kārD lege?
which card do you want to use? (to man/woman)
kawnsā kārD dege/degī?
Mastercard/Visa
yes, sir jī hā̃
what's the number? iskā nambar kyā hA?
and the expiry date? awr Khatam hōne kī tārīKh?

crisps krisp
crockery chīnī ke bartan
crocodile magar macchh
(freshwater) ghaRiyāl
crossing (by sea) samundar pār karnā
crossroads chawrāhā
crowd bhīR
crowded bharā
crown (on tooth) khōl
cruise pānī ke jahāz kī sAr
crutches Tek
cry (verb) rōnā
cucumber khīrā
cup pyālā
a cup of ..., please ek pyālā ... de dījiye
cupboard almārī
cure (verb) ilāj karnā

curly ghughrālā
current lahar
curtains parde
cushion gaddā
custom dastūr, prathā (H)
Customs chungī

On entering India you may be required to register anything valuable on a Tourist Baggage Re-Export Form to make sure you take it home with you. There is a ban on the export of antiques and ivory and other animal products.

cut (noun) kāT
  (verb) kāTnā
I've cut myself mujhe chōT lag gayī
cutlery chhurī-kāTe
cycle shop sāikil kī dukān
cycling sāikil chalānā
cyclist (man/woman) sāikil vālā/vālī

D

dad pitā (H), abbā (U)
daily (adverb) rōzānā, pratidin (H)
  (adj) rōzānā kā, pratidin kā
dam bāadh
damage (verb) bigaRnā
  damaged bigRī
I'm sorry, I've damaged this māf kījiye, ye mujh se bigaR gayī

damn! dhat tere kī!
damp (adj) gīlā
dance (noun) nāch, nrity (H)
  (verb) nāchnā
would you like to dance? (to man/woman) āp Dans karege/karegī?
dangerous Khatarnāk, bhayānak (H)
Danish Denish
dark (adj: colour) gahrā
  (hair) kālā
it's getting dark ab andherā hō rahā hA
date*: what's the date today? āj kyā tārīKh hA?
let's make a date for next Monday ham agle somvār ko mile?
dates (fruit) khajūr
daughter beTī
daughter-in-law bahū
dawn bahut subah, ushā kāl (H)
at dawn bahut subah kō
day din
the day after kal
the day after tomorrow parsō
the day before kal
the day before yesterday parsō
every day har rōz
all day sāre din
in two days' time dō din me

The exact meaning of 'kal' and 'parsō' will be clear from the context in which they are used. For example, the tense of the verb would tell you whether the meaning is 'the day after tomorrow' or 'the day before yesterday'.

day trip din bhar kī sAr
dead (man/woman) marā huā/marī huī
deaf bahrā
deal (business) sawdā
  it's a deal sawdā pakkā
death mawt
decaffeinated coffee binā kAfīn kī kawfī
December disambar
decide tay karnā
  we haven't decided yet hamne abhī ye tay nahī kiyā
decision fAslā, nirnay (H)
deck (on ship) DAk
deckchair DAk kursī
deep gahrā
definitely zarūr
  definitely not bilkul nahī
degree (qualification) Digrī
delay (noun) der
deliberately jān būjh kar
delicious mazedār, svādishT (H)
deliver de denā
delivery (of mail) bāT
Denmark Denmārk
dental floss dāt sāf karne kā reshā
dentist dātōō kā DākTar

If you are going on a long trip, have a dental check-up before you leave home – you don't want to go down with unexpected tooth trouble in India. If you do, and it feels serious, head for Delhi, Bombay or Calcutta, and ask a foreign consulate to recommend a dentist.

dialogue

> **it's this one here** yahā par hA
> **this one?** ye?
> **no, that one** jī nahī, vō dūsrā
> **here?** yahā?
> **yes** jī hā

dentures naklī dāt
deodorant DioDarenT
department mahakmā, vibhāg (H)
department store DipārTmenT sTōr
departure ravāngī, prasthān (H)
departure lounge Dipārchar lawnj
depend: it depends ye nirbhar hA (H), ye munhasir hA (U)
  it depends on ... ... par nirbhar kartā hA (H), ... par munhasir kartā hA (U)
deposit (as security) zamānat (as part payment) jamā
dessert miThāi
destination jāne kī jagah

develop baRhānā

dialogue

could you develop these films? āp ye filme dhō dege?
yes, certainly jī hā, zarūr
when will they be ready? kab tAyār hō jāyegī?
tomorrow afternoon kal dōpahar kō
how much is the four-hour service? chār ghanTe me tAyār karne ke kitne pAse lagege?

diabetic (noun) madhumeh kā bīmār
dial (verb) Dāyal karnā
dialling code Dāyal karne kā kōD

The country code for India is 91. The codes for the main Indian cities are – Delhi 011, Bombay 022, Calcutta 033 and Madras 044.

diamond hīrā
diaper bacche kā pōtRā
diarrhoea pechish
do you have something for diarrhoea? āp ke pās pechish kī kōī davā hA?
diary Dāyrī
dictionary shabdkōsh (H), lugat (U)
didn't* nahī

see not
die marnā
diesel Dīzal
diet Khurāk
I'm on a diet merī Khurāk bandhī hA
I have to follow a special diet mujhe ek Khās Khurāk lenī paRtī hA
difference fark
what's the difference? kyā fark hA?
different alag, muKhtalif (U)
this one is different ye alag hA
a different table dūsrī mez
difficult mushkil, kaThin (H)
difficulty mushkilāt, kaThināyī (H)
dining room khāne kā kamrā
dinner (evening meal) shām kā khānā
to have dinner khānā khāne
direct (adj) sīdhā
is there a direct train? kōī sīdhī gāRī hA?
direction taraf
which direction is it? kis taraf hA?
is it in this direction? kyā is taraf hA?
directory enquiries pūchh tāchh kī phōn lāin

In most cities directory enquiries is 197 and operators speak English, but their information is often out of date.

dirt gandagī
dirty gandā
disabled apāhij
  is there access for the disabled? kyā apāhijō ke liye āne jāne kī sahūliyate hA?
disappear gāyab hōnā
  it's disappeared ye gāyab hōgayā
disappointed māyūs, nirāsh
disappointing nirāshājanak
disaster musībat
disco Diskō
discount kaTawtī
  is there a discount? kīmat me koī kaTawtī hA?
disease bīmārī
disgusting Kharāb
dish (meal) khānā
  (bowl) pyālā
dishcloth bartan pōchhne kā kapRā
disinfectant kīRe mārne kī davā
disk (for computer) Disk
disposable nappies, disposable diapers nApī
distance dūrī
  in the distance dūr se
district zilā
disturb pareshān karnā
diversion (detour) dūsrā rāstā
diving board gōtā lagāne kā phaTTā
divorced talāKshudā
dizzy: I feel dizzy muje chakkar ārahā hA
do (verb) karnā
  what shall we do? ham kyā

kare?
  how do you do it? (to man/woman) ye kAse karte/kartī hA?
  will you do it for me? kyā ye mere liye kar dege?

dialogues

how do you do? kyā hāl hA?
nice to meet you āp se milkar baRī Khushī huī
what do you do? (to man/woman) āp kyā kām karte/kartī hA?
I'm a teacher, and you? mA Tīchar hū, awr āp?
I'm a student mA sTuDent hū
what are you doing this evening? (to man/woman) āj shāmkō āp kyā kar rahe/rahī hA?
we're going out for some tea, do you want to join us? ham chāy-pānī ki liye bāhar jāyege, kyā āp hamāre sāth āyege?

do you want milk? āpkō dūdh chāhiye?
I do, but she doesn't jī hā mujhe chāhiye, magar ise nahī

doctor (man/woman) DākTar/DākTarnī
  we need a doctor hame

DākTar kī zarūrat hA
please call a doctor DākTar
kō bulāiye

In the light of the potential
health risks involved in a
trip to India, travel
insurance is too important to ignore.
To claim, you need supporting
evidence of medical treatment in the
form of bills, though with some
policies doctors and hospitals will
be able to bill your insurers direct.
Pharmacies can usually advise on
minor medical problems, and most
doctors in India speak English. Many
hotels keep a doctor on call.
Hospital standards vary. Private
clinics and mission hospitals are
often better than state-run ones, but
may not have the same facilities;
hospitals in the big cities are
generally pretty good, and university
or medical school hospitals are the
best of all. Indian hospitals usually
require patients (even emergency
cases) to buy necessities such as
plaster casts and vaccines, and to
pay for X-rays, before procedures
are carried out. However, charges
are usually so low that for minor
treatment the cost may well be less
than the initial 'excess' on your
insurance.

dialogue

where does it hurt? kahā
dard kartā hA?

right here yahī
does that hurt now? kyā
abhī bhī dard hA?
yes jī hā
take this to the pharmacy
ye davā kī dukān par
lejāiye

document dastāvez
dog kuttā
doll guRiyā
domestic flight DomesTik
flāiT, antardeshīy uRān (H)
donkey gadhā
don't!* mat!
  don't do that! ye mat kījiye!
  see not
door darvāzā
doorman darbān
double Dabal
double bed Dabal bistar
double room Dabal kamrā
down nīche
  down here yahā par
  put it down over there vahā
  rakh dījiye
  it's down there on the right ye
  vahā dāyī taraf hA
  it's further down the road isī
  saRak par thōRā āge
downmarket (restaurant etc)
bāzārū
downstairs nīche kī ōr
dozen darzan
  half a dozen ādhā darzan
drain (in sink, road) nālī
draught beer pīpe kī bīyar
draughty: it's draughty ye
havādār hA

drawer darāz
drawing khākā, rekhā chitr (H)
dreadful bahut burā
dream (noun) sapnā
dress (noun) pōshāk

Indians are generally very conservative about dress and women are expected to dress modestly, with limbs and shoulders covered. Although you may see naked **sādhūs**, their nakedness is tolerated as a sign of their asceticism. Nude bathing is frowned upon even if seemingly tolerated in places like Goa. You are obliged to cover your limbs and head when entering mosques and Sikh temples. Cleanliness is a key factor in dress acceptability – even the destitute try to maintain their dignity with regular washing.

dressed: to get dressed kapRe pahannā
dressing (for cut) marham-paTTī
(for salad) salād chaTnī
dressing gown chōgā
drink (noun: alcoholic) sharāb
(non-alcoholic) pīne kō kuchh
(verb) pīnā
a cold drink pīne kō kuchh ThanDā
can I get you a drink? pīne ke liye kuchh lāū?
what would you like (to drink)? āp kyā lege (pīne ke

liye)?
no thanks, I don't drink jī nahī, mA sharāb nahī pītā
I'll just have a drink of water mujhe sirf pānī chāhiye
see bar

drinking water pīne kā pānī
is this drinking water? kyā ye pīne kā pānī hA?
see water

drive (verb) kār chalānā
we drove here ham yahā kār me āye
I'll drive you home (said by man/woman) mA āpko kār me le jāūgā/jāūgī

It is much more usual for tourists in India to be driven than it is for them to drive; car rental firms operate on the basis of supplying chauffeur-driven vehicles, and taxis are available at cheap daily rates. Rental can be arranged through tourist offices, local car rental firms, or branches of Hertz, Budget or Europcar. The driver sleeps in the car. The big international chains are the best bet for self-drive car rental; in India they charge around thirty per cent less than chauffeur-driven, with a 1,000 rupees deposit against damage, though if you pay in your home country it can cost a whole lot more. In one or two places, motorbikes or mopeds may be rented out for local use but if you're biking around the country it's a

much better idea to buy.
In any case, driving in India is not for beginners. If you do drive yourself, expect the unexpected, and expect other drivers to take whatever liberties they can get away with. Country roads are narrow and badly maintained, and during the monsoon roads can become flooded and dangerous.
Accident rates are high, and you should be on your guard at all times, taking special care after dark – not everyone uses lights, and bullock-carts don't have any.
see **bicycle** and **motorbike**

driver Drāivar
driving licence kār chalāne kā lāisens
drop: just a drop, please (of drink) bahut ThōRā dījiye
drug davā
drugs (narcotics) nashīlī davā
drunk (adj) nashe me chūr
dry (adj) sūkhā
dry-cleaner Drāiklīnar kī dukān
duck (meat) battaKh kā gōsht
due: he was due to arrive yesterday vō kal ānevālā Thā
when is the train due? gāRī ke āne kā vakt kyā hA?
dull (pain) bejān
(weather) dhudhlā
dummy (baby's) bacche kī chūsnī
during ke dawrān

dust dhūl
dustbin kūRedān
dusty dhūl bharā
Dutch Dach
duty-free (goods) binā mahsūl kā (sāmān)
duty-free shop binā mahsūl kī dukān
duvet razāi
dysentery pechish

E

each har ek
how much are they each? har ek kā dām kyā hA?
ear kān
earache: I have earache mere kān me dard hA
early jaldī
early in the morning savere-savere
I called by earlier (said by man/woman) mA pahle bhī āyā thā/thī
earrings bālī
east pūrab (H), mashrik (U)
in the east pūrab me
Easter īsTar
eastern pūrabī (H), mashrikī (U)
easy āsān
eat khānā
we've already eaten, thanks ham khā chuke hA, shukriyā
eau de toilette itar
economy class sastī klās

egg anDā
eggplant bAgan
either: either ... or ... ... yā ...
either of them dōnō me se ek
elastic (noun) lachīlā
elastic band lachīlā fītā
elbow kōhnī
electric bijlī kā
electrical appliances bijlī kā sāmān
electric fire bijlī kī angīThī
electrician bijlī kā mistrī
electricity bijlī
  see voltage
elephant hāthī
elevator lifT
else: something else awr kuchh
  somewhere else awr kahī

dialogue

would you like anything else? āpkō awr kuchh chāhiye?
no, nothing else, thanks jī nahī, kuchh nahī

e-mail īmel
embassy dūtāvās (H), sifārat Khānā (U)
emerald pannā
emergency Khatre kī hālat
  this is an emergency! ye khatre kī hālat hA!
emergency exit Khatre me bāhar jāne kā rāstā
empty Khālī
end (noun) āKhir

(verb) Khatm hōnā
  at the end of the street galī ke āKhir me
  when does it end? ye kab Khatm hōtā hA?
engaged (toilet, telephone) istemāl me hA
  (to be married) sagāi hō chukī hA
engine (car) injan
England inglAnD
English angrezī
  I'm English mA angrez hū
  do you speak English? (to man/woman) āp angrezī bōlte/bōltī hA?
enjoy: to enjoy oneself mazā lenā

dialogue

how did you like the film? āpkō 'film' kAsī lagī?
I enjoyed it very much, did you enjoy it? mujhe bahut acchhī lagī, āpkō acchhī lagī?

enjoyable mazedār
enlargement (of photo) baRā banānā
enormous bahut baRā
enough kāfī
  there's not enough ye kāfī nahī
  it's not big enough ye kam baRī hA
  that's enough ye kāfī hA
entrance (noun) andar āne kā

rāstā, pravesh (H)

envelope lifāfā

epileptic mirgī kā bīmār

equipment sāmān

error galtī

especially Khāskar

essential zarūrī

  it is essential that ... ye
  zarūrī hA ki ...

Europe yūrōp

European yūrōpian

even (even the ...) bhī

  even if ... chāhe ...

evening shām

  this evening āj shām kō

  in the evening shām kō

evening meal shām kā khānā

eventually āKhir kār

ever kabhī

dialogue

  have you ever been to
  Jaipur? (to man/woman) āp
  kabhī jApur gaye/gayī
  hA?
  yes, I was there two years
  ago (said by man/woman) jī
  hā, mA vahā dō sāl pahle
  thā/thī

every har ek

every day har rōz

everyone har ek

everything har chīz

everywhere har kahī

exactly! bilkul!

example misāl, udāharan (H)

  for example misāl ke tawr

par

excellent baRhiyā

  excellent! bahut Khūb!

except ke sivā

excess baggage had se zyādā
sāmān

exchange rate sikke badalne
kī dar

exciting mazedār

excuse me (to get past, to say
sorry) māf kījiye
  (to get attention) suniye

exhausted (man/woman) thakā
huā/thakī huī

exhibition numāish,
pradarshinī (H)

exit bāhar jāne kā rāstā, nikās
(H)

  where's the nearest exit? sab
  se nazdīk bāhar jāne kā
  rāstā kahā hA?

expect (wait for) rāh dekhnā
  (hope) ummīd karnā

expensive mahangā

experienced anubhavī (H),
tajrabā kār (U)

explain batlānā

  can you explain that? (to
  man/woman) kyā āp batlā
  sakte/saktī hA?

express (mail) Akspres Dāk
  (train) Dāk gāRī

extension (telephone) phōn kā
AksTAnshan

  extension 221, please
  AksTAnshan do saw ikkīs
  dījiye

extension lead bijlī ke tār kā
AksTAnshan

extra: can we have an extra one? hame ek awr chāhiye
do you charge extra for that? kyā iskā dām alag hA?
extraordinary ajīb
extremely bahut
eye ākh
will you keep an eye on my suitcase for me? mere sūTkes kī nigrānī rakhe
eyebrow pencil bhawhõ kō savārne kī pAnsil
eye drops ākh me Dālne kī davā
eyeglasses (spectacles) chashmā
eyeliner vilāyatī kājal
eye make-up remover ākh ka mekap haTāne kī chīz
eye shadow ākh ke nīche lagāne kā pāwDar

F

face chehrā
factory kārKhānā
Fahrenheit fâranhāiT
faint (verb) behōsh hō jānā
she's fainted vō behōsh hōgayī
I feel faint mujhe chakkar ārahe hA
fair (funfair) melā
(trade) hāT-bāzār
(adj) gōrā
fairly īmāndārī se
fake (imitation) naklī
(forgery) jālī

fall (verb) girnā
(US: noun) patjhaR (H), Khizā (U)
in the fall patjhaR me
she's had a fall vō gir paRī
false jhūThā
family parivār (H), kunbā (U)
famous mashhūr
fan (electrical) bijlī kā pankhā
(handheld) hāTh kā pankhā
(sport etc) shaukīn
fantastic (good) bahut baRhiyā
far dūr

dialogue

is it far from here? kyā yahā se dūr hA?
no, not very far jī nahī, bahut dūr nahī
well, how far? acchhā, kitnī dūr?
it's about 20 kilometres Karīb bīs kilōmīTar hA

fare (for bus etc) kirāyā
farm kheT
fashionable fAshan parast
fast Tez
fat (person) mōTā
(noun: on meat) charbī
father pitā (H), vālid (U)
father-in-law sasur
faucet TōTī
fault galtī
sorry, it was my fault māf kījiye, ye merī galtī thī
it's not my fault merī galtī

nahī hA
faulty (equipment) nuKs vālā
favourite dilpasand
fax (noun) fAks
  (verb: person) fAks karnā
  (document) fAks kar denā
February farvarī
feel: I feel hot mujhe garmī
lag rahī hA
I feel unwell merī tabiyat
Thīk nahī hA
I feel like going for a walk
(said by man/woman) mA
ghūmne jānā chāhtā/chāhtī
hū
how are you feeling? (to
man/woman) āp kAse/kAsī hA?
I'm feeling better mA behtar
hū

feet
When entering a temple
you are required to leave
your shoes outside. The same
applies to mosques, where taps or
special fountains are provided for
visitors to wash their hands and feet
before entering. It's considered rude
to show the soles of your feet and
should never be done to a deity –
when sitting down in a temple it's
best to tuck your feet under you.

felt-tip (pen) reshe ke nōk
vālī kalam
fence bāRā
fender bampar
ferry kishtī
festival tyōhār

**festivals and special
events**
Virtually every temple in
every town or village across the
country has its own festival. The
biggest and most spectacular
include Puri's Rath Yatra festival in
June or July, Pushkar's camel fair in
November, Kullu's Dussehra, and
Madurai's three annual festivals.
While mostly religious in nature,
merrymaking rather than solemnity
is generally the order of the day, and
onlookers are usually welcome.
You may, while in India, have the
privilege of being invited to a
wedding. These are jubilant affairs
with great feasting, always
scheduled on auspicious days. A
Hindu bride wears red for the
ceremony, and puts a **bindā** on her
forehead for the rest of her married
life. Although the practice is officially
illegal, large dowries change hands.
These are usually paid by the bride's
family to the groom, and can be the
subject of dispute; poor families feel
obliged to save for years to get their
daughters married.
Funeral processions are much more
sombre affairs, and should be left in
peace. In Hindu funerals, the body is
normally carried to the cremation
site within hours of death by white-
shrouded relatives (white is the
colour of mourning). The eldest son
is expected to shave his head and
wear white following the death of a
parent. At Varanasi and other places,

you may see cremations; such occasions should be treated with respect and not photographed.

fetch le ānā
 I'll fetch him (said by man/woman) mA use le āūgā/āūgī
 will you come and fetch me later? āp ākar bād me mujhe le jāye
feverish harārat
few: a few ThōRā
 a few days ThōRe din
fiancé/fiancée mangetar
field mAdān
fight (noun) laRāi
figs anjīr
fill in bharnā
 do I have to fill this in? kyā mujhe ye bharnā paRegā?
fill up bhar denā
 fill it up, please ise bhar dījiye
filling (in cake, sandwich) bharne kī chīz
 (in tooth) dāt me bharne kā masālā
film 'film'

dialogue

> **do you have this kind of film?** āpke pās is kism kī 'film' hA?
> **yes, how many exposures?** jī hā, kitne phōTō khīchne vālī?
> **36** chhattīs

film processing 'film' dhōnā
filthy (room etc) gandā
find (verb) milnā
 I can't find it mujhe nahī mil rahā
 I've found it mujhe mil gayā
find out patā karnā
 could you find out for me? āp mere liye patā kar le?
fine (weather) acchhā
 (punishment) jurmānā

dialogues

> **how are you?** (to man/woman) āp kAse/kAsī hA?
> **I'm fine thanks** Thīk hū, shukriyā

> **is that OK?** kyā ye Thīk hA?
> **that's fine thanks** jī hā, yi Thīk hA

finger unglī
finish Khatm hōnā
 (doing something) Khatm karnā
 I haven't finished yet mAne abhī Khatm nahī kiyā
 when does it finish? ye kab Khatm hōtā hA?
fire āg
 (blaze) tez āg
 fire! āg lagī hA!
 can we light a fire here? (said by man/woman) kyā ham yahā āg jalā sakte/saktī hA?
 it's on fire is me āg lagī hA
fire alarm āg lagne ke Khatre kī ghanTī

fire brigade damkal

fire escape āg se bachne kā rāstā

fire extinguisher āg bujhāne kā purzā

first pahlā

  I was first (said by man/woman) mA sabse pahle Thā/Thī

  at first pahle

  the first time pahlī bār

  first on the left bāyī taraf pahlā

first aid fasT eD

first-aid kit fasT eD kā baksā

first class (travel etc) pahlā darjā

first floor pahlī manzil; (US) nichlī manzil

first name shuru kā nām

fish (noun) machhlī

fishmonger's machhlī vālā

fit (attack) dawrā

  it doesn't fit me ye mujhe Thīk nahī bAThtā

fitting room kapRe ājmāne kā kamrā

fix (verb: arrange) pakkā karnā

  can you fix this? (repair) is kī marammat kar sakte hA?

fizzy Tharre vālā

flag jhanDā

flannel (facecloth) chhōTā tawliyā

flash (for camera) kAmre kī flAsh

flat (noun: apartment) flAT (adj) chapTā

  I've got a flat tyre mere pahiye kī havā nikal gayī

flavour zāykā (U), svād (H)

flea pissū

flight uRān

flight number uRān kā nambar

flippers flipar

flood bāRh, sAlāb (U)

floor (of room) farsh (storey) manzil

  on the floor farsh par

florist phūl vālā

flour āTā

flower phūl

flu flū

fluent: he speaks fluent Hindi vō pharrāTe se hindī bōlta hA

fly (noun) uRān (verb) havāi jahāz se jānā

  can we fly there? kyā ham vahā havāi jahāz se jā sakte hA?

fly in havāi jahāz se ānā

fly out havāi jahāz se jānā

fog kuhrā

foggy: it's foggy kuhrā chhāyā hA

folk dancing lōk nritya

folk music lōk sangīt

follow pīchhe ānā

  follow me mere pīchhe āye

food khānā

food and drink
India is renowned the world over for its aromatic cooking and vast repertory of dishes. Excellent vegetarian food can be found

throughout India, where the quality of meat is often suspect. In the north **dāl** (lentils), rice and **roṭī** (unleavened bread) are the staples, while in the south it is mostly rice. Restaurant food is dominated by rich Mughlai cuisine, featuring spices mixed with a cream sauce, but regional variations are infinite. Stomach upsets are common and it is best to avoid drinking water other than the bottled mineral variety – check the seal and date first. Steer clear of salads except in the best restaurants, as the vegetables will invariably be washed in tap water; fruit with edible skins should be peeled first. Coca Cola and Pepsi are available in the towns and cities, along with several brands of Indian soft drink; fruit juice in cartons, such as mango-based Fruiti, can be found in most places.

food poisoning Kharāb khāne se pAdā huī bīmārī
food shop/store khāne kī chīzō kī dukān
foot (of person) pAr (measurement) fuT
on foot pAdal
football fuTbāl
football match fuTbāl mAch
for: do you have something for ...? (headache, diarrhoea etc) āpke pās ... ke liye kuchh hA?

Fo

dialogues

who's the sag gosht for? ye sāg gōsht kiske liye hA?
that's for me ye mere liye hA
and this one? awr ye?
that's for her ye iske liye

where do I get the bus for Chandigarh? mujhe chanDīgaRh ke liye bas kahā milegī?
the bus for Chandigarh leaves from Sadar Bazar chanDīgaRh ke liye bas sadar bāzār se chhūTtī hA

how long have you been here? āp yahā kitne din se hA?
I've been here for two days, how about you? mA yahā dō din se hū, awr āp?
I've been here for a week mA yahā ek hafte se hū

forehead māthā
foreign pardesh
foreigner pardeshī
forest jangal
forget bhūl jānā
I forget mA bhūl jātā hū
I've forgotten (said by man/woman) mA bhūl gayā/gayī

fork (for eating) kāTā
(in road) rāstā baT jānā
form (document) fāram
formal (dress) pōshāk
fortnight dō hafte
fortunately Khush kismatī se
**forward: could you forward my
mail?** āp merī Dāk āge bhej
dege?
forwarding address āge
bhejne kā patā
foundation cream fāunDeshan
krīm
fountain (ornamental) fuvvārā
(for drinking water) chashmā
foyer DyawDhī
fracture (noun) TūTī haDDī
France frāns
free āzād, svatantra (H)
(no charge) muft
is it free (of charge)? kyā ye
muft hA?
freeway khulī saRak
freezer frīzar
French frānsīsī
French fries tale ālū ke katle
frequent bār bār
**how frequent is the bus to
Agra?** āgrā ke liye bas kab
kab jātī hA?
fresh tāzā
fresh orange juice santare kā
tāzā ras
Friday shukr vār (H), zummā
(U)
fridge friz
fried talā huā
fried egg talā huā anDā
friend dōst

friendly dōstānā
from se
**when does the next train
from Amritsar arrive?**
amritsar se aglī gāRī kab ātī
hA?
from Monday to Friday
sōmvār se shukrvār tak (H),
pīr se zumme tak (U)
from next Thursday agle
brihaspativār se (H), agle
zumme rāt se (U)

dialogue

> **where are you from?** āp
> kahā se hA?
> **I'm from Slough** mA
> Slough se hū

front (part) aglā hissā
in front sāmne
in front of the hotel hōTal ke
sāmne
at the front bilkul sāmne
frost pālā
frozen jamā huā
frozen food jamā huā khānā
fruit phal

 What fruit is available
varies from region to
region and season to
season, but there's always a wide
choice. Ideally, you should peel all
fruit, or soak it in a strong iodine or
potassium permanganate solution
for half an hour. Roadside vendors
sell fruit which they often cut up and

serve sprinkled with salt or even **masālā**.

Mangoes of various kinds are usually on offer, but not all are sweet – some are used for pickles or curries. Indians are picky about their mangoes, which they feel and smell before buying; if you're not familiar with the art of choosing mangoes, you could be sold the leftovers. Bananas of one sort or another are also on sale all year round, and oranges and tangerines are generally easy to come by, as are melons and watermelons.

fruit juice phal kā ras
frying pan kaRhāi
full bharā
  it's full of ... ye ... se bharā hA
  I'm full merā peT bharā hA
full board sab khāne
fun: it was fun ye hasī-mazāK Thī
funeral antyeshTi sanskār (H), janāzā (U)
funny (strange) ajīb
  (amusing) mazāKiyā
furniture mez kursī vagArā
further āge
  it's further down the road isī saRak par awr āge hA

dialogue

  how much further is it to Chandni Chauk? chādnī chawk awr kitnī dūr hA?

about 5 kilometres Karib pāch kilōmīTar

fuse (noun) bijlī kā fyuz
  the lights have fused battī chalī gayī
fuse box fyūz kā baksā
fuse wire fyūz kī Tār
future bhavishya (H), mustakbil (U)
  in future āge

G

gallon gAlan
game (match, cards etc) khel
  (meat) shikār
garage (for fuel) peTrōl sTashan
  (for repairs, parking) gArāj
garden bāg
garlic lahsan
gas gAs
gas can peTrōl kā kanasTar
gas cylinder gAs silanDar
gasoline (US) peTrōl
gas permeable lenses gAs parmiebal lAns
gas station peTrōl sTashan
gate phāTak
  (at airport) rāstā
gay (homosexual) lawnDebāz, samlingī (H)
gearbox giyar baksā
gear lever giyar badalne kī chhaR
gears giyar
general (adj) ām, sādhāran (H)

general delivery chiTThī jamā karne vālā DākKhānā
gents' toilet purush shawchālay (H), mardānā pākhānā (U)
genuine (antique etc) aslī
German jarman
Germany jarmanī
get (fetch) lānā
 could you get me another one, please? mere liye ek awr lāiye
 how do I get to ...? mA ... kAse jāū?
 do you know where I can get them? āpko mālūm hA ki ye mujhe kahā milege?

dialogue

> can I get you a drink? pīne ke liye kuchh lāū?
> no, I'll get this one, what would you like? (to man/woman) jī nahī, ye mere par hA, āp kyā lege/legī?
> a glass of red wine ek gilās rAD vāin

get back (return) vāpas ānā
get in (arrive) pahuchnā
get off utarnā
 where do I get off? (off bus etc) mA kahā utrū?
get on (to train etc) chaRhnā
get out (of car etc) bāhar nikalnā
get up (in the morning) uThnā

gift tōhfā
gift shop tōhfe ke chīzō kī dukān
gin jin
 a gin and tonic, please jin awr Tawnik lāiye
girl laRkī
girlfriend (sweetheart) mahbūbā (woman's female friend) sahelī
give denā
 can you give me some change? mujhe kuch rezgārī dege?
 I gave it to him mAne ye use de diyā
 will you give this to ...? āp ye ... kō dege?

dialogue

> how much do you want for this? āp iske kitne pAse lege?
> 60 rupees sāTh rupaye
> I'll give you 50 rupees (said by man/woman) mA pachās rupaye dūgā/dūgī

give back vāpas denā
glad Khush, prasann (H)
glass (material) kāch (for drinking) gilās
 a glass of red wine ek gilās rAD vāin
glasses (spectacles) chashmā
gloves dastāne
glue (noun) gōd
go jānā
 we'd like to go to the Taj

Mahal hame tājmahal jānā
hA

where are you going? (to
man/woman) āp kahā jā
rahe/jā rahī hA?

where does this bus go? ye
bas kahā jātī hA?

let's go! chalō chale!

she's gone vō chalī gayī

where has he gone? vō kahā
gayā hA?

I went there last week (said by
man/woman) mA vahā pichhle
hafte gayā/gayī

samosa to go samōse bāhar
le jāne ke liye

go away chale jānā

 go away! chale jāō!

go back (return) vāpas jānā

go down (the stairs etc) nīche
jānā

go in (enter) andar jānā

go out (in the evening) bāhar
jānā

 **do you want to go out
tonight?** (to man/woman) āj
shām kahī bāhar jānā
chāhte/chāhtī hA?

go through ... ... se hō kar
jānā

go up (the stairs etc) ūpar jānā

goat bakrī

god devtā

God īshvar (H), allah (U)

goddess devī

goggles dhūp kā chashma

gold sōnā

golf gōlf

golf course gōlf kā mAdān

good acchhā

 good! bahut acchhā!

 it's no good ye bekār hA

goodbye namaste (H), Khudā
hāfiz (U)

good evening namaste (H),
assalam ālekam (U)

good morning namaste (H),
assalam ālekam (U)

good night namaste (H),
Khudā hāfiz (U)

goose bataKh

got: we've got to leave hame
jānā hA

 have you got any ...? āpke
pās kōī ... hA?

government sarkār

gradually dhīre dhīre, āhistā
āhistā (U)

grammar vyākaran (H),
Kavāyad (U)

gram(me) grām

granddaughter pōtī

grandfather dādā

grandmother dādī

grandson pōtā

grapefruit chakōtrā

grapefruit juice chakōtre kā
ras

grapes angūr

grass ghās

grateful ehsānmand

gravy shōrbā

great (excellent) baRhiyā

 that's great! bahut baRhiyā!

 a great success baRī
kāmyābī

Great Britain briTen

Greece yūnān

greedy lālchī
Greek yūnānī
green harā
greengrocer's sabzī vālā

greeting people
The most common form of Hindu greeting is **namaste**, when palms are joined together in front of the chest. The gesture is often accompanied by the word **namaskār** or **namaste** but can also be made in silence. The greeting is made to an equal or an older person and is rarely made to a child or younger person, except in response. If somebody wants to show particular respect – to parents, grandparents or teacher, for example – they will bend down in a gesture of touching the other person's feet before joining palms. Muslims do not not say namaste but instead greet each other with **salām ālekām** (peace be with you), the response to which is **ālekām salām**; a less formal and more familiar greeting is simply **kyā hāl hA?** (how are you?). When parting, Muslims wish each other well with **khudā hāfiz** (God be with you).

grey bhūrā
grilled sikā huā
grocer's pansārī
ground zamīn
 on the ground zamīn par
ground floor nichlī manzil
group Tōlī, dal (H)

guarantee (noun) gāranTī
 is it guaranteed? kyā iskī gāranTī hA?
guest mehmān
guesthouse Thaharne kī jagah
 see **hotel**
guide (noun) gāiD
guidebook gāiD buk
guided tour gāiD ke sāth sAr
guitar gitār
Gujarati gujrātī
gum (in mouth) masūRā
gun bandūk
gym kasrat kī jagah, vyāyām shālā (H)

H

hair bāl
hairbrush bālō kā burush
haircut bāl kaTāi
hairdresser's (men's) nāi, hajjām (U)
 (women's) heyar Dresar
hairdryer heyar Drāyar
hair gel heyar jAl
hairgrips heyar pin
hair spray heyar spre
half* ādhā
 half an hour ādhā ghanTā
 half a litre ādhā liTar
 about half that is ādhā
 half board ek vakt kā khānā
 half-bottle ādhī bōtal
 half fare ādhā kirāyā
 half-price ādhī kīmat
ham sūar kā ublā gōsht

hamburger hAmbargar
hammer hathawRā
hand hāth

The left hand is considered unclean since it is traditionally used for washing after defecating. Traditionally the belief was so strong that the upper two castes of Hindu society, the Brahmins and the Kshatriyas, were known as the 'right-handed' castes. Never eat with your left hand and do not pass or touch food with it. When eating food with your hands, try to use just the tips of the fingers of the right hand, and certainly not your palm.

handbag hAnD bAg
handbrake hAnD brek
handkerchief rumāl
handle (on door) hatthā
(on suitcase etc) hAnDal
hand luggage hāth me le jāne vālā sāmān
hangover Khumār
I've got a hangover mujhe Khumār chaRhī hA
happen hōnā
what's happening? kyā hō rahā hA?
what has happened? kyā hōgayā?
happy Khush
I'm not happy about this mujhe is se tasallī nahī hA
harbour bandargāh
hard saKht

(difficult) mushkil
hard-boiled egg Khūb ublā anDā
hard lenses mazbūt lAns
hardly shāyad hī
hardly ever shāyad hī kabhī
hardware shop lōhe ke sāmān kī dukān
hat Tōp
hate (verb) nafrat karnā
have* hōnā
(take) lenā
can I have a ...? (said by man/woman) kyā mA ... le saktā/saktī hū?
do you have ...? āpke pās ... hA?
what'll you have? (drink: to man/woman) āp kyā lege/legī?
I have to leave now mujhe ab jānā hōgā
do I have to ...? kyā mujhe ... hōgā?
can we have some ...? hame kuchh ... milegā?
hayfever mawsamī bukhār
hazelnuts pahāRī bādām
he* (person nearby) ye
(person further away) vō
head sir
headache sir dard
headlights āge kī baRī battī
headphones hADphōn

health
A lot of visitors fall ill in India, and some of them get very ill. However, if you are careful, you should be able to get

through the country with nothing worse than a dose of diarrhoea. When mild and not accompanied by other major symptoms, it may just be your stomach reacting to unfamiliar food. Accompanied by cramps and vomiting, it could well be food poisoning. In either case, it will probably pass of its own accord in 24-48 hours without treatment. If symptoms persist for more than a few days, a course of antibiotics may be necessary; this should be seen as a last resort, following medical advice.

A few common-sense precautions are in order. Be particularly wary of prepared dishes that have to be reheated. Anything that is boiled or fried in your presence is usually all right, though meat can sometimes be dodgy; anything that has been left out for any length of time is definitely suspect. Raw unpeeled fruit and vegetables should always be viewed with suspicion, and you should avoid salads unless you know they have been soaked in iodine or potassium permanganate solution.

Be vigilant about personal hygiene. Wash your hands often, especially before eating; keep all cuts clean, treat them with iodine or antiseptic, and cover them to prevent infection. Be fussier about sharing things like drinks and cigarettes than you might be at home. It is also inadvisable to go round barefoot – and best to wear flip-flop sandals even in the shower.

healthy (person) svasTh (H), tandurast (U)
(food, climate) svāsThyprad (H), sehat bakhsh (U)
hear sunnā

dialogue

can you hear me? āpko sunāi detā hA?
I can't hear you, could you repeat that? mujhe sunāi nahĪ detā, āp phir kahiye

hearing aid sunne me madad dene kī mashīn
heart dil
heart attack dil kā dawrā
heat garmī

heat trouble
The sun and the heat can cause a few unexpected problems. Many people get a bout of prickly heat rash before they've acclimatized. A cool shower, zinc oxide powder and loose cotton clothes should help. Dehydration is another possible problem, so make sure you're drinking enough fluids, and take rehydration salts frequently, especially when hot and/or tired.

A high-factor sun-block is vital on exposed skin, especially when you first arrive, and on areas newly exposed by haircuts or a change of clothes. A light hat is also a very good idea, especially if you're doing

a lot of walking around in the sun.
Finally, be aware that getting
overheated can cause heat-stroke,
which can be fatal. Signs are a very
high body temperature with no
feeling of fever accompanied by
headaches and disorientation.
Getting your body temperature down
(by taking a tepid shower for
example) is the first step in
treatment.

heater hīTar
heating hīting
heavy bhārī
heel (of foot) eRī
  (of shoe) jūte kī eRī
  could you heel these? jūte
  me eRī lagā dō
heelbar eRī lagāne kā
  kāwnTar
height (of person) kad
  (of mountain) ūchāi
hello namaste (H), salām (U)
  (on phone) halō
helmet (for motorcycle) hifāzat
  kā Tōp
help (noun) madad
  (verb) madad karnā
  help! bachāō!
  can you help me? (to
  man/woman) kyā āp merī
  madad karege/karegī?
  **thank you very much for your
  help** āp kī madad ke liye
  bahut shukriyā
helpful madad gār
hepatitis hepTāiTis
her* (direct object: nearby) ise

  (further away) use
  (possessive: person nearby) inkā
  (person further away) unkā
  I haven't seen her mAne ise
  nahī dekhā hA
  to her iskō
  with her iske sāTh
  for her iske liye
  that's her ye vahī hA
herbal tea jaRī būTī kī chāy
herbs jaRī būTiyā
here yahā
  here is/are ... ye hA/hA ...
  here you are (offering) ye
  lījiye
hers* (referring to person nearby)
  iskā
  (referring to person further away)
  uskā
  that's hers ye iskā hA
hey! are!
hi! halō!
hide chhipnā
  (something) chhipānā
high ūchā
highchair bacche kī ūchī
  kursī
highway khulī saRak
hill pahāRī
him* (person nearby) ise
  (person further away) use
  to him iskō
  with him iske sāTh
  for him iske liye
  I haven't seen him mAne ise
  nahī dekhā hA
  that's him ye vahī hA
Himalayas himālay pahāR
Hindi hindī

Hindu hindū
hip kūlhā
hire kirāye par lenā
 for hire kirāye ke liye
 where can I hire a bike?
 kirāye par sāikil kahā
 milegī?
 see rent
his* (referring to person nearby)
 iskā
 (referring to person further away)
 uskā
 that's his ye iskā hA
hit (verb) mārnā
hitch-hike muft savārī karnā
hobby shawk
hold (verb) pakaRnā
hole chhed
holiday chhuTTī
 on holiday chhuTTī par
home ghar
 at home (in my house etc) ghar
 par
 (in my country) apne ghar jAsā
 we go home tomorrow (said by
 man/woman) ham kal apne
 mulk jāyege/jāyegī
honest īmāndār
honey shahad
honeymoon suhāgrāt
hood (US: of car) bāneT
hope ummīd, āshā (H)
 I hope so mujhe Asī ummīd
 hA
 I hope not mujhe ummid
 hA Asā nahī hōgā
hopefully ummīd hA
horn (of car) bhōpū
horrible bahut burā

horse ghōRā
horse-drawn carriage ghōRā
 gāRī, tāgā
horse riding ghuR savārī
hospital aspatāl
hospitality mehmāndārī
 thank you for your hospitality
 āpkī mehmāndārī ke leye
 shukriyā
hot garam
 (curry etc) tez
 I'm hot mujhe garmī lag
 rahī hA
 it's hot today āj garam hA
 is it very hot? (curry etc) kyā is
 me tez mirch hA?
 not too hot (curry etc) zyādā
 tez nahī
hotel hōTal

At the top of the hotel range are the prestigious five-star hotels where tourists are required to pay in foreign currency. Far more common are mid-priced hotels, which often include a choice of air-conditioned rooms, air-cooled rooms (where air is blown through moistened matting) and ordinary rooms with fans only. Guest houses are common in centres frequented by tourists; they are usually low- to mid-priced, and can be anything from a grubby doss-house to something quite decent. Tourist lodges are inexpensive but usually poorly managed; some include dormitories.
Like most other things in India, the

Ho

price of a room may well be open to negotiation. If you think the price is too high, or if all the hotels in the town are empty, try haggling. You may get nowhere – but nothing ventured, nothing gained.

hotel room hōTal kā kamrā
hour ghanTā
house (home) ghar
  (building) makān
how kAse
  how many? kitne?
  how do you do? kyā hāl hA?

dialogues

  how are you? (to man/woman) āp kAse/kAsī hA?
  fine, thanks, and you? mA Thīk hū̃, shukriyā, awr āp Thīk hA?

  how much is it? is kī kīmat kyā hA?
  100 rupees sau rupaye
  I'll take it (said by man/woman) mA ise le lū̃gā/le lū̃gī

humid sīlā
hungry bhūkhā
  are you hungry? (kyā) āpkō bhūkh lagī hA?
hurry (verb) jaldī karnā
  I'm in a hurry mujhe jaldī hA
  there's no hurry jaldī kī kōī bāt nahī

hurry up! jaldī karō!
hurt (injure) chōT lagnā
  it really hurts ye dard kartā hA
husband pati (H), Khāvind (U)

I

I mA
ice barf
  with ice barf ke sāTh
  no ice, thanks barf nahī, shukriyā
ice cream āiskrīm
ice-cream cone āiskrīm kōn
iced tea barfīlī chāy
ice lolly chūsne vālī āiskrīm
idea Khayal, vichār (H)
idiot buddhū
if agar
ill bīmār
  I feel ill merī tabiyat Thīk nahī
illness bīmārī
imitation (leather etc) naklī
immediately fawran, turant (H)
important zarūrī
  it's very important ye bahut zarūrī hA
  it's not important ye zarūrī nahī
impossible nāmumkin, asambhav (H)
impressive rōbdār, prabhāv shālī (H)
improve behtar banānā
  I want to improve my Hindi

mА apnī hindī behtar banānā chāhtā/chāhtī hū̃

in: it's in the centre ye bīch me hA

in my car merī kār me

in Kanpur kānpur me

in two days from now dō din bād

in five minutes pā̃ch minaT me

in May mayī me

in English angrezī me

in Hindi hindī me

is he in? kyā vō yahā̃ hA?

inch 'inch'

include shāmil

  does that include meals? (kyā) is me khānā bhī shāmil hA?

  is that included? kyā ye bhī shāmil hA?

inconvenient nāmunāsib, asuvidhā janak (H)

incredible (very good) tājjub kā

India bhārat

Indian bhārtīy

Indian Ocean hind mahāsāgar

indicator (on car) inDikaTar

indigestion badhazmī

indoor pool bhītar kā tālāb

indoors makān ke andar

inexpensive sasTā

infection phAlne vālī bīmārī

infectious phAlne vālā

inflammation sūjan

informal sādā, anōpchārik (H)

information jānkārī, sūchnā (H)

  do you have any information

about ...? āpkō ... ke bare me kōī jānkārī hA?

information desk jānkārī kī jagah

injection injekshan

injured ghāyal

  she's been injured vō ghāyal hōgAi

in-laws sasurāl vāle

inner tube Tāyar kī Tyūb

innocent (not guilty) begunāh, nirdōsh (H)

insect kīRā

insect bite kīRā kāTnā

  do you have anything for insect bites? āpke pās kīRe kī kāT ke liye kōī davā hA?

insect repellent kīRe mārne kī davā

inside andar

  inside the hotel hōTal ke andar

  let's sit inside chaliye, andar bAThe

insist āgrah (H), isrār (U)

  I insist merā āgrah (H)/isrār (U) hA

insomnia nīd na ānā

instant coffee fawran banne vālī kāfī, 'instant' kāfī

instead kī bazāy

  give me that one instead iskī bazāy vō dījiye

  instead of ... kī bazāy ...

insulin 'insulin'

insurance bīmā

intelligent tez

interested: I'm interested in ... merī ... me dilchaspī hA

interesting dilchasp

that's very interesting ye bahut dilchasp hA

international antar-rāshTrīy (H), bAnul aKvāmī (U)

Internet inTarneT

interpret anuvād karnā (H), tarzumā karnā (U)

interpreter dubhāshiyā

intersection chawrāhā

interval (at theatre) inTarval

into ke andar

I'm not into ... merā ... me rujhān nahī hA

introduce milānā, parichay karānā (H)

may I introduce ...? ... se miliye

invitation dāvat, nimantran (H)

invite dāvat denā, nimantran denā (H)

Ireland āyarlAnD

Irish āyarish

I'm Irish (said by man/woman) mA āyarlAnD kā rahne vālā/vālī hū

iron (for ironing) istarī

can you iron these for me? (to man/woman) kyā mere liye inpar istarī kar dege/degī?

is* hA

island Tāpū

it ye

it is ... ye ... hA

is it ...? kyā ye ... hA?

where is it? ye kahā hA?

it's him ye vahī hA

it was ... ye ... Thā

Italian iTāliyan

Italy iTalī

itch: it itches is me khujlī hōtī hA

J

jacket jākeT

Jainism jAn dharm

jam murabbā

jammed: it's jammed ye dab gayā

January janvarī

jar martbān

jaw jabRā

jazz jāz sangīt

jealous shakkī

jeans jīn

jellyfish jelī fish

jersey jarsī

jetty ghāT

jeweller's jawharī

jewellery javāhirāt

Jewish yahūdī

job kām

jogging dhīre dhīre dawRnā

to go jogging dawRne kī kasrat karnā

joke mazāk

journey safar, yātrā (H)

have a good journey! KhAriyat se jāye!

jug jag

a jug of water pānī kā jag

juice ras

July julāi

jump (verb) kūdnā

jumper jampar

junction jankshan

June jūn
just (only) sirf
  just two sirf dō
  just for me sirf mere liye
  just here yahī
  not just now abhī nahī
  we've just arrived ham abhī āye hA

K

keep rakhnā
  keep the change rezgārī rakhiye
  can I keep it? (said by man/woman) kyā mA ise rakh saktā/saktī hū?
  please keep it āp ise rakh lījiye
ketchup chaTnī
kettle ketlī
key chābī
  the key for room 201, please kamrā nambar do so ek kī chābī
keyring chābī kā chhallā
kidneys gurdā
kill mārnā
kilo kilō
kilometre kilōmīTar
  how many kilometres is it to ...? ... kitne kilōmītar hA?
kind (generous) meharbān, udār (H)
  (helpful) dayālu (H), madadgār (U)
  that's very kind āpkī baRī meharbānī

dialogue

which kind do you want?
āpkō kis kism kā chāhiye?
I want this kind mujhe is kism kā chāhiye

king rājā
kiosk būth
kiss (noun) chummā
  (verb) chūmnā

kissing
Kissing and embracing are considered highly sexual and should be avoided in public – indeed, even holding hands with a member of the opposite sex is taboo. However, it is not unusual to see Indian men (even policemen) walking down the road hand-in-hand as a sign of brotherliness.

kitchen rasōī
kitchenette chhōTī rasōī
Kleenex® kāgaz ke rumāl
knee ghuTnā
knickers nikar
knife chākū
knock (verb) Thōknā
knock down (in road accident) ke nīche ānā
  he's been knocked down vō gāRī ke nīche āgayā
knock over (object) Takrā jānā
know jānanā
  I don't know mujhe mālūm nahī, mujhe pata nahī

I didn't know that mujhe ye mālūm nahī Thā
do you know ...? kyā āp jānate hA ...?

L

label lebal
ladies' compartment (on train) janānā Dibbā

Ladies' compartments exist on all trains for women travelling unaccompanied; they are usually small and can be full of noisy kids, but can give untold relief to women travellers who would otherwise have to endure incessant staring in the open section of the carriage. Some stations also have ladies-only waiting rooms.

ladies' room, ladies' toilets janānā gusal Khānā, mahilā shawchālay (H)
ladies' wear awrtō ke kapRe
lady mahilā (H), KhāTūn (U)
lager lāgar bīyar
 see **beer**
lake jhīl
lamb (meat) bheR kā gōsht
lamp battī
lane (of motorway) rāsTā
 (alley) galī
language bhāshā (H), zabān (U)
language course bhāshā

pāThy kram (H), lAngvez kōrs
large baRā
last āKhirī
 (previous) pichhlā
last week pichhle hafte
last Friday pichhle shukrvār kō (H), jumme kō (U)
last night kal rāt
what time is the last train to Varanasi? vārānasī ke liye āKhirī gāRī kitne baje jāyegī?
late der
sorry I'm late māf kījiye, mujhe der hōgayī
the train was late gāRī der se āyī
we must go — we'll be late hame chalnā chāhiye nahī tō der hōjāyegī
it's getting late ab der hō rahī hA
later bād me
 (again) phir
I'll come back later (said by man/woman) mA phir āugā/āugī
later on bād me
see you later on bād me milege
latest āKhirī
by Wednesday at the latest zyādā se zyādā budhvār tak
laugh (verb) hasnā
launderette, laundromat dhulāī kī dukān
laundry (clothes) dhulāi ke kapRe

(place) dhulāi ghar

In India nobody goes to the laundry: if they don't do their own, they send it out to a **dhobī**. Wherever you are staying, there will either be an in-house dhobī or one very close by to call on. The dhobī will take your dirty washing to the **dhobī ghāt**, a public clothes-washing area (the bank of a river for example), where it is sorted, soaped and given a good thrashing to beat the dirt out of it. Then it is hung out in the sun and once dry, taken to the ironing sheds. Your clothes will come back from the dhobi absolutely spotless, though this kind of violent treatment does take it out of them: buttons get lost and eventually the cloth starts to fray. Dry-cleaners are available in larger towns.

lavatory shawchālay (H), pāKhānā (U)
law kānūn
lawn ghās kā mAdān
lawyer vakīl
laxative julāb
lazy sust
lead (electrical) bijlī kā tār
(verb) āge le jānā
  where does this lead to? kis ōr le jātā hA?
leaf pattā
leaflet pannā
leak (noun) chhed
(verb) chūnā

the roof leaks chhat chū rahī hA
learn sīkhnā
least: not in the least hargiz nahī
  at least kam se kam
leather chamRā
leave (go away) chhūTnā
(leave behind) chhōRnā
  I am leaving tomorrow (said by man/woman) mA kal jā rahā/jārahī hū
  he left yesterday vō kal chalā gayā
  when does the bus for Shimla leave? shimlā ke liye bas kab chhuTTī hA?
  may I leave this here? (said by man/woman) kyā mA ise yahā chhōr sakTā/sakTī hū?
  I left my coat in the bar merā koT bār me chhūT gayā
leeks gandanā
left bāyā
  on the left bāyī taraf
  to the left bāyī taraf
  turn left bāyī taraf muRe
  there's none left kuchh nahī bachā
left-handed khabbā
left luggage (office) chhuTe sāmān kā daftar
leg Tāg
lemon nībū
lemonade lemaneD
lemon tea nībū vālī chāy
lend udhār denā
  will you lend me your ... ? āp mujhe āpnā ... udhār dege?

lens (of camera) lAns
lesbian lAsbiyan
less kam
    less than se kam
    less expensive kam
    mahangā
lesson sabaK, pāTh (H)
let (allow) karne denā
    will you let me know? (to
    man/woman) āp mujhe batā
    dege/degī?
    I'll let you know (said by
    man/woman) mA āpkō batā
    dūgā/dūgī
    let's go for something to eat
    chaliye, kuchh khāne chale
    let off: will you let me off at ...?
    āp mujhe ... par chhōR
    dege?
letter chiTThī, patr (H)
    do you have any letters for
    me? mere liye kōī chiTThī
    hA?
letterbox Dāk baks
lettuce salād
lever (noun) kamānī
library lAibrerī, pustakālay (H)
licence lāisAns
lid Dhaknā
lie (verb: tell untruth) jhūTh
    bōlnā
lie down leTnā
life zindagī, jīvan (H)
lifebelt jān bachāne kī peTī
lifeguard (man/woman) jān
    bachāne vālā/vālī
life jacket jān bachāne kī
    jākeT
lift (in building) lifT

could you give me a lift?
    mujhe savārī dege?
    would you like a lift? āpkō
    savārī karnī hA?
light (noun) rōshnī
    (not heavy) halkā
    do you have a light? (for
    cigarette) āpke pās māchis
    hA?
light green halkā harā
light bulb bijlī kā laTTū
    I need a new light bulb
    mujhe nayā laTTū chāhiye
lighter (cigarette) lāiTar
lightning bijlī
like (things) pasand karnā
    (people and things) acchhā
    lagnā
    I like it mujhe ye pasand hA
    I like going for walks mujhe
    ghūmne jānā pasand hA
    I like you (to a man) mujhe āp
    acche lagate hA
    (to a woman) mujhe āp acchī
    lagTī hA
    I don't like it mujhe ye
    pasand nahI
    do you like ...? āpkō ...
    pasand hA?
    I'd like a beer mujhe bīyar
    chāhiye
    I'd like to go swimming (said
    by man/woman) mA tArne jānā
    chāhtā/chāhtī hū
    would you like a drink? āpkō
    pīne ke liye kuchh chāhiye?
    would you like to go for a
    walk? (to man/woman) āp
    ghūmne jānā chāhte/

chāhtī hA?

what's it like? ye kAsā hA?

I want one like this mujhe Asā hī chāhiye

lime kāgzī nībū

lime cordial nībū kā sharbat

line (on paper) lakīr

(phone) phōn kī lāin

could you give me an outside line? mujhe bāhar kī lāin dege?

lips ōTh

lip salve ōTh par lagāne kī marham

lipstick lipsTik

liqueur likyōr

listen sunnā

litre liTar

a litre of white wine ek litar vāiT vāin

little thōRā

just a little, thanks thōRā sā, shukriyā

a little milk thōRā dūdh

a little bit more thōRā awr

live (verb) rahnā

we live together ham sab sāth rahte hA

dialogue

where do you live? (to man/woman) āp kahā rahte/rahtī hA?

I live in London (said by man/woman) mA landan me rahtā/rahtī hū

lively (person) zindādil

(town) chahalpahal vālā

liver (in body) jigar

(food) kalejī

loaf Dabal rōTī

lobby (in hotel) barāmdā

lobster baRī jhīngā machhlī

local sthānīy (H), mukāmī (U)

can you recommend a local restaurant? ās-pās me kōī acchhā restarā hA?

lock (noun) tālā

(verb) tālā band karnā

it's locked tālā band hA

lock in andar band kar dena

lock out bāhar se tālā na khulnā

I've locked myself out merī chābī andar chhūT gayī hA

locker (for luggage etc) tālevālī almārī

lollipop lawli pāp miThāi

London landan

long lambā

how long will it take to fix it? is kī marammat me kitnī der lagegī?

how long does it take? kitnī der lagegī?

a long time bahut der

one day/two days longer ek din/dō din awr zyādā

long-distance call dūr kī telīphōn kāl

look: I'm just looking, thanks (said by man/woman) mA sirf dekh rahā/rahī hū, shukriyā

you don't look well āp Thīk nahī lagte

look out! dekhte rahnā!

can I have a look? (said by man/woman) kyā mA dekh saktā/saktī hū?
look after dekhbhāl karnā
look at kō dekhnā
look for talāsh karnā
I'm looking for ... mA ... kī talāsh me hū
look forward to intzār karnā
I'm looking forward to it (said by man/woman) mA is kā intzār kar rahā/rahī hū
loose (handle etc) Dhīlā
lorry lārī
lose khōnā
I've lost my way (said by man/woman) mA rastā khō gayā/khō gayī
I'm lost, I want to get to ... (said by man/woman) mA bhaTak gayā/gayī mujhe ... jānā hA
I've lost my bag merā jhōlā khō gayā
lost property (office) khōye sāmān kā daftar
lot: a lot, lots bahut zyādā
not a lot zyādā nahī
a lot of people bahut lōg
a lot bigger kāfī baRā
I like it a lot mujhe ye bahut pasand hA
lotion lōshan
loud ūchā
lounge (in house, hotel) bAThak
(in airport) ārāmghar
love (noun) pyār, prem (H)
(verb) pyār karnā
I love India mujhe bhārat

bahut acchhā lagtā hA
lovely sundar
low (prices) kam
(bridge) nīchā
luck kismat, bhāgy (H)
(good fortune) achhī kismat, achhā bhāgy (H)
good luck! merī duā!
luggage sāmān
luggage trolley sāmān le jāne vālī Trālī
lump (on body) gumTā
lunch dōpahar kā khānā
lungs phephRe
luxurious Ash-ārām deh
luxury Ash-ārām

M

machine mashīn
mad (insane) pāgal
(angry) āgbabūlā
magazine paTrikā (H), risālā (U)
maid (in hotel) nawkrānī
maiden name shādī se pahle kā nām
mail (noun) Dāk
(verb) Dāk me Dālnā
is there any mail for me? merī kōī Dāk hA?
could you mail this for me? ye Dāk me Dāl dege?
see **post**
mailbox Dāk baks
main sabse baRā, Khās
main course Khās khānā
main post office baRā Dāk

Khānā
main road baRī saRak
mains switch baRā svich
make (brand name) mek
(verb) banānā
 I make it ... (amount) mere
 hisāb se ... bante h**A**
 what is it made of? ye kis
 chīz kā banā h**A**?
make-up banāv-singār
malaria maleriyā

The malaria-carrying
anopheles mosquito is
particularly common in
humid areas with an abundance of
wetlands along the sub-Himalayan
belt known as the terrai. Most
mosquitoes, however, are harmless
if irritating, and the percentage of
visitors who contract malaria is
small. Precautions include mosquito
nets over the bed, mosquito
repellents for the skin, smoke coils,
and electric repellents. Visitors are
advised to check with their doctor
prior to departure and to take any
suggested precautionary medicine.

man ādmī
manager mAnejar
 can I see the manager?
 mujhe mAnejar se milnā
 h**A**?
manageress mAnezarānī
mango ām
manual (with manual gears) hāth
 se chalne vāle gīyar
many bahut

not many bahut nahī
map (city plan) Khākā
 (road map, geographical) nakshā
 network map saRkō̃ kā
 nakshā
March mārch
margarine marjarīn
market bāzār
 see **bargaining**
marmalade marmleD
married: I'm married m**A**
 shādīshudā hū̃
 are you married? āp
 shādishudā h**A**?
mascara maskārā
match (football etc) m**A**ch
matches māchis
material (fabric) kapRā
matter: it doesn't matter kōī
 bāt nahī
 what's the matter? kyā bāt
 h**A**?
mattress gaddā
May mayī
may: may I have another one?
 ek awr dījiye
 may I come in? m**A** andar
 āū̃?
 may I see it? (said by
 man/woman) m**A** ise dekh
 saktā/saktī hū̃?
 may I sit here? (said by
 man/woman) m**A** yahā̃ b**A**Th
 saktā/saktī hū̃?
maybe shāyad
mayonnaise mayōnez
me* mujhe
 that's for me ye mere liye
 h**A**

send it to me ye mujhe bhej denā
me too mujhe bhī
meal khānā, bhōjan (H)

dialogue

did you enjoy your meal?
āpkō khānā acchhā lagā?
it was excellent, thank you
bahut baRhiyā, shukriyā

mean (verb) matlab hōnā
what do you mean? is sab kā kyā matlab hA?

dialogue

what does this word
mean? is shabd kā kyā matlab hA? (H), is lafz kā kyā matlab hA? (U)
it means ... in English is kō angrezī me ... kahte hA

measles khasrā
German measles khasrā
meat gōsht, mās (H)
mechanic misTrī
medicine davā
medium (adj: size) bīch kā
medium-sized bīch ke māp kā
meet milnā
nice to meet you āp se milkar baRī Khushī huī
where shall I meet you? āpse kahā milū?
meeting mulaKāt

meeting place milne kī jagah
melon Kharbūzā
men ādmī
mend marammat karnā
could you mend this for me?
is kī marammat kar dege?
men's room purush shawchālay (H), mardānā pākhānā (U)
menswear mardāne kapRe
mention (verb) zikr karnā
don't mention it! bas, rahne dījiye!
menu menyū
may I see the menu, please?
mujhe menyū dikhāiye
see menu reader page 222
message sandesā (H), pAgām (U)
are there any messages for me? mere liye kōī sandesā hA?
I want to leave a message for ... (said by man/woman) mA ... ke liye ek sandesā denā chahtā/chāhtī huī
metal dhāt
metre mīTar
microwave (oven) māikrōvev
midday dōpahar
at midday dōpahar ko
middle: in the middle bīch me
in the middle of the night ādhī rat kō
the middle one bīch vālā
midnight ādhī rāt
at midnight ādhī rāt kō
might: I might shāyad
I might not shāyad nahī

I might want to stay another **day** shāyad ek din awr Thaharnā chāhūgā

migraine ādhāsīsī

mild (taste: not hot) kam mirch vālā

(weather) suhāvnā

mile mīl

milk dūdh

millimetre milīmīTar

mind: never mind! jāne dījiye!

I've changed my **mind** merā irādā badal gayā

dialogue

do you **mind** if I open the window? āpkō kōī etrāj na hō tō mA khiRkī khōl dū?

no, I don't **mind** jī nahī, mujhe kōī etrāj nahī

mine* merā

it's **mine** ye merā hA

mineral water bōtal vālā pānī

mints piparminT

minute minaT

in a **minute** ek minaT me

just a **minute!** ek minaT rukō!

mirror āīnā

Miss kumārī (H), muhtarmā (U)

miss: I missed the bus bas chhūT gayī

missing gāyab

one of my ... is **missing** merā ... gāyab hōgayā

there's a suitcase **missing** baksa gāyab hōgayā

mist kuhrā

mistake galtī

I think there's a **mistake** mere Khyāl me kahī galtī hA

sorry, I've made a **mistake** māf kījiye, mujh se galtī hōgayī

misunderstanding galatfahmī

mix-up: sorry, there's been a mix-up māf kījiye, kuchh gaRbaRī hōgayī

mobile phone mōbāil phōn

modern ājkal kā, ādhunik (H)

modern art gallery ādhunik chitrshālā

moisturizer namī dene vālā

moment: I won't be a moment (said by man/woman) mA abhī āyā/āyī

Monday sōmvār (H), pīr (U)

money pAsā

monkey bandar

monsoon barsāt kā mawsam

month mahīnā

monument yādgār, smārak (H)

moon chād

moped chhōTī mōTar sāikil

more* zyādā, awr

can I have some **more** water, please? mujhe kuchh awr pānī chāhiye

more expensive/interesting zyādā mahangā/dilchasp

more than 50 pachās se zyādā

more than that is se zyādā

a lot **more** awr zyādā

dialogue

would you like some
more? (to man/woman) āp
thōRā awr lege/legī?
no, no more for me, thanks
bas, awr nahī, shukriyā
how about you? awr
āpkō?
I don't want any more,
thanks mujhe awr nahī
chāhiye, shukriyā

morning subah
 this morning āj subah
 in the morning subah kō
mosque masjid
mosquito macchhar
 see bite
mosquito net macchhardānī
mosquito repellent macchhar
 mārne ki davā
most: I like this one most of all
 mujhe ye sabse zyādā
 pasand hA
 most of the time zyāda vakt
 most tourists zyādā sAlānī
mostly zyādātar
mother mā, matā (H), vālidā
 (U)
mother-in-law sās
motorbike mōTar sāikil

 It's worth considering
buying a motorbike,
scooter or moped as a
way of getting round India. Garages
and repair shops are a good place to
find them. You can expect to pay half

to two-thirds the original price for a
bike in reasonable condition and,
given the right bargaining skills, you
can sell it again later for a similar
price – perhaps to another foreign
traveller. A certain amount of
bureaucracy is involved in
transferring vehicle ownership, but a
garage should be able to put you on
to a broker ('auto consultant') who,
for a modest commission, will help
you find a seller or buyer and do the
necesssary paperwork.

motorboat injan se chalnevālī
 kishtī
motorway khulī saRak
mountain pahāR
 in the mountains pahāR par
mountaineering pahāR kī
 chaRhāī karnā,
 parvatārōhan (H)
mouse chūhā
moustache mūchh
mouth muh
mouth ulcer muh kā chhālā
move (remove) hatānā
 (go away) chalā jānā
 he's moved to another room
 vō dūsre kamre me chalā
 gayā
 could you move your car?
 apnī kār haTā lījiye
 could you move up a little?
 āge baRh jāiye
 where has it moved to? yahā
 se badalkar kahā chalā
 gayā?
 where has it been moved to?

ise kahā le gaye?
movie 'film'
movie theater sinemā
  see **cinema**
Mr shrī (H), janāb (U)
Mrs shrīmatī (H), muhtarmā
  (U)
much bahut
  much better/worse zyādā
  behtar/zyādā Kharāb
  much hotter zyādā garam
  not much zyādā nahī
  not very much bahut zyādā
  nahī
  I don't want very much
  mujhe zyādā nahī chāhiye
mud kīchaR
mug (for drinking) pyālā
  I've been mugged mujhe lūt
  liyā
mum mā
mumps mamps
museum ajāyab ghar

Most museums are open
on Sundays but are closed
one day during the week
and on public holidays. Entry is
either free or very cheap.

mushrooms khumbī
music sangīt
musician (man/woman) gāne
  vālā/vālī, sangīt kār (H)
Muslim (adj) 'muslim',
  musalmān
mussels sīp kā jhīngar
must*: I must do it mujhe
  karnā chāhiye

I mustn't drink alcohol mujhe
  sharāb nahī pīnī chāhiye
mustard sarsō
my* merā
  it's my car ye merī kār hA
  that's my towel ye merā
  tawliyā hA
myself: I'll do it myself (said by
  man/woman) mA ise Khud
  karūgā/karūgī
  by myself Khud

N

nail (finger) nākhūn
  (metal) kīl
nailbrush nākhūn sāf karne
  kā burush
nail varnish nākhūn kī pālish
name nām
  my name's John merā nām
  Jōhn hA
  what's your name? āpkā nām
  kyā hA?
  **what is the name of this
  street?** is galī kā nām kyā hA?
napkin nApkin
nappy bacche kā pōtRā
narrow (street) tang
nasty bahut burā
national rāshTrīy (H), Kawmī
  (U)
nationality rāshTrīytā (H),
  Kawmiat (U)
natural kudratī, prākritik (H)
nausea matlī
navy (blue) gahrā nīlā
near nazdīk, ke pās

is it near the city centre? kyā ye bīch shahar ke pās hA?

do you go near the Kutub Minar? kyā āp kutub mīnār ke nazdīk jāte hA?

where is the nearest ...? sab se nazdīk ... kahā hA?

nearby pās me

nearly lagbhag (H), taKrīban (U)

necessary zarūrī

neck gardan

necklace gale kā hār

necktie Tāī

need: I need ... mujhe ... chāhiye

do I need to pay? kyā mujhe pAsā denā hõgā?

needle suī

negative (film) negATiv

neither: neither (one) of them dõnõ me se koī nahī

neither ... nor ... na ... na ...

Nepal nApāl

Nepali nApālī

nephew (brother's son) bhatījā
(sister's son) bhānjā

net (in sport) jāl

Netherlands hālenD

never kabhī nahī

dialogue

have you ever been to Goa? (to man/woman) āp kabhī goā gaye/gayī hA?
no, never, I've never been there (said by man/woman) jī nahī, kabhī nahī gayā/gayī

new nayā

news (radio, TV etc) Khabar, samāchār (H)

newsagent's aKhbār vālā

newspaper aKhbār

newspaper kiosk aKhbār kā sTāl

New Year nayā sāl

Happy New Year! nayā sāl mubāraK!

New Year's Eve nav varsh ki purv sandhyā (H)

New Zealand nyuzīlAnD

New Zealander: I'm a New Zealander (said by man) mA nyuzīlAnD kā rahnevālā hū
(said by woman) mA nyuzīlAnD ki rahnevālī hū

next aglā
(after that) ke bād

the next turning/street on the left bāyī taraf aglā mõR/aglī galī

at the next stop agle sTāp par

next week agle hafte

next to ke pās

nice acchhā

niece (brother's daughter) bhatījī
(sister's daughter) bhānjī

night rāt

at night rāt kõ

good night namaste (H), khudā hāfiz (U)

dialogue

do you have a single room for one night? āpke pās ek

rāt ke liye singal kamrā
hA?
yes, madam jī hā,
memsāhib
how much is it per night?
ek rāt kā kyā kirāyā hA?
**it's 100 rupees for one
night** ek rāt ke saw
rupaye
thank you, I'll take it
shukriyā, mA ise le lūgī

nightclub nāit klab
nightdress rāt kī pōshāk
night porter rāt kā darbān
no nahī
  I've no change mere pās
  rezgārī nahī
  there's no ... left kōī ... nahī
  rahā
  no way! hargiz nahī!
  oh no! (upset) hāy re!
nobody kōī nahī
  there's nobody there vahā
  kōī nahī hA
noise shōr
noisy: it's too noisy ye bahut
  shōr bharā hA
non-alcoholic binā sharāb
  vālā
none kōī nahī
nonsmoking compartment
  bīRī sigreT manāhī vālā
  Dibbā
noon dōpahar
  at noon dōpahar kō
no-one kōī nahī
nor: nor do I mA bhī nahī
normal sādhāran

north uttar (**H**), shumāl (**U**)
  in the north uttar me
  to the north uttar kī taraf
  north of Delhi dillī ke uttar
  me
northeast uttar pūrvī (**H**),
  shumāl mashrīKī (**U**)
northern uttarīy (**H**), shumālī
  (**U**)
Northern Ireland uttarī
  āyarlAnD (**H**), shumālī
  āyarlAnD (**U**)
northwest uttar pashchim
  (**H**), shumāl magribī (**U**)
Norway nārve
Norwegian nārvejian
nose nāk
not* nahī
  no, I'm not hungry jī nahī,
  mujhe bhūkh nahī lagī
  I don't want any, thank you
  mujhe kuchh nahī chāhiye,
  shukriyā
  it's not necessary ye zarūrī
  nahī
  I didn't know that majhe ye
  mālūm nahī thā
  not that one – this one vō
  nahī ye vālā
note (banknote) nōT
notebook nōTbuk
notepaper (for letters) chiTThī
  kā kāgaz
nothing kuchh nahī
  nothing for me, thanks mere
  liye kuchh nahī, shukriyā
  nothing else awr kuchh nahī
novel nōval, upanyās (**H**)
November navambar

now ab
number nambar
(figure) gintī, sankhyā (H)
I've got the wrong number mAne galat nambar lagāyā
what is your phone number? āpkā phōn nambar kyā hA?
number plate nambar pleT
nurse nars
nut (for bolt) Dhibrī
nuts girīdār mevā

O

occupied (toilet, telephone) Khālī nahī
o'clock* baje
October akTūbar
odd (strange) ajīb
of* kā
off (lights) band
it's just off ... ... se saTā huā hA
we're off tomorrow ham kal chale jāyege
offensive (language, behaviour) burā
office (place of work) daftar
officer (said to policeman) thānedār sāhab
often aksar
not often aksar nahī
how often are the buses? base kitnī bār ātī hA?
oil tel
ointment marham
OK Thīk
are you OK? āp Thīk hA?

is that OK with you? kyā ye Thīk hA?
is it OK to ...? kyā ... Thīk hA?
that's OK, thanks ye Thīk hA, shukriyā
I'm OK (nothing for me) mere liye kāfī hA
(I feel OK) mA Thīk hū
is this train OK for ...? kyā ye gāRī ... ke liye Thīk rahegī?
I said I'm sorry, OK? mA ne māfī māg lī, Thīk hA nā?
old (man/woman) būRhā/buRhiyā
(thing) purānā

dialogue

> **how old are you?** āpkī umar kyā hA?
> **I'm 25** (said by man/woman) mA pacchīs sāl kā/kī hū
> **and you?** awr āp?

old-fashioned purāne Dharre kā
old town shahar kā purānā hissā
in the old town shahar ke purāne hisse me
omelette āmleT
on* par
on the street galī par
on the beach samandar ke kināre par
is it on this road? kyā ye isī saRak par hA?
on the plane havāī jahāz me

on Saturday shanivār kō
on television Telīvizan par
I haven't got it on me mere
pās nahī̃ hA
this one's on me (drink) ab
merī bārī hA
the light wasn't on battī nahī̃
jal rahī Thī
what's on tonight? āj rāt kō
kyā chal rahā hA?
once (one time) ek bār
at once (immediately) fawran
one* ek
the white one safed vālā
one-way ticket singal Tikat
see ticket
onion pyāj
only sirf, keval (H)
only one sirf ek
it's only 6 o'clock sirf chhA
baje hA
I've only just got here (said by
man/woman) mA abhī yahā̃
āyā/āyī hū̃
open (adj) khulā
(verb: something) khōlnā
(of shop etc) khulnā
when do you open? āp kab
khōlte hA?
I can't get it open mujh se ye
nahī̃ khultā
in the open air khule mAdān
me
opening times khulne kā
vaKt
open ticket khulā TikaT
opera āperā, gīt nāTy (H)
operation (medical) āpreshan
operator (telephone) āpreTar

opposite: the opposite
direction sāmne kī taraf
the bar opposite sāmne kā
bār
opposite my hotel mere
hōTal ke sāmne
optician Anak banāne vālā
or yā
orange (fruit) santarā
(colour) nārangī
fizzy orange gAs vālā santare
kā ras
orange drink santare kā
sharbat
orange juice santare kā ras
orchestra awrkesTrā, vādy
manDalī (H)
order: can we order now? (in
restaurant) āp khāne kā ārDar
lẽge?
I've already ordered, thanks
mAne ārDar de diyā,
shukriyā
I didn't order this mAne ye
nahī̃ mãgā
out of order Thīk-Thāk nahī̃
ordinary māmūlī, sādhāran
(H)
other dūsrā
the other one dūsrā
the other day hāl hī me
I'm waiting for the others mA
awr lōgõ kī intzār me hū̃
do you have any others?
āpke pās awr kōī hA?
otherwise varnā
our* hamārā
ours* hamārā
it's ours ye hamārā hA

out: he's out vō bahar gayā hA

three kilometres out of town shahar se Tīn kilō mīTar dūr

outdoors bahar khule me

outside ke bāhar

can we sit outside? chaliye, bāhar bAThe?

oven bhaTTī

over: over here idhar

over there udhar

over 500 pāch saw se zyādā

it's over ye Khatm hōgayā

overcharge: you've overcharged me āpne zyādā pAse liye hA

overcoat ōvarkōT

overlooking: I'd like a room overlooking the courtyard mujhe Asā kamrā chāhiye jahā se āngan dīkh sake

overnight (travel) rāt bhar kā safar

overtake bagal se āge nikal jānā

owe: how much do I owe you? mujhe āpko kitne pAse dene hA?

own: my own ... merā apnā ...

are you on your own? (to man/woman) kyā āp akele/akelī hA?

I'm on my own (said by man/woman) mA akelā/akelīa hū

owner (man/woman) mālik/mālkin

P

pack (verb) sāmān bādhnā

a pack of ... ... kā banDal

package (parcel) pārsal

package holiday pAkej hōliDe

packed lunch Dibbe me band dōpahar kā khānā

packet: a packet of cigarettes sigreT kā pAkeT

padlock kunDe me lagāne vālā tālā

page (of book) pannā, prishTh (H)

could you page Mr ...? meharbānī karke janāb ... kō bulāiye?

pain dard

I have a pain here mujhe yahā dard hA

painful dardnāk

painkillers dard miTāne kī davā

paint (noun) rōgan

painting tasvīr, chitr (H)

pair: a pair of ... ... kā jōRā

Pakistan pākistān

Pakistani pākistānī

palace mahal

pale pīlā

pale blue halkā nīlā

pan patīlā

panties jāghiyā

pants (underwear) jāghiyā (US) patlūn

pantyhose TāiTs

paper kāgaz

(newspaper) aKhbār

a piece of paper kāgaz kā pannā

paper handkerchiefs kāgaz ke rumāl

parcel parsal

pardon me? (didn't understand) phir kahiye?

parents mābāp

parents-in-law sās sasur

park (noun) pārk
(verb) gāRī khaRī karnā
can I park here? (said by man/woman) kyā mA yahā gāRī khaRī kar saktā/saktī hū?

parking lot kār pārk

part (noun) hissā

partner (boyfriend, girlfriend etc) sāthī

party (group) Tōlī
(celebration) dāvat

pass (in mountains) darrā

passenger musāfir, yātrī (H)

passport pāspōrT

 A valid passport is essential and you should keep it with you at all times, tucked away safely in a body belt or something similar. It is advisable to take photocopies of the first two or three pages and to keep these separate from the original as a safeguard in the event that your passport is lost or stolen.

past*: in the past gujre jamāne me

just past the information **office** jānkārī ke daftar ke pare

path rāstā

pattern Dhāchā

pavement paTrī
on the pavement paTrī par

pay (verb) pAse denā
can I pay, please? (said by man/woman) kyā mA pAsa de saktā/saktī hū?
it's already paid for iske pAse de diye hA

dialogue

who's paying? kawn pAse degā?
I'll pay (said by man/woman) mA dūgā/dūgī?
no, you paid last time, I'll pay (said by man/woman) nahī nahī, āpne pichhli bār diye the, ab mA dūgā/dūgī

payphone sikke lene vālā sārvajanik phōn

peaceful shānt (H), pur-aman (U)

peach āRū

peanuts mūngphalī

pear nāshpātī

pearl mōtī

peas maTar

peculiar (taste, custom) ajīb

pedestrian crossing pAdal pār karne kā rāstā

peg (for washing) kapRō kī

chimTī

(for tent) KhūTī

pen Kalam

pencil pAnsil

penfriend pAnfrAnD

penicillin pAnsilin

penknife chōTā chākū

pensioner (man/woman)

penshan pāne vālā/vālī

people lōg

the other people in the hotel

hōTal me dūsre lōg

too many people bahut lōg

pepper (spice) kālī mirch

(vegetable) shimlā mirch

peppermint (sweet)

piparminT

per: per night ek rāt kā

how much per day? har rōz

(kā) kitnā?

per cent fī sadī

perfect bilkul sahī

perfume itar

perhaps shāyad

perhaps not shāyad nahī

period (of time) muddat, avdhi

(H)

(menstruation) māhvārī, māsik

dharm (H)

perm parm

permit (noun) parmiT

person vyakti (H), shaKhs (U)

personal stereo nijī sTīriō

petrol peTrōl

petrol can peTrōl kā

kanasTar

petrol station peTrōl sTashan

pharmacy davāKhānā

Pharmacies can usually advise on minor medical problems. Most medicines are available without prescription (always check the sell-by date).

phone (noun) Telīphōn

(verb) Teliphōn karnā

It's becoming increasingly easy to make phone calls to and from India, where even small towns now have phone booths from which you can make direct international calls. However, as antiquated systems are being replaced by new technology, this can lead to confusing changes to phone numbers. Booths often provide a list of changes to the telephone prefix numbers. The quickest and most reliable way to make a call is from an attended phone booth, where you pay after finishing your call.

phone book Telīphōn kī
kitāb

phone box Teliphōn būTh

phonecard Telīphōn kārD

phone number phōn namber

photo phōtō

excuse me, could you take a photo of us? suniye, kyā āp hamārī phōtō khīch dege?

photography

It is always best to ask permission before taking

a picture of somebody. Orthodox Muslims believe that only God can create an image and find representational art objectionable. Hindus do not like pictures of idols and photography in temples is not tolerated; neither is photography of anything 'sensitive' or 'strategic', such as bridges, airports and military bases. The general rule is – if in doubt, don't.

phrase book fiKrō kī kitāb
piano piyānō
pickpocket (man/woman) jeb katrā/katrī
pick up: will you be there to pick me up? āp vahā se mujhe le jāyege?
picnic piknik
picture tasvīr, chitr (H)
pie pakvān
piece TukRā
  a piece of ... ... kā ek TukRā
pill gōlī
  I'm on the pill mA gōlī khā rahī hū
pillow takiyā
pillow case takiye kā gilāf
pin (noun) ālpin
pineapple anānās
pineapple juice anānās kā ras
pink gulābī
pipe (for smoking) pāip
  (for water) nalī
pistachio pistā
pity: it's a pity! baRe afsōs kī bāt hA!

pizza pītzā
place jagah
  at your place āp ke yahā
  at his place uske yahā
plain (not patterned) sādā
plane havāī jahāz
  by plane havāī jahāz se
plant pawdhā
plaster cast palastar kī Dhāl
plasters palastar
plastic plāsTik
  (credit cards) bAnk kārD
plastic bag plāsTik kā thAlā
plate plet
  (metal) thālī
platform pletfāram
  which platform is it for Jaipur? jApur ke liye kawnsā pleTfāram hA?
play (verb) khelnā
  (noun: in theatre) nāTak
playground khel kā mAdān
pleasant suhāvnā
please meharbānī karke, kripayā (H)
  yes, please jī hā
  could you please ...? meharbānī karke ...
  please don't ye mat kījiye
  can I have some ..., please? mujhe ..., chāhiye
  two beers, please dō bīyar, dījiye
pleased: pleased to meet you āp se milkar baRī Khushī huī
pleasure: my pleasure koī bāt nahī
plenty: plenty of ... kāfī ...

there's plenty of time kāfī
vaKT hA

that's plenty, thanks bas, ye
kāfī hA, shukriyā

pliers chimTī

plug (electrical) bijlī kā plag
(for car) injan kā plag
(in sink) DāT

plumber nalsāz

pm dōpahar ke bād

pocket jeb

point: two point five do
dashamlav pāch
there's no point is me kōī
tuk nahī

poisonous jahrilā

police pulis
call the police! pulis bulāō!

policeman pulis kā sipāhī

police station thānā

policewoman pulis kī mahilā
sipāhī (H)

polish (noun) pālish

polite vinamr (H), salīKedār
(U)

polluted mAlā, dūshit (H)

pony TaTTū

pool (for swimming) tArne kā
tālāb

poor (not rich) garīb
(quality) ghaTiyā

pop music pawp sangīt

pop singer (man/woman) pawp
gānā gānevālā/gānevālī

popular lōkpriy (H), ām
pasand (U)

population ābādī

pork sūar kā gōsht

port (for boats) bandargāh

(drink) pōrt sharāb

porter (in hotel) darbān

portrait tasvīr

posh (restaurant, people) shāndār

possible mumkin, sambhav
(H)
is it possible to ...? kyā ...
mumkin hA?
as ... as possible jitnā ...
hōsake

post (noun: mail) Dāk
(verb) Dāk me Dālnā
could you post this for me?
ye Dāk me Dāl dege?

Mail can take anything
from three days to four
weeks to get to or from
India, depending largely on where
exactly you are; two weeks is about
the norm. Ideally, you should have
mail franked in front of you. Most
post offices are open Mon–Fri
10am–5pm and Sat 10am–noon, but
big city post offices keep longer
hours (Mon–Fri 9.30am–6pm, Sat
9.30am– 1pm). You can also buy
stamps at big hotels.
Poste Restante services throughout
the country are pretty reliable,
though how long individual offices
hang on to letters is more or less at
their own discretion; if a letter is
likely to be waiting a month or more
for you, it makes sense for your
expected arrival date to be marked
on it. Letters are filed alphabetically;
in larger offices you sort through
them yourself. To avoid misfiling,

Pl

104

your name should be printed clearly, with the surname in large capitals and underlined, but it is still a good idea to check under your first name too, just in case. Have letters addressed to you c/o Poste Restante, GPO (if it's the main post office you want), and the name of the town and state.

Sending a parcel out of India can be quite a performance. First you have to have it cleared by customs at the post office (they often don't bother, but check), then you take it to a tailor and agree a price to have it wrapped in cheap cotton cloth (which you will have to go and buy yourself), stitched up and sealed with wax. Next, take it to the post office, fill in and attach the relevant customs forms (it's best to tick the box marked 'gift' and give its value as less than 1,000 rupees or 'no commercial value', to avoid bureaucratic entanglements), buy your stamps, watch the parcel being franked, and dispatch it. Parcels should not be more than a metre long or weigh more than 20kg. Surface mail is incredibly cheap but takes an average of six months to arrive.

postbox Dāk baks
postcard pōsTkarD
postcode Dāk kā kōD
poster pōsTar
poste restante chiTThī jamā karne vālā Dāk-Khānā
post office Dāk-Khānā
potato ālū

potato chips krisp
pots and pans bhānDe-bartan
pottery miTTī ke bartan
pound (money) pawnD (pAsā) (weight) pawnD (vazan)
power cut bijlī kī katawtī
power point bijlī kā sakeT
practise: I want to practise my Hindi (said by man/woman) mA apnī hindī istemāl karnā chāhtā/chāhtī hū
prawns jhīngā
prefer: I prefer ... mujhe ... jyādā pasand hA
pregnant garbhvatī (H), hāmilā (U)
prescription (for medicine) nusKhā
present (gift) tōhfā
president (of country) rāshTrpati (H), sadar (U)
pretty Khūbsuarat
it's pretty expensive ye kāfī mahangā hA
price kīmat
priest purōhit (H), imām (U)
prime minister pradhān mantrī (H), vazīre-āzam (U)
printed matter chhapī huī chīz
prison jel
private nijī
private bathroom nijī gusalKhānā
probably shāyad
problem maslā, samasyā (H)
no problem! kōī dikkat nahī!
program(me) (noun) prōgrām,

kārykram (H)

promise: I promise (said by man/woman) mA vādā kartā/kartī hū

pronounce: how is this pronounced? iskō kAse bōltē hA?

properly (repaired, locked etc) Thīk tarah se

Protestant prōTAsTAnT īsāī

public convenience shawchālay (H), pāKhānā (U)

public holiday sarkārī chhuTTī

 The following are public holidays in India:

January/February **īdulfitar** end of Ramadan

26 January **gantantra divas** Republic Day

February/March **hōlī** Festival of Colours

April/May **īdmilād** Id-e-Milad (Muslim festival)

July/August **rakshā bandhan** Raksha Bandhan (Hindu festival)

15 August **svatantratā divas** Independence Day

August/September **janmāshtamī** Krishna's birthday

2 October **gāndhījayantī** Mahatma Gandhi's birthday

September/October **dashaharā** Dussehra (Hindu festival marking the triumph of good over evil)

October/November **divālī** Festival of Lights

October/November **gurūnānak janmdivas** Guru Nanak's birthday

25 December **krismas** Christmas

See **Hindi Signs** page 184 and **Urdu Signs** page 202.

pudding (dessert) miThāī

pull khīchnā

pullover sveTar

puncture panchar

Punjabi panjābī

purple bAjnī

purse (for money) baTuā (US) hAnD bAg

push dhakkā denā

pushchair bacchā gāRī

put rakhnā

where can I put ...? (said by man/woman) mA ... kahā rakh saktā/saktī hū?

could you put us up for the night? āpke pās ek rāt Thaharne ke liye jagah hōgī?

pyjamas pāyjāmā

Q

quality Khāsiyat, gun (H)

quarantine kvāranTīn

quarter chawthāi hissā

quayside: on the quayside jahāz kī gōdī par

question savāl, prashn (H)

queue (noun) Katār, pankti (H)

quick jaldī

that was quick ye bahut jaldī kar liyā

what's the quickest way

there? vahā bahut jaldi kAse
jāye?

fancy a quick drink? thōRī
der ke liye kuchh pīne
chalege?

quickly jaldī se

quiet (place, hotel) shānt

 quiet! chup rahō!, Khāmōsh!
 (U)

quite (fairly) kuchh had tak
 (very) kāfī

 that's quite right ye bilkul
 Thīk hA

 quite a lot kāfī sārā

R

rabbit Khargōsh

race (for runners, cars) dawR

racket (tennis, squash) ballā

radiator (of car, in room)
 reDiyeTar

radio reDiō

 on the radio reDiō par

rail: by rail gāRī se

railway relve

rain bārish

 in the rain bārish me

 it's raining bārish hō rahī hA

raincoat barsātī

rape (noun) balātkār (H),
 zabardastī (U)

rare (uncommon) birlā

rash (on skin) Khārish

raspberry rasbharī

rat chūhā

rate (for changing money) dar

rather: it's rather good ye tō

acchā hA

 I'd rather ... acchhā hō ki
 mA ...

razor ustarā

razor blades ustare kā bleD

read paRhnā

ready tayyār

 are you ready? āp tayyār hA?

 I'm not ready yet mA abhī
 tayyār nahī

dialogue

> **when will it be ready?** ye
> kab tayyār hōgā?
> **it should be ready in a
> couple of days** dō din me
> tayyār hō jāyegā

real aslī

really vāKai

 I'm really sorry mujhe bahut
 afsōs hA

 that's really great bahut
 baRhiyā

 really? (doubt) sachmuch!
 (polite interest) acchhā tō!

rear lights pichhlī battiyā

rearview mirror pīchhe
 dekhne kā āinā

reasonable (prices etc) zāyaz

receipt rasīd

recently hāl hī me

reception (in hotel) risepshan
 DAsk

 (party) dāvat

 at reception risepshan me

reception desk risepshan

receptionist risepshanisT

recognize pahchānnā
recommend: could you recommend ...? āp batāyege ...?
record (music) rikārD
red lāl
red wine rAD vāin
refund (noun) pAse kī vāpsī
can I have a refund? merā pAsā vāpas kar de
region ilāKā
registered: by registered mail rajisTrī Dāk se
registration number rajisTreshan nambar
relative (noun) rishtedār
religion dharm (H), mazhab (U)

It's important always to show due respect to religious buildings, shrines, images, and people at prayer. When entering a temple or mosque, remove your shoes and leave them at the door (socks are OK and protect your feet from the burning hot ground). Some temples – Jain ones in particular – do not allow you to enter wearing or carrying leather articles. Dress conservatively and try not to be obtrusive. In a mosque, you'll not normally be allowed in at prayer time; in a Hindu temple, you are not usually allowed into the inner sanctum; and at a Buddhist **stūpa** or monument you should always walk round clockwise. Hindus are very

superstitious about taking photographs of images of deities and inside temples; if in doubt, desist. Do not take photos of funerals or cremations.

remember: I don't remember mujhe yād nahī
I remember mujhe yād hA
do you remember? āpkō yād hA?
rent (noun: for apartment etc) kirāyā
(verb: car etc) kirāye par lenā
for rent kirāye ke liye

dialogue

I'd like to rent a car mujhe kirāye par kār chāhiye
for how long? kītnī der ke liye?
two days dō din
this is our range hamāre pās ye sab hA
I'll take the ... (said by man/woman) mA ... le lūgā/le lūgī
is that with unlimited mileage? jitnī dūr chāhe ise le jā sakte hA?
it is jī hā
can I see your licence please? apnā lāisens dikhāiye
and your passport awr apnā pāspōrt
is insurance included? kyā is me bīmā bhī shāmil

hA?
**yes, but you pay the first
1,000 rupees** jī hā, magar
āp pahle ek hazar rupaye
dījiye
**can you leave a deposit of
500 rupees?** āp pāch saw
rupaye zamānat ke tawr
par de sakte hA?

rented car kirāye kī kār
repair (verb) marammat karnā
  can you repair it? āp iskī
  marammet kar dege?
repeat phir kahnā
  could you repeat that? phir
  kahiye
reservation rizarveshan
  I'd like to make a reservation
  kyā mere liye rizarv kar
  dege?

dialogue

I have a reservation merā
rizarveshan hA
yes sir, what name please?
jī hā, āpkā nām?

reserve rizarv karnā

dialogue

**can I reserve a table for
tonight?** mere liye āj
shām kō ek mez rizarv
kar dege?
**yes madam, for how many
people?** jī hā, kitne lōgō

for two dō ke liye
and for what time? kitne
baje ke liye?
for eight o'clock āTh baje
ke liye
**and could I have your
name please?** āpkā nām
kyā hA?

rest: I need a rest mujhe
ārām karnā hA
  the rest of the group bāKī
  lōg
restaurant restōrā

There are hundreds of
eating places to suit most
budgets, ranging from the
cheap roadside **Dhābā** or café,
where the choice is limited but the
food wholesome, to plush air-
conditioned restaurants serving
Indian, Chinese and continental
cuisine. More cosmopolitan dining is
available in cities such as Delhi and
Bombay, especially in five-star
hotels. Tourist restaurants in the
more popular centres cater for
budget travellers by serving
pancakes, porridge, omelettes,
milkshakes and other Western food,
although the quality is often
disappointing.

restaurant car restōrā kā
  Dibbā
rest room shawchālay (**H**),
  pāKhānā (**U**)

where is the rest room?
shawchālay kahā hA?

I have to go to the rest room
mujhe shawchālay jānā hA

(politer) mujhe bāth rūm
jānā hA

retired: I'm retired (said by
man/woman) mA riTāyar
hogayā/hogayī

return: a return to ... ... ke liye
ek vāpsī

return ticket vāpsī TikaT
see **ticket**

reverse charge call rivars
chārj kawl

reverse gear rivars gīyar

revolting ghinōnā

rib paslī

rice chāval

(cooked) bhāt

rich (person) amīr

(food) charbī vālā

rickshaw rikshā

cycle rickshaw sāikil rikshā
see **taxi**

ridiculous betukā

right (correct) Thīk

(not left) dāyā

you were right āpne Thīk
kahā

that's right ye Thīk hA

this can't be right ye Thīk
nahī mālūm hōtā

right! Thīk!

is this the right road for ...?
kyā ... ke liye ye sahī rāstā
hA?

on the right dāyī taraf

to the right dāyī taraf

turn right dāyī taraf muRe

right-hand drive dāyī taraf ke
sTīyring vālī kār

ring (on finger) angūThī

I'll ring you (said by man/woman)
mA āpkō phōn
karūgā/karūgī

ring back vāpas phōn karnā

ripe (fruit) pakā

rip-off: it's a rip-off chūnā lagā
diyā

rip-off prices man-māne
dām

risky jōKhim bharā

river nadī

road saRak

is this the road for ...? kyā ...
ke liye yahī rāsta hA?

down the road ThōRā āge

roadsign rāstā batāne kā
taKhtā

rob: I've been robbed mujhe
lūt liyā

rock chaTTān

(music) rāk sangīt

on the rocks (with ice) barf
Dālkar

roll (bread) gōl Dabal rōTī

roof chhat

roof rack kār ke ūpar kā
janglā

room kamrā

in my room mere kamre me

dialogue

do you have any rooms?
(kyā) āpke pās kamre
khālī hA?

for how many people?
kitne lōgõ ke liye?
for one/for two ek/dō ke
liye
yes, we have rooms free jī
hā, hamāre pās kamre
khālī hA
**for how many nights will it
be?** kitnī rāt Thahrege?
just for one night sirf ek
rāt
how much is it? kirāyā
kyā hA?
**... with bathroom and ...
without bathroom**
gusalKhāne vālā aur ...
binā gusalKhāne vālā
**can I see a room with
bathroom?** gusalKhāne
vālā kamrā dikhāiye
OK, I'll take it (said by
man/woman) Thīk hA, mA
ye lelūgā/lelūgī

room service rūm sarvis
rope rassā
rosé (wine) rōze vāin
roughly (approximately) lagbhag
(H), taKrīban (U)
round: it's my round ab merī
bārī hA
roundabout (for traffic) gōl
chakkar
round trip ticket vāpsī TikaT
see ticket
route rāstā
what's the best route? sabse
acchhā rāstā kawnsā hA?
rubber rabaR

rubber band rabaR kā
chhallā
rubbish (waste) kuRā karkaT
(poor quality goods) ghaTiyā
māl
rubbish! (nonsense) ye sab
bakvās hA!
ruby rūbī
rucksack piTThā
rude gustāKh
ruins khanDhar
rum ram
rum and Coke® ram awr
kōkā kōlā®
run (verb: person) dawRnā
how often do the buses run?
base kitnī kitnī der me jātī
hA?
I've run out of money mere
pās kuchh pAsā nahī bachā
rush hour bhīR ke vaKt
Russia rūs
Russian rūsī

S

sad udās
saddle (for bike) gaddī
(for horse) zīn
safe (not in danger) sahī salāmat
(not dangerous) Khatarnāk
nahī
safety pin sefTī pin
sail (noun) pāl
salad salād
salad dressing salād kā
masālā
sale: for sale bikrī ke liye

salmon sāman machhlī
salt namak
same: the same vahī
the same as this vAsā hī
the same again, please vahī phir dījiye
it's all the same to me mere liye sab ek jAsā hA
sand ret
sandals chāppal
sandwich sAnDvich
sanitary napkins/towels awrat**ō** ke sAniTarī Tāvel
sapphire nīlam
Saturday shanīchar, hafta (U)
sauce chaTnī
saucepan Degchī
saucer tashtarī
sauna sawnā
sausage sāsej
say kahnā
how do you say ... in Hindi? ... ko hindī m**e** kyā kahte h**A**?
what did he say? usne kyā kahā?
she said ... usne kahā ki ...
could you say that again? phir kahiye
scarf (for neck) maflar
(for head) sāfā
scenery nazārā
schedule (US) Tāim Tebal
scheduled flight fehrisht m**e** dī gayī flāit
school skūl
scissors: a pair of scissors kAnchī
scooter skūTar
scotch viskī
Scotch tape® selōTep®
Scotland skāTlAnD
Scottish skāTlAnD kā
I'm Scottish (man/woman) mA skāTlAnD kā rahne vālā/vālī h**ū**
scrambled eggs ph**e**Te anDe
scratch (noun) khar**ō**ch
screw (noun) p**e**ch
screwdriver pechkash
sea samandar
by the sea samandar ke kināre
seafood daryāyī khānā
search (verb) khōjnā
seasick: I feel seasick mujhe matlī ārahī hA
I get seasick mujhe jahāz m**e** matlī ātī hA
seaside: by the seaside samandar ke kināre
seat sīT
is this seat taken? kyā is sīT par kōī bAThā hA?
seat belt sīT par lagī peTī
seaweed daryāyī ghāspāt
secluded ekānt
second (adj) dūsrā
(of time) sekanD
just a second! zarā Thahrō!
second class (travel etc) sekanD klās
second floor dūsrī manzil
(US) pahlī manzil
second-hand purānā
see dekhnā
can I see? mujhe dikhāiy**e**
have you seen ...?

āpne ... dekhā hA?

I saw him this morning mAne
use āj subah dekhā

see you! phir milege!

I see (I understand) mA samjhā

self-catering apartment Khud
khānā banāne ke bandōbast
vālā makān

self-service Khud-bakhud
lenā

sell bechnā

do you sell ...? kyā
āp ... bechte hA?

Sellotape® selōTep®

send bhejnā

I want to send this to England
mujhe ye inglAnD bhejnā
hA

senior citizen buzurg

separate alag

separated: I'm separated mA
judā hū

separately (pay, travel) alag se

September sitambar

septic pīp paRā hA

serious gambhīr (H), sangīn
(U)

service charge sarvis chārj

service station sarvis kī jagah

serviette nApkin

set menu fiks mīnu

several kaī

sew sīnā

could you sew this back on?
is kī silāī kar dege?

sex (gender) ling (H), jins (U)

sexy sAksī

shade: in the shade chāh me

shake: let's shake hands

acchha, hāth milāye

shallow (water) uthlā

shame: what a shame! ye
afsōs kī bāt hA!

shampoo shAmpū

shampoo and set bāl dhōnā
awr bAThānā

share (verb: room, table etc) sāth
lenā

sharp (knife, taste) tez

shattered (very tired) bahut
thakā

shaver bijlī kā ustarā

shaving foam hajāmat kī
jhāgvālī krīm

shaving point bijlī ke ustare
kā plag

she* (person nearby) ye
(person further away) vō

sheet (for bed) chādar

shelf tāk

shellfish ghōnghā

sherry shArī sharāb

ship jahāz

by ship jahāz se

shirt kamīz

shit! bakvās!

shock (noun) dhakkā
(electric) jhaTkā

**I got an electric shock from
the ...** mujhe ... se bijlī kā
jhaTkā lagā

shocking nā-gavār

shoe jūtā

a pair of shoes ek jōRī jūtā
see feet

shoelaces tasme

shoe polish jūte kī pālish

shoe repairer mōchī

shop dukān

 In general, shops are open Mon–Sat 9.30am–6pm, but in large towns and cities they tend to stay open till around 8pm.

shopping: I'm going shopping (said by man/woman) mA Kharīdārī ke liye jā rahā/rahī hū

shopping centre bāzār

shore kinārā

short (person) chhōTā (time, journey) thōRā

shortcut chhōTā rāstā

shorts jāghiyā

should: what should I do? mA kyā karū?

you should ... āp ... kare

you shouldn't ... āp ... mat kare

he should be back soon vō jaldī vāpas ājāyegā

shoulder kandhā

shout (verb) chillānā

show (in theatre) shō

could you show me? kyā mujhe dikhā dege?

shower (of rain) bawchhār (in bathroom) shāvar

with shower shāvar ke sāth

shower gel shāvar krīm

shut (verb: of shop etc) band hōnā

(something) band karnā

when do you shut? āp kab band karte hA?

when does it shut? ye kab band hōtā hA?

the shop is shut dukān band hA

I've shut myself out merā darvājā band hōgayā

shut up! chup!

shutter (on camera) shaTar (on window) jhilmilī

shy sharmīlā

sick (ill) bīmār

I feel sick merī tabiyat Thīk nahī

I'm going to be sick (vomit) mujhe matlī ā rahī hA

side taraf

the other side of the street saRak kī dūsrī taraf

side lights bāzū kī battiyā

side salad sāth kā salād

side street sāth kī galī

sidewalk paTrī

on the sidewalk paTrī par

sight: the sights of ... ... kā nazārā

sightseeing: we're going sightseeing ham sAr ke liye jā rahe hA

sightseeing tour sAr

sign (roadsign etc) rāste kā nishān

signature hastākshar (H), dastKhat (U)

signpost nishān kā taKhtā

Sikh sikh

silence Khāmōshī

silk resham

silly nāsamajh

silver chāndī

similar ke jAsā

simple (easy) āsān

since: since last week pichhle hafte se

since I got here (said by man/woman) jab se mA yahā āyā/āyī

sing gānā

singer (man/woman) gāne vālā/vālī

single: a single to ... ... ke liye singal

I'm single (said by man/woman) mA akelā/akelī hū

single bed singal bistar

single room singal kamrā

single ticket singal TikaT

sink (in kitchen) 'sink'

sister bahan

sister-in-law (wife's sister) sālī (brother's wife) bhābhī (husband's sister) nanad

sit: can I sit here? (kyā) mA yahā bATh saktā/saktī hū?

is anyone sitting here? yahā kōī bAThā hA?

sit down bAThnā

sit down! bATh jāō!

size māp

skin chamRī

skin-diving skin Dāiving

skinny dublā

skirt skarT

sky āsmān

sleep (verb) sōnā

did you sleep well? āp Thīk se sōye?

sleeper (on train) slīpar

sleeping bag slīping bAg

sleeping car slīpar

sleeping pill nīd kī gōlī

sleepy: I'm feeling sleepy mujhe nīd ārahī hA

sleeve āstīn

slide (photographic) phōTō slāiD

slippery fisalne vālā

slow dhīmā

slow down! raftār kam kījiye!

slowly dhīre dhīre (H), āhistā āhistā (U)

very slowly bahut dhīre

small chhōTā

smell: it smells (smells bad) is me badbū ārahī hA

smile (verb) muskarānā

smoke (noun) dhuā

do you mind if I smoke? mere sigreT pīne me āpkō kōī etrāz hA?

I don't smoke mA sigreT nahī pītā

do you smoke? āp sigreT pīte hA?

snack: just a snack sirf halkā khānā

snake sāp

sneeze (noun) chhīk

snorkel pānī ke andar sās lene kī nalī

snow (noun) barf

it's snowing barf gir rahī hA

so: it's so good ye bahut acchhā hA

it's so expensive ye bahut mahangā hA

not so much itnā zyādā nahī

not so bad itnā burā nahī

so am I mA bhī Asā hī hū

so do I (said by man/woman) mA bhī Ase hī kartā/kartī hū

so-so Asā–vAsā

soaking solution (for contact lenses) bhigōne kā ghōl

soap sābun

soap powder chūredār sābun

sober (not drunk) hōsh me

sock mōzā

socket bijlī kā sākeT

soda (water) sōDa vāTar

sofa sōfā

soft (material etc) mulāyam

soft-boiled egg halkā ublā anDā

soft drink ThanDā

 Widely available soft drinks include Indian colas such as **Campa Cola**, **Thums Up**, **Gold Spot** (fizzy orange), and **Limca** (rumoured to contain dubious additives). All contain a lot of sugar but little else. More recommendable are straight water (treated, boiled or bottled) and cartons of **Frooti** and similar brands of fruit juice drinks, which come in mango, guava, apple and lemon varieties. At larger stations, there will be a stall on the platform selling **Himachali** apple juice. Better still, green coconuts are cheaper than any of these, and sold on the street by vendors who will hack off the top for you with a machete and give you a straw to suck up the coconut

water (you then scoop out the flesh and eat it). You will also find street stalls selling freshly made sugar-cane juice: delicious, and not in fact very sweet, but not always healthy. India's greatest cold drink, **lassī**, is made with curd and drunk either sweetened with sugar, salted, or mixed with fruit. It varies widely from smooth and delicious to insipid and watery, and is sold at virtually every cafe, restaurant and canteen. Freshly made milk shakes are also available. You may also be sold something called "fruit juice", which is usually fruit, water and sugar (or salt) liquidized and strained. With all such drinks, however appetizing they may seem, you should exercise great caution in deciding whether or not to drink them; try to find out where the water came from.

soft lenses sawfT lAns

sole (of shoe, of foot) talī

could you put new soles on these? in me nayī talī lagā dege?

some: can I have some water/rolls? mujhe thōRā pānī/thōRī gōl Dabal rōTī chāhiye

can I have some? (said by man/woman) kyā mA thōRā le saktā/saktī hū?

somebody, someone kōī

something kuchh

something to eat khāne ke liye kuchh

sometimes kabhī kabhī
somewhere kahī
son beTā
song gānā
son-in-law dāmād
soon jaldī
  I'll be back soon (said by man/woman) mA jaldī vāpas āũgā/āũgī
  as soon as possible jitnī jaldī hōsake
sore: it's sore is me dard hA
sore throat galā Kharāb hA
sorry: (I'm) sorry māf kījiye
  sorry? (didn't understand) kyā kahā?
sort: what sort of ...? kis kism kā ...?
soup shōrbā
sour (taste) khaTTa
south dakshin (H), janūb (U)
  in the south dakshin me
South Africa dakshin afrīkā (H), janūb afrīkā (U)
South African dakshin afrīkā kā (H), janūb afrīkā kā (U)
  I'm South African (man/woman) mA dakshin afrīkā kā/kī hū
southeast dakshin-pūrv (H), janūb-mashrik (U)
southern dakshinī (H), janūbī (U)
southwest dakshin-pashchim (H), janūb-magrib (U)
souvenir yādgār nishānī
Spain spen
Spanish spenī
spanner pānā
spare part purjā

spare tyre phāltū Tāyar
speak: do you speak English? (to man/woman) āp angrezī bōlte/bōltī hA?
  I don't speak ... (said by man/woman) mA ... nahī bōltā/bōltī
  can I speak to ...? (said by man/woman) kyā mA ... se bāt kar saktā/saktī hū?

dialogue

  can I speak to Ashok?
  Ashōk jī se bāt karnī hA
  who's calling? kawn bōl rahā hA?
  it's Patricia mA Patricia hū
  I'm sorry, he's not in, can I take a message? māf kījiye, vō yahā nahī hA, āpkō kuchh kahnā hA?
  no thanks, I'll call back later jī nahī, mA phir phōn karūgī
  please tell him I called unse kah dījiye ki mAne phōn kiyā thā

spectacles chashmā
speed (noun) raftār
speed limit raftār kī had
spell: how do you spell it? is ke hijje kAse karte hA?
spend kharch karnā
spice masālā
spicy masāle dār
  (hot) mirch masāle vālā
spider makRī

spirits

Spirits usually take the form of 'Indian Made Foreign Liquor' (IMFL), rough local varieties of whisky, gin and brandy. In Goa, **fene** is a spirit distilled from coconut or cashew fruit. Steer well clear of illegally distilled **arak**, which often contains methanol (wood alcohol) and other poisons. A look through the press, especially at festival times, will soon reveal numerous cases of blindness and death as a result of drinking bad hooch. Licensed locally made alcohol, sold in several states under such names as **banglā**, is an acquired taste. In the Himalayas, the Bhotia people, who are of Tibetan stock, drink **chang** (a beer made from millet) and one of the nicest drinks of all, **tumba**: fermented millet topped up with hot water and drunk through a bamboo pipe from a bamboo flask.

splinter tukRā
spoke (in wheel) spōk
spoon chammach
sport khel
sprain: I've sprained my ... mere ... me mōch āgayī
spring (of car, seat) 'spring' (season) vasant (H), bahār (U)
in the spring vasant/bahār me
square (in town) chawk
Sri Lanka shrī lankā

Sri Lankan shrī lankā kā
stairs sīRhiyā
stale bāsī
stamp (noun) TikaT

dialogue

a stamp for England, please inglAnD ke liye Dāk kā TikaT dījiye
what are you sending? āp kyā bhej rahe hA?
this postcard ye pasTkārD

standby (flight) uRān ke vakt hāzir
star tārā
(in film) filmī sitārā
start (noun) shuruāt
(verb: film, play etc) shuru hōnā
(doing something) shuru karnā
when does it start? ye kab shuru hōtā hA?
the car won't start kar nahī chaltī
starter (food) pahlā dawr
starving: I'm starving mujhe bhūkh lagī hA
state (country) desh (H), mulk (U)
the States (USA) amrīkā
station sTeshan
statue mūrti (H), but (U)
stay: where are you staying? āp kahā Thahre hA?
I'm staying at ... (said by man/woman) mA ... me Thahrā/Thahrī hū
I'd like to stay another two

nights (said by man/woman) mA dō rāt awr Thaharnā chāhtā/chāhtī hū
steal churānā
 my bag has been stolen merā thAlā chōrī hōgayā
steep (hill) Dhalvā
step: on the steps sīRhī par
stereo sTīriō
sterling briTish pāunD
steward (on plane) sTuarD
stewardess sTuarDes, parichārikā (H)
still: I'm still here mA abhī bhī yahā hū
 is he still there? kyā vō abhī bhī vahā hA?
 keep still! hilō Dulō nahī!
sting: I've been stung mujhe Dank mār diyā
stockings mōzā
stomach peT
stomach ache peT dard
stone patthar
stop (verb) ruknā
 please, stop here (to taxi driver etc) yahā rukiye
 do you stop near ...? āp ... ke pās rukege?
 stop it! band karō!
stopover paRāv
storm tūfān
straight (whisky etc) Khālis
 it's straight ahead yahā se sīdhe jāiye
straightaway fawran
strange (odd) ajīb
stranger ajanbī
 I'm a stranger here mA yahā

ajanbī hū
strap paTTā
strawberry sTrābarī
stream dhārā
street galī
 on the street saRak par
streetmap saRkō kā nakshā
string rassī
strong zōrdār
stuck phasā
 it's stuck ye phasā hA
student sTuDAnT
stupid bevkūf
suburb muhallā
suddenly achānak
suede sveD
sugar chīnī
suit (noun) sūT
 it doesn't suit me (jacket etc) ye mujhe Thīk nahī bAThtā
 it suits you ye Thīk lagtā hA
suitcase sūTkes
summer garmī
 in the summer garmiyō me
sun sūraj
 in the sun dhūp me
 out of the sun chhāh me
sunbathe dhūp seknā
sunblock dhūp se bachne kī krīm
sunburn dhūp me jhulasnā
sunburnt dhūp me jhulsā
Sunday itvār
sunglasses dhūp kā chashmā
sun lounger dhūp me bAThne ke liye ārām kursī
sunny: it's sunny dhūp niklī hA
sunroof khulne vālī chhat

sunset sūraj Dūbne kā vaKt, sūryāsT (H)

sunshade chhāyā (H), sāyā (U)

sunshine dhūp

sunstroke lū lagnā

suntan sanTan

suntan lotion sanTan lōshan

suntanned dhūp se chamRī kā badlā huā rang

suntan oil sanTan tel

super baRhiyā

supermarket supar mārkeT

supper shām kā khānā

supplement (extra charge) awr kharchā

sure: are you sure? āpkō pakkā mālūm hA?

sure! sach!

surname dūsrā nām

swearword gālī

sweater svATar

sweatshirt svATsharT

Sweden svīDan

Swedish svīDan kā

sweet (taste) mīThā
(noun: dessert) miThāī

sweets miThāī

swelling sūjan

swim (verb) tArnā

I'm going for a swim (said by man/woman) mA tArne jā rahā/rahī hū

let's go for a swim chalō, tArne chale

swimming costume tArne kī pōskāk

swimming pool tArne kā tālāb

swimming trunks tArne kā jāghiyā

switch (noun) svich

switch off band karnā

switch on (engine, TV) chalū karnā
(lights) jalānā

swollen sūjā huā

T

table mez

a table for two dō lōgō ke liye ek Tebal

tablecloth mezpōsh

table tennis Tebal TAnis

table wine Tebal vāin

tailor darjī

take (verb: lead) le jānā
(accept) lenā

can you take me to the ...? mujhe āp ... le jāyege?

do you take credit cards? āp krediT kārD lete hA?

fine, I'll take it (said by man/woman) Thīk hA, mA ise le lūgā/lūgī

can I take this? (leaflet etc: said by man/woman) mA ise le saktā/saktī hū?

how long does it take? kitnā vaKt lagegā?

it takes three hours tīn ghanTe lagege

is this seat taken? kyā ye sīt khālī hA?

samosa to take away samōse bāhar le jāne ke liye

can you take a little off here?

(to hairdresser) yahā par se
zarā bāl chāT dījiye

talcum powder TAlkam
pāuDar

talk (verb) bātchīt karnā

tall (person) lambā
(building) ūchā

tampons TAmpān

tan (noun) sāvlā rang
to get a tan sāvlā karnā

tap TōTī

tape (cassette) Tep

tape measure nāpne kā fītā

tape recorder Tep RikārDar

taste (noun) svād (H), zāykā
(U)
can I taste it? (said by
man/woman) mA ise chakh
saktā/saktī hū?

taxi TAksī
will you get me a taxi? mere
liye TAksī bulā dege?
where can I find a taxi?
mujhe TAksī kahā milegī?

dialogue

to the airport/to the Ashok
Hotel, please havāi
aDDe/ashōk hōTal le
chaliye
how much will it be? kitne
pAse lagege?
500 rupees pāch saw
rupaye
that's fine right here,
thanks bas yahī par Thīk
hA shukriyā

Taxi drivers should use
the meter, but the usual
compromise is to agree a
fare for the journey before you get
in. From places such as main
stations, you may be able to find
other passengers to share a taxi to
the town centre, while large airports
operate pre-paid taxi schemes with
set fares that you pay at the airport;
more expensive pre-paid limousines
are also available.

That most Indian of vehicles, the
auto-rickshaw, is the front half of a
motor-scooter with a couple of seats
mounted on the back. Cheaper than
taxis, better at nipping in and out of
traffic, and usually metered, auto-
rickshaws are a little unstable and
their drivers often rather reckless,
but that's all part of the fun.
Agreeing a price before the journey,
which you should always do if
there's no meter, will not necessarily
stop your rickshaw wallah reopening
discussion when the journey is
under way, or at its end.

One or two cities also have larger
versions of auto-rickshaws known
as **tempos**, with six or eight seats
behind, which usually ply fixed
routes at flat fares. Here and there
you'll also come across horse-drawn
carriages or **tāngās**.

Slower and cheaper still is the cycle
rickshaw – basically a glorified
tricycle. Foreign visitors often feel
squeamish about travelling this way,
and with good reason; except in the

major tourist cities, cycle rickshaw wallahs are invariably emaciated pavement dwellers who earn only a pittance for their pains. In the end, though, they'll earn even less if you don't use them. Only in Calcutta do the rickshaw wallahs continue to haul the city's pukka rickshaws on foot.

taxi-driver TAksī Drāivar
taxi rank TAksī aDDā
tea (drink) chāy
 tea for one/two please ek chāy/dō chāy dījiye

India sometimes seems to run on tea, which is sold by **chai-vālās** on just about every street corner. It is usually made by putting tea dust, milk and water in a pan, boiling it all up, straining it into a cup or glass with lots of sugar and pouring back and forth from one cup to another to stir. Special chai might be made with ginger and/or cardamoms. If you're quick off the mark, you can get them to hold the sugar. Occasionally, you might get a pot of European-style tea, generally consisting of a tea bag in lukewarm water – you'd do better to stick to the pukka Indian variety.

teabags Tī bAg
teach: could you teach me? mujhe sikhā degē?
teacher (man/woman)

māsTar/masTarānī
tea house chāy kī dukān
team Tīm
teaspoon chāy kī chammach
tea towel rasōī kā tawliyā
teenager nawjavān
telegram tār
telephone Telīphōn
 see **phone**
television Telivizan, dūr darshan (H)
tell: could you tell him ...? unse kah de ki ...
temperature (weather) Temprechar, tāpmān (H) (fever) buKhār
temple (Sikh) gurdvārā (Hindu, Jain) mandir
 see **religion**
tennis TAnis
tent tambū
term (at university, school) Tarm
terminus (rail) rel kā āKhirī sTeshan
terrible bahut burā
terrific bahut baRhiyā
Thai thāilAnD kā
Thailand thāilAnD
than* se
 smaller than se chhōTā
thank: thank you shukriyā, dhanyvād (H)
 thanks shukriyā
 thank you very much bahut bahut shukriyā
 thanks for the lift lift ke liye shukriyā
 no, thanks jī nahī

dialogue

thanks shukriyā

that's OK, don't mention it
Thīk hA, kōī bāt nahī

that: that boy vō laRkā
  that girl vō laRkī
  that one vō vālā
  I hope that ... mujhe ummīd
  hA ki ...
  that's nice bahut Khūb
  is that ...? kyā vō ...?
  that's it (that's right) ye Thīk
  hA

the*

theatre ThiyeTar

their* (referring to people nearby)
inkā
  (referring to people further away)
  unkā
  it's their car ye inkī kār hA

theirs* (referring to people nearby)
inkā
  (referring to people further away)
  unkā

them* (referring to people nearby)
inhe
  (referring to people further away)
  unhe
  for them inke liye
  with them inke sāth
  to them inkō
  who? – them kawn? – ye

then (at that time) tab
  (after that) uske bād

there vahā
  over there vahā
  up there ūpar

is there ...? kyā ...?
are there ...? kyā ...?
there is ... ek ...
there are ... kul ...
there you are (giving something)
ye lījiye

thermometer tharmāmīTar

Thermos® flask tharmas
bōtal

these*: **these men** ye ādmī
  these women ye awrate
  I'd like these mujhe ye
  chahiye

they* (nearby) ye
  (further away) ve

thick mōTā
  (stupid) mōTī aKl kā

thief chōr

thigh jāgh

thin patlā

thing chīz
  my things merī chīze

think sōchnā
  I think so merā Asā hī Khyāl
  hA
  I don't think so mere Khyāl
  me Asā nahī
  I'll think about it (said by
  man/woman) mA is par sōch
  vichār karūgā/karūgī

thirsty: I'm thirsty mujhe pyās
lagī hA

this: this boy ye laRkā
  this girl ye laRkī
  this one ye vālā
  this is my wife ye merī bībī
  hA
  is this ...? kya ye ... hA?

those: those men ve ādmī

those women ve awrate
which ones? — those kawnse? — ve
thread (noun) dhāgā
throat galā
throat pastilles gale ke liye chūsne kī gõlī
through (via) hõkar
(by means of) ke zariye
does it go through ...? (train, bus) kyā ye ... hõkar jātī hA?
throw pheknā
throw away phek denā
thumb angūThā
thunderstorm garaj kaRak kā tūfān
Thursday brihaspat vār (H), jumme rāt (U)
ticket TikaT

dialogue

> **a return ticket to Rishikesh** rishikesh kā ek vāpasī TikaT
> **coming back when?** kab vāpas ānā hA?
> **today/next Tuesday** āj/agle mangal vār kõ
> **that will be 300 rupees** tīn saw rupaye lagege

ticket office TikaT ghar
tie (necktie) Tāī
tiger bāgh
tight (clothes etc) tang
it's too tight ye bahut tang hA
tights TāiTs

till (cash desk) kAsh kāunTar
time* vaKt, samay (H)
what's the time? kyā vaKt hA?, kitne baje hA?
this time is vaKt
last time pichhlī bār
next time aglī bār
three times tīn bār
timetable Tāim Tebal
tin (can) Tin
tinfoil Tin kī paTrī
tin-opener Tin khõlne kī chābī
tiny bahut chhõTā
tip (to waiter etc) baKhshīsh

tipping
As a presumed-rich **sahab** or **memsahab**, you will, like wealthy Indians, be expected to be liberal with the **bakshīsh**, which takes three main forms.

The most common form is tipping: a small reward for a small service done by anyone from a waiter or porter to someone who lifts your bags onto the roof of a bus or keeps an eye on your vehicle for you. Large amounts are not expected – five rupees should satisfy all the aforementioned. Taxi drivers and staff at cheaper hotels and restaurants do not necessarily expect tips, but they always appreciate them, of course, and tips can keep people sweet for the next time you call. Some may take liberties in demanding bakshīsh, but it's often better just to go along with it rather than cause offence over trifling sums.

More expensive than plain tipping is paying people to bend the rules, many of which seem to have been invented for precisely that purpose. Examples might include letting you into a historical site after hours, finding you a seat or a sleeper on a train that is 'full', or speeding up some bureaucratic process. This should not be confused with bribery, a more serious business with its own risks and etiquette, which is best not entered into.

The last type of bakshish is alms giving. In a country without social security, this is an important social custom. People with disabilities and mutilations are the traditional recipients, and it seems right to join local people in giving out small change to them. Kids demanding money, pens or the like are a different case, pressing their demands only on tourists. In return for a service it is fair enough, but giving in to any request encourages them to go and pester others. Think twice before you do.

tired thakā
  I'm tired (said by man) mA
  thakā huā hū
  (said by woman) mA thakī huī
  hū
tissues kāgaz ke rumāl
to: to Delhi/London

dillī/landan (kō)
  to India/England
  bhārat/inglAnD (kō)
  to the post office Dāk-Khāne
  (kō)
toast (bread) TōsT
tobacco tambākū
today āj
toe pAr kā angūthā
together ek sāth
  we're together (in shop etc)
  ham ek sāth hA
toilet shawchālay (H),
  pākhānā (U)
  where is the toilet?
  shawchālay kahā hA?
  I have to go to the toilet
  mujhe shawchālay jānā hA
  (politer) mujhe bāth rūm
  jānā hA

 A visit to the toilet is not one of India's more pleasant experiences: toilets are often filthy and major potential breeding grounds for disease. Paper, if used, often goes in a bucket next to the loo rather than down it. Indians use a jug of water and their left hand, a method you may also come to prefer. If you do use paper, keep some handy – it isn't usually supplied.

There are several words for toilet: **shawchālay** (H) and **pākhānā** (U) mean toilet or public toilet. In some areas, these words might not be understood and you may have to ask for **peshāb ghar** (urinals) or **TaTTi**.

125

The latter word is not very polite, but you may come across it when trekking. In someone's home, it is best to ask to use the bathroom: **bāth rūm**.

toilet paper TāyleT pepar
tomato TamāTar
tomato juice TamāTar kā ras
tomato ketchup TamāTar kī chaTnī
tomb maKbarā
tomorrow kal
  tomorrow morning kal subah
  the day after tomorrow parsõ
toner (cosmetic) Tōnar
tongue jībh
tonic (water) Tānik vāTar
tonight āj rāt
tonsillitis Tānsil
too (excessively) bahut adhik (also) bhī
  too hot bahut garam
  too much bahut zyādā
  me too mujhe bhī
tooth dāt
toothache dāt me dard
toothbrush dāt sāf karne kā brash
toothpaste tūth pest
top: on top of ... ... ke ūpar
  at the top sabse ūpar
top floor sabse ūpar kī manzil
topless nangī
torch bATarī vālī Tārch
total (noun) kul
tour (noun) sAr
  is there a tour of ...?

kyā ... ke liye Tūr hA?
tour guide (man/woman) Tūr kā gāiD/Tūr kī gāiD
tourist sAlānī
tourist information office TūrisT jānkārī kā daftar, paryaTan kāryālaya (H)

 Government offices, including most tourist offices, stay open Mon–Fri 9.30am–5pm and Sat 9.30am–1pm; all government offices are closed on the second Saturday of each month.

Inside India, both national and local governments run tourist information offices providing general travel advice and handing out an array of printed material, from city maps to glossy leaflets on specific destinations. The Indian government's tourist department has branches in most regional capitals. These, however, operate independently of the information counters and bureaux run by the state tourism development corporations, usually referred to by their initials (MPTDC, RTDC, etc), which offer a wide range of travel facilities, including guided tours, car rental, and their own hotels.

For the latest up-to-the-minute information on hotels, restaurants, transport and problems on the road, however, your best source may well be your fellow travellers.

tour operator Tūr chalāne
vālā
towards kī taraf
towel tawliyā
town shahar
  in town shahar me
  just out of town shahar ke
  bahār hī
town centre shahar kā bīch
town hall Tāun hāl
toy khilawnā
track (US) pletfãram
  which track is it for Jaipur?
  jApur ke liye kawnsā
  pleTfãram hA?
tracksuit TrAk sūT
traditional purāne tawr tarīke
kā
traffic TrAfik, yātāyāt (H)
traffic jam TrAfik kī rukāvat
traffic lights TrAfik lāiT
trailer (US) kārvā
trailer park kārvā kī jagah
train relgāRī, gāRī
  by train relgāRī se

 India's train network is
one of the most extensive
in the world and is the
best means of exploring most of the
country. Broadly speaking there are
six types of train: super-fast inter-
city trains known as **shatābdi**, used
on runs of up to around eight hours;
rājdhāni or super-fast long distance
inter-city trains; fast express trains
which may stop frequently; mail
trains which are generally, but not
always, slower; passenger trains
that stop at every station; and
commuter trains, which can be
unbearably crowded. Although there
are just two classes – first and
second – on most (except passenger
and commuter trains), sleepers and
air-conditioning are available. Air-
conditioned (AC) chair cars are
available on some trains, while
shatābdi trains have nothing else.
Reserving seats or berths on trains
in the major cities and tourist
centres is quite painless – there are
special tourist desks for this. An
Indrail Pass is a very good
investment.

dialogue

**is this the train for
Bangalore?** (kyā) ye gāRī
banglawr ke liye hA?
sure jī hā
**no, you want that platform
there** jī nahī, āp us
pleTfãram par jāiye

trainers (shoes) khelne ke jūte
train station relve sTeshan
tram Trām
translate anuvād karnā (H),
  tarzumā karnā (U)
  could you translate that? is
  kā anuvād/tarzumā kar
  dege?
translation anuvād (H),
  tarzumā (U)
translator anuvādak (H),
  tarzumān (U)

trash (waste) kuRā karkaT
(poor quality goods) ghaTiyā
māl
trashcan kūRedān
travel sAR karnā
we're travelling around ham
ghūmne phirne āye hA
travel agent's TrAval ejAnT
traveller's cheque TrAvlar
chAk
do you take traveller's
cheques? (to man/woman) āp
TrAvlar chAK lete/letī hA?
tray Tre
tree peR
trek (noun) pAdal safar
trekking pAdal ghummā
phirnā
tremendous bahut baRhiyā
trendy naye fAshan kā
trim: just a trim please (to
hairdresser) mere bāl zarā
chhāT dījiye
trip (excursion) sAr
I'd like to go on a trip
to ... (said by man/woman)
mA ... kī sAr ke liye jānā
chāhtā/chāhtī hū̃
trolley Trālī
trouble (noun) dikkat
I'm having trouble with ...
(said about man/woman) mujhe
... dikkat de rahā/de rahī
hA
trousers patlūn
true sach
that's not true ye sach nahī̃
trunk (US: of car) sāman
rakhne kī peTī

try (verb) āzmānā
can I try it? (said by man/woman)
mA ise āzmā ke dekh
saktāl/saktī hū̃?
try on pahan kar dekhnā
can I try it on? pahan kar
dekhū̃?
T-shirt Tī sharT
Tuesday mangalvār
tuna Tūnā machhlī
tunnel gufā
turban pagRī
turn: turn left bāyī taraf muRe
turn right dāyī taraf muRe
turn off: where do I turn off?
mA kahā se muR jāū̃?
can you turn the heating off?
āp hīTing band kar de
turn on: can you turn the
heating on? āp hīTing chalā
de
turning (in road) mōR
TV 'TV'
tweezers chimTī
twice dō bār
twice as much itnā hī
dubārā
twin beds sāth me lage dō
bistar
twin room dō bistarõ vālā
kamrā
twist: I've twisted my ankle
mere Takhne me mōch
āgayī
type (noun) kism
another type of ... dūsrī kism
kā ...
typical apnī kism kā
tyre Tāyar

U

ugly badsūrat
UK briTen
ulcer nāsūr
umbrella chhātā
uncle (father's younger brother)
  chāchā
  (father's older brother) tāyā
  (mother's brother) māmā
unconscious behōsh
under (in position) nīche
  (less than) se kam
underdone (meat) adhpakā
underpants jāghiyā
understand: I understand mA
  samjhā
I don't understand mA nahī
  samjhā
do you understand? āp
  samjhe?
unemployed berōzgār
unfashionable fAshan me
  nahī
United States amrīkā
university yūnivarsiTī,
  vishvavidyālay (H)
unleaded petrol binā lAd kā
  petrōl
unlimited mileage dūr tak
  lejāne me kōī bandish nahī
unlock tālā khōlnā
unpack sāmān khōlnā
until jab tak
unusual anōkhā
up ūpar
  up there vahā ūpar
  he's not up yet (not out of bed)

vō abhī uThā nahī
what's up? (what's wrong?) kyā
  huā?
upmarket ūche kism kā
upset stomach peT me
  gaRbaRī
upside down ulTā pulTā
upstairs ūpar kī manzil me
up-to-date naye Dhang kā
Urdu urdū
urgent zarūrī
us* hame
  with us hamāre sāth
  for us hamāre liye
USA yū As e
use (verb) istemāl karnā
  may I use ...? (said by man/
  woman) kyā mA ... istemāl
  kar saktā/saktī hū?
useful kām kā
usual ām
  the usual (drink etc) hameshā
  vālā

V

vacancy: do you have any
  vacancies? āpke pās kamre
  khālī hA?
  see room
vacation chhuTTī
  on vacation chhuTTī par
vaccination Tīkā
vacuum cleaner vAkum
  klīnar
valid (ticket etc) sahī
  how long is it valid for? is kī
  miyād kab tak hA?

valley ghāTī
valuable (adj) kīmtī
  can I leave my valuables
  here? (said by man/woman) kyā
  mA apnī kīmtī chīze yahā
  chhōR saktā/saktī hū?
value (noun) kīmat
van vAn
vanilla vAnilā
  a vanilla ice cream vAnilā
  āiskrīm
vary: it varies ye badaltā rahtā
  hA
vase phūldān
vegetables sabziyā
vegetarian (noun) shākāhārī
vending machine bikrī
  mashīn
very bahut
  very little for me mere liye
  bahut thōRā
  I like it very much mujhe
  bahut pasand hA
vest (under shirt) baniyān
via ke rāste
video (noun: film) vīDiō
video recorder vīDiō
  rekārDar
view nazārā
village gāv
vinegar sirkā
visa vīzā

To enter India, you must
be in possession of a
visa, which you can get
from the Indian embassy or
consulate in your country. Apply in
person, and it will be ready the

following day; apply by post and it
can take two to three weeks.

visit (verb: person) milne jānā
  (place) dekhne jānā
  I'd like to visit ... (said by
  man/woman) mA ... dekhne
  jānā chāhtā/chāhtī hū
vital: it's vital that ... ye zarūrī
  hA ki ...
vodka vōdkā
voice āvāz
voltage vōltej

Generally voltage is 220V
50Hz AC, though direct
current supplies also
exist, so check before plugging in.
Most sockets are double round-pin
but sizes vary. British, Irish and
Australasian plugs will need an
adaptor, preferably universal;
American and Canadian appliances
will need a transformer too, unless
multi-voltage. Power cuts and
voltage variations are very common.

vomit ulTī ānā

W

waist kamar
waistcoat vāskaT
wait intzār karnā
  wait for me merī intzār kare
  don't wait for me merī intzār
  mat kare
  can I wait until my wife gets

here? apnī bībī ke āne tak mA yahā intzār kar saktā hū?

can you do it while I wait? (said by man/woman) āp abhī kar dījiye, mA intzār kartā/kartī hū

could you wait here for me? yahā par merā intzār kare

waiter bArā

waiter! bArā!

wake: can you wake me up at 5.30? mujhe sāRe pāch baje jagā de

wake-up call jagāne kī ghanTī

Wales vels

walk: is it a long walk? (kyā) ye lambā rāstā hA?

it's only a short walk ye thoRī dūr hA

I'll walk (said by man/woman) mA pAdal chalūgā/chalūgī

I'm going for a walk (said by man/woman) mA ghūmne jārahā/jārahī hū

wall dīvār

wallet baTuā

wander: I like just wandering around mujhe idhar-udhar ghūmne-phirne kā shawk hA

want: I want a ... mujhe ... chāhiye

I don't want any ... mujhe koī ... nahī chāhiye

I want to go home (said by man/woman) mA ghar jānā chāhtā/chāhtī hū

I don't want to ... (said by

man/woman) mA ... nahī chāhtā/chāhtī

he wants to ... vō ... chāhtā hA

what do you want? āpkō kyā chāhiye?

ward (in hospital) vārD

warm garam

I'm so warm mujhe bahut garmī lag rahī hA

was*: he was vō thā

she was vō thī

it was ye thā

wash (verb) dhōnā

can you wash these? āp inko dhō dege?

washer (for bolt etc) vāshar

washhand basin hāth muh dhōne kī chilamchī

washing (clothes) kapRe dhōnā

washing machine vāshing mashīn

washing powder kapRe dhōne kā pāuDar

washing-up: to do the washing-up bartan sāf karnā

washing-up liquid bartan dhōne kā sābun

wasp tatAyā

watch (wristwatch) hāth kī ghaRī

will you watch my things for me? merī chīzō kī nigrānī rakhe

watch out! khabar dār!

watch strap ghaRī kā fītā

water pānī

may I have some water?

mujhe ThoRā pānī chāhiye

It is generally not a good idea to drink tap water, although in big cities it is usually chlorinated. However, it is almost impossible in practice to avoid untreated tap water completely: it is used to make ice (which may appear in drinks without being asked for), **lassīs** are made with it, utensils are washed with it, and so on. Bottled water is widely available. Always check that the seal is intact, as refilling bottles is not uncommon. Carbonated water is generally safer, as it is more likely to be genuine.

If you plan to go somewhere with no access to bottled drinks – which really only applies to travellers venturing well off the beaten track – find an appropriate method of treating water.

Purification, a two-stage process involving both filtration and sterilization, gives the most complete treatment, and you can buy portable water purifiers that will fit in your pocket.

waterproof (adj) vāTarprūf
waterskiing vātar skī
wave (in sea) lahar
way: it's this way idhar hA
 it's that way udhar hA
 is it a long way to ...?
 kyā ... bahut dūr hA?
 no way! hargiz nahī!

dialogue

> **could you tell me the way to ...?** ... ke liye kis rāste se jāū?
> **go straight on until you reach the traffic lights**
> TrAfik kī battī tak sīdhe jāye
> **turn left** bāyī taraf muRe
> **take the first on the right**
> dāyī taraf kī pahlī sarak le see **where**

we* ham
weak (person) kamzōr
 (drink) halkā
weather mawsam

dialogue

> **what's the weather forecast?** mawsam kAsā rahegā?
> **it's going to be fine** acchhā rahegā
> **it's going to rain** bārish hōgī
> **it'll brighten up later** bād me dhūp niklegī

wedding shādī
wedding ring shādī kī angūThī
Wednesday budhvār
week haftā
 a week (from) today āj se ek hafte bād
 a week (from) tomorrow kal

se ek hafte bād
weekend shanivār awr itvār
 at the weekend shani awr
 itvār kō
weight vazan
weird ajīb
welcome: you're welcome
 (don't mention it) kōī bāt nahī̃
well: I don't feel well meri
 tabiyat Thīk nahī̃
 she's not well inkī tabiyat
 Thīk nahī̃
 you speak English very well
 (to man/woman) āp bahut
 acchhī angrezī bōlte/bōltī
 hA
 well done! shābāsh!
 this one as well ye bhī
 well, well! are vāh!

dialogue

> **how are you? (to**
> **man/woman)** āp kAse/kAsī
> hA?
> **very well, thanks, and you?**
> Thīk hū̃, shukriyā, awr āp?

well-done (meat) khūb pakā
Welsh velsh
 I'm Welsh (man/woman) mA
 vels kā/kī hū̃
were* the
west pashchim (H), magrib
 (U)
 in the west pashchim me
West Indian vest inDīz kā
western pashchimī (H),
 magribī (U)

wet gīlā
what? kyā?
 what's that? ye kyā hA?
 what should I do? ma kyā
 karū̃?
 what a view! kyā nazārā hA!
 what bus do I take? mA
 kawnsī bas lū̃?
wheel pahiyā
wheelchair pahiyōvālī kursī
when? kab?
 when we get back jab ham
 vāpas āyẽge
 when's the train/ferry?
 gāRī/nāv kab jāyegī?
where? kahā̃?
 I don't know where it is
 mujhe mālūm nahī̃ ki ye
 kahā̃ hA

dialogue

> **where is the temple?**
> mandir kahā̃ hA?
> **it's over there** vahā̃ par hA
> **could you show me where**
> **it is on the map?** mujhe
> nakshe me dikhāiye ki ye
> kahā̃ par hA?
> **it's just here** yahā̃ par hA
> **see way**

which: which bus? kawnsī
bas?

dialogue

> **which one?** kawnsā?
> **that one** vo vālā

this one? ye vālā?
no, that one jī nahī, vō vālā

while: while I'm here jabtak
mA yahā hū
whisky viskī
white safed
white wine vāiT vāin
who? kawn?
who is it? kawn hA?
the man who ... vō ādmī
jō ...
whole: the whole week sāre
hafte
the whole lot sāre kā sārā
whose: whose is this? ye
kiskā hA?
why? kyō?
why not? kyō nahī?
wide chawRā
wife: my wife merī bībī
will*: will you do it for me? kyā
mere liye ye kar dege?
wind (noun) tez havā
window khiRkī
near the window khiRkī ke
pās
in the window (of shop)
khiRkī me
window seat khiRkī vālī sīT
windscreen vinD skrīn
windscreen wiper vinD skrīn
vāipar
windsurfing vinD sarfing
windy: it's so windy bahut tez
havā chal rahī hA
wine vāin
can we have some more
wine? thōRī awr vāin dījiye

The choice of wine in
India is limited. Imported
wines are expensive and
not widely available except in the
big cities. Wine made in Goa,
Maharashtra and Andhra Pradesh
from local grapes is available but
varies tremendously in quality and
price.

wine list vāin lisT
winter jāRā
in the winter jāRe me
winter holiday jāRe kī
chhuTTiyā
wire tār
(electric) bijlī kā tār
wish: best wishes
mubāraKbād, shubh
kāmnāye (H)
with ke sāth
I'm staying with ... (said by
man/woman) mA ... ke sāth
Thahrā/ThahRī hū
without binā
witness gavāh
will you be a witness for me?
merī gavāhī dege?
woman awrat

women
Women travelling alone
will encounter sexual
harassment, or 'eve teasing', all over
the north and wherever there are
large concentrations of tourists – it
is especially rampant in Delhi.
Harassment is usually limited to
comments and lewd suggestions but

can occasionally take the form of groping, since Western women are often stereotyped as being loose, a myth perpetuated by Bombay films. Women travelling alone with small children invariably get sympathy; a woman travelling with a man to whom she is not married will invite unhealthy curiosity, which can be avoided by playing married.

worm kīRā
wonderful bahut baRhiyā
won't*: it won't start ye chālu nahī hōtā
  see **not**
wood (material) lakRī
  (forest) jangal
wool ūn
word shabd (H), lafz (U)
work (noun) kām
  it's not working ye thīk nahī chal rahī
world duniyā
worry: I'm worried mA pareshān hū
worse: it's worse ye zyādā Kharāb hA
worst sabse Kharāb
worth: is it worth a visit? kyā ye dekhne lāyak hA?
would: would you give this to ...? ye ... kō de de
wrap: could you wrap it up? ise kāgaz me lapeT de
wrapping paper lapeTne kā kāgaz
wrist kalāī
write likhnā

could you write it down? ise likh de
how do you write it? ise kis tarah likhte hA?
writing paper likhne kā kāgaz
wrong: it's the wrong key ye galat chābī hA
  this is the wrong train ye galat gāRī hA
  the bill's wrong bil galat hA
  sorry, wrong number māf kījiye, galat nambar
  sorry, wrong room māf kījiye, galat kamrā
  there's something wrong with ... ... me kuchh gaRbaR hA
  what's wrong? kyā gaRbaRī hA?

X

X-ray Aks-re

Y

yacht nawkā
yard (place) āngan
year sāl
yellow pīlā
yes hā
yesterday kal
  yesterday morning kal subah
  the day before yesterday parsō
yet abhī tak

dialogue

is it here yet? abhī tak
yahā nahī āyā?
no, not yet jī nahī, abhī tō
nahī
**you'll have to wait a little
longer yet** āpkō thōRī der
tak awr intzār karnī
paRegā

yoghurt dahī
yoga yōg
you* (pol) āp
(fam) tum
this is for you (pol) ye āpke
liye hA
(fam) ye tumhāre liye hA
with you (pol) āpke sāth
(fam) tumhāre sāth

 The familiar **tum** forms
for 'you' or 'your' are
used among people who
are equal in age and status. They
indicate either intimacy or
disrespect and are best avoided by
non-native speakers. To avoid
embarrassment it is safer to use the
polite **āp** form in all situations,
unless you are sure that you are on
familiar/equal terms with the person
addressed.

young javān
your* (pol) āpkā
(fam) tumhārā
yours* (pol) āpke
(fam) tumhāre

that's yours ye
āpke/tumhāre hA
youth hostel yūth hōsTal

Z

zero sifar, shūny (H)
zip zip
could you put a new zip on?
āp nayī zip lagā dege?
zipcode Dāk kā kōD
zoo chiRiyāghar

Hindi/Urdu

→

English

Colloquialisms

You might well hear the following expressions, but on no account should you use any of the stronger ones – local people will not be amused or impressed by your efforts.

abe! swine!
andhā hA kyā? are you blind?
are! really!, hey!, well!
badmāsh wicked person; naughty child
bakvās nonsense
bāp re bāp! good heavens!
bhāR me Jāye he/she/it can go to hell
buddhū idiot; stupid
chal sāle nikal ya hāse! get lost!
chālū cunning, crafty
chōr kahī kā! bloody thief!
dhat tere kī! damn it!
gadhā kahī kā! stupid idiot!
harāmi/harāmkhōr good-for-nothing, layabout
hāy marā I've had it
kaminā! low life!
kuttā kahī kā! low life!
kuttā kamina! bloody low life!
kyā Khūb! that's great!
lambū beanpole
mōTi chiRiyā moneybags
nīch! low life!
mar sāle! go to hell!
mujhe banātā hA? do you think I'm stupid?
pāgal crazy, mad
sankī eccentric, crazy
sālā jhūThā kahī kā bloody liar
shābāsh! well done!
sālā kuttā! bloody low life!
suvar (kā bachhā) bastard (literally: piglet)
tīs mār Khā show-off
ullū kā paTThā absolute idiot
vāh great, terrific

In this section, alphabetical order is as follows:

a, ā, A, b, ch, d, D, e, f, g, h, i, ī, j, k, K, l, m, n, ō, p, r, R, s, t, T, u, ū, v, y, z

a

ab now
abbā dad
abhāgā unlucky
abhinetā actor
abhinetrī actress
abhī! just a second!
abhī bhī yahā still
abhī tak yet
acchhā good, nice, fine
acchhā hō ki mA ... I'd rather ...
acchhā lagnā to like
acchhā tō! really?
achānak suddenly
achhe se achhe best
achraj bharā astonishing
adālat court
adhpakā underdone, not cooked
afrīkī African
afsōs: mujhe bahut afsōs hA I'm really sorry
   afsōs ki bāt hA it's regrettable
agar if
agast August
aglā next; front
agle hafte next week
aglī bār next time

aglā hissā front (part)
agrim (H) advance (money)
ajanabī stranger
ajāyab ghar museum
ajīb funny, odd, weird
akasmāt unexpectedly, by chance
akāran for no reason
akelā alone; single, unmarried; on my own
akelāpan loneliness
aksar often
   aksar nahī not often
akTūbar October
aKhbār newspaper
aKhbār kā sTāl newspaper kiosk
aKhbār vālā newsagent's
alag separate; different
alag kisam ke different types
alag se separately
allah (U) God
allāh kā shukr hA! (U) bless you!
almārī cupboard
amīr rich (person)
amrīkā America
amrīkī American
andar inside
andar āiye come in
andar āne kā rāstā entrance
andar band hōnā to lock in
andar jānā to go in, to enter
andar ki bāt secret
andāz estimate; style
andāzan approximately
andāzā approximation
andhā blind
andhera darkness

angrezī English
 angrezī me in English
angūThā thumb
angūThī ring (on finger)
anivārya unavoidable
anjān unknown, unfamiliar;
 unaware
anōkhā unusual
anōpchārik (H) informal
ant end
antardeshīy uRān (H)
 domestic flight
antar-rāshTrīy (H)
 international
antyeshTi sanskār (H) funeral
anubhavī (H) experienced
anuchit unfair; unacceptable
anuvād (H) translation
anuvādak (H) translator
anuvād karnā (H) to translate
apāhij disabled
apne āp by myself
apnī kism kā typical
aprAl April
are! really!, hey!, well!
 are vāh! well well!
arthī bier

arthī uThānā to die
aRsaTh sixty-eight
aRtālīs forty-eight
aRtīs thirty-eight
asabhya uncivilized
asahya unbearable
asambhav (H) impossible
asbāb (U) baggage
aslī real, genuine
aspatāl hospital
assalam ālekam (U) good
 morning; good evening

assī eighty
asuvidhā janak (H)
 inconvenient
asvasth unhealthy
aTAchī briefcase
aThattar seventy-eight
aTThā-īs twenty-eight
aTThānve ninety-eight
aTThārā eighteen
aTThāsī eighty-eight
aTThāvan fifty-eight
avdhi (H) period
awr and; more
 awr sunāō tell us more
awrat woman
awratō ke sAniTarī Tāvel
 sanitary towels, sanitary
 napkins
awr kahī somewhere else
awr kharchā supplement,
 extra charge
awr kuchh something else
 awr kuchh? anything else?
 awr kuchh nahī nothing else
awrtō ke kapRe ladies' wear

ā

āapd (U) population
ābādī population
ābhār thanks
ādat habit
ādhā half
ādhā ghanTā half an hour
ādhā kirāyā half fare
ādhī kīmat half-price
ādhī rāt midnight
 ādhī rāt kō at midnight; in
 the middle of the night

ādhunik (H) modern

ādhunik chitrshālā modern art gallery

ādi et cetera

ādmī man; men

āg fire

āgan forecourt

āgbabūlā angry

āge further; in the future

āge bhejne kā patā forwarding address

āge le jānā to lead

āge pīchhe dekhō watch where you're going

āg lagī hA! fire!

āgrah (H) insist

āhistā āhistā gradually; (U) slowly

āinā mirror

āiye welcome

āj today

  āj se ek hafte bād a week (from) today

āj dōpahar this afternoon

ājkal kā modern

āj shām this evening

āj subah this morning

āj rāt tonight

ākāshvāni radio

ākh eye

āKhir end

āKhirī last; latter

āKhir kār eventually

ālpin pin

ām usual; general (adj); mango

ām pasand (U) popular

ānā to come

āntarrāshtrīya havāī aDDā

international airport

āp you

āp hA you are

āpkā your

āpke yours

āpke bād after you

āpreshan operation (medical)

āpreTar operator

āp the you were

ārām rest

ārām deh comfortable

ārāmghar lounge (in airport)

āsān easy, simple

āshā (H) hope

āshchary janak (H) amazing, astonishing

āshram sanctuary; monastery

āsmān sky

āstīn sleeve

āțō kī sūjan appendicitis

āTh eight

āūgā to call back; to call round

āvāz voice

āyarish Irish

āyarlAnD Ireland

āyu (H) age

āzād free

āzmānā to try

A

AgzhawsT nalī exhaust pipe

Akspres Dāk express mail

Alarjī allergic

Alarjī kī davā antihistamine

AmbulAns ambulance

Ampiyar amp

Anak glasses, eyeglasses
Anak banāne vālā optician
Asā of this sort
Asā-VAsā so-so
Ash-ārām luxury
Ash-ārām deh luxurious

b

bacchā baby (male); child (male)
bacchā gāRī pushchair, buggy
bacche children
bacche kā khānā baby food
bacche kā pōtRā nappy, diaper
bacche kī bōtal baby's bottle
bacche kī chūsnī dummy (baby's)
bacche kī ūchī kursī highchair
bacchī baby (female); child (female)
bachāō! help!
badalnā to change
badbū bad smell
badhazmī indigestion
badhāi! (H) congratulations!
badsūrat ugly
bahan sister
bahattar seventy-two
bahādūr brave
bahānā excuse
bahār (U) spring
bahrā deaf
bahut much; many; very, extremely
　bahut nahī not many

bahut acchhā! good!
bahut adhik too (excessively)
bahut bahut shukriyā thank you very much
bahut baRā enormous
bahut baRhiyā great, wonderful
bahut burā awful, horrible
bahut chhōTā tiny
bahut der a long time
bahut Khūb that's nice
　bahut Khūb! excellent!
bahut subah dawn
　bahut subah kō at dawn
bahut zyādā a lot, lots; too much
　bahut zyādā nahī not very much
bahū daughter-in-law
baje o'clock
bakhār village barn, storehouse
bakrī goat
baks box
baksā bag; case
bakvās: bakvās! nonsense!
　ye sab bakvās hA! rubbish!
bakvās band karō stop talking rubbish
bakhshīsh tip (to waiter etc)
balātkār rape
balki moreover
ballā racket (tennis, squash)
bambai Bombay
banā huā make, brand name
banānā to make
banāv-singār make-up
band closed; blocked; switched off

bandagī salutation; greetings
bandar monkey
bandargāh harbour, port
band hōnā to close, to shut
bandī prisoner
band karnā to close, to shut; to switch off
band karō! stop it!
bandūk gun, rifle
bangalā bungalow
bangālī Bengali
baniyā grocer; merchant
baniyān vest (under shirt)
bansī flute
ban Than ke well-dressed
barāmdā lobby; veranda
barāt wedding procession
barf ice; snow
barmā Burma
barmī Burmese
barsātī raincoat
barsāt kā mawsam monsoon
bartan dhōne kā sābun washing-up liquid
bartan pōchhne kā kapRā dishcloth
bartāniyā Britain
bartānvī British
barth berth; couchette
baRā big, large
baRā banānā enlargement
baRā din Christmas
  baRā din mubārak! merry Christmas!
baRā Dāk Khānā main post office
baRhānā to develop
baRhiyā great, super
baRī dūkān department store

baRī saRak main road
bas bus; coach
bas: bas, rahne dījiye! don't mention it!
  bas, ye kāfī hA, shukriyā that's plenty, thanks
bas kā aDDā bus station, coach station
bas kī sAr coach trip
bas sTāp bus stop
bas sTeshan bus station
batānā to tell
batlānā to explain
battī lamp
battīs thirty-two
baTan button
baTuā wallet; purse
bavanDar violent storm
bawchhār shower
bawddh Buddhist
bayālīs forty-two
bayān description
bayāsī eighty-two
bābuji gentleman; sir
bād after
bādal cloud
bādh dam
bād me later on, afterwards
bādshāh king
bāg garden
bāgh tiger
bāh arm
bāhar: vō bāhar gayā hA he's out
bāhar jānā to go out
bāhar jāne kā rāstā exit
bāhar khule me outdoors
bāhar nikalnā to get out (of car etc)

bāhar se tālā na khulnā to lock out

bā-īs twenty two

bājā musical instrument

bāje vālī Tōlī orchestra

bākā crooked; showy

bākī the rest

bāl hair

bālak child

bālbachhe children

bālig adult

bālī earrings

bāl kaTāi haircut

bāl krishna young Lord Krishna

bālō kā burush hairbrush

bāltī bucket

bānve ninety-two

bāp dad

bārā twelve

bār bār frequent

bārish rain

  bārish hō rahī hA it's raining

bāRā fence

bāRh flood

bās bamboo

bāsaTh sixty-two

bāsī stale

bāt talk

  kyā bāt hA? what's the matter?

bātchīt karnā to talk

bāT delivery (of mail)

bāTnā to deliver

bāvan fifty-two

bāyā left

bāyī taraf on the left; to the left

bāyī taraf muRe turn left

bāzār market; shopping centre

bāzārū downmarket

bāzū arm

bAgnī purple

bAlgaRi ox cart

bAnk kārD credit card

bArā waiter

bAsākhī crutches

bAtul Khalā (U) toilet, restroom

bATarī battery

bATarī vālī Tārch torch

bAThak lounge (in house, hotel)

bATh jāiye! sit down!

bATh jāō! sit down!

bAThnā to sit

bechnā to sell

begunāh innocent

behōsh unconscious

behōsh hō jānā to faint

behtar better

behtar banānā to improve

bejān dull (pain)

berōzgār unemployed

beshak of course

betukā ridiculous

beTā son

beTī daughter

bevkūf stupid

bhagvān God

bhagvān āpkā bhalā kare! (H) bless you!

bhagvān kā shukriyā! thank God!

bhakti religious devotion

bhalā well; good

  āpkā bhalā hō may God bless you

bhalāi goodness
bhale hi it doesn't matter
bharā full, crowded
bhar denā to fill up
bharnā to fill in
bhatījā nephew (brother's son)
bhatījī niece (brother's daughter)
bhaTThī oven
bhavishya (H) future
bhayānak (H) dangerous
bhābhī sister-in-law (brother's wife)
bhāda fare
bhāDā pot
bhāgō bhāgō! run, run!
bhāgya (H) luck
bhāi brother
bhāiō awr bahnō! ladies and gentlemen!
bhāi sāhab! mister!
bhānDe-bartan pots and pans
bhāng hashish
bhānjā nephew (sister's son)
bhānjī niece (sister's daughter)
bhārat India
bhārī heavy
bhārtīya Indian
bhāshā (H) language
bhāshā pāThya kram (H) language course
bhejnā to send
bhikhārī beggar
bhī too, also; even
bhīR crowd
bhīR ke vaKt rush hour
bhītar kā tālāb indoor pool
bhōjan (H) meal
bhōlā bhālā simple
bhrashTāchār corruption

bhunānā to change (money)
bhūkhā hungry
bhūl jānā to forget
bhūrā brown; grey
bigaRnā to break down; to damage
bigRī damaged
bijlī electricity; lightning
bijlī kā electric
bijlī kā balb light bulb
bijlī kā fyūz fuse
bijlī kā laTTū light bulb
bijlī kā mistrī electrician
bijlī kā pankhā fan (electrical)
bijlī kā plag plug (electrical)
bijlī kā sākeT socket, power point
bijlī kā sāmān electrical appliances
bijlī kā tār lead, wire
bijlī kā ustarā shaver
bijlī kī katawtī power cut
bikrī sale
bikrī ke liye for sale
bilding apartment block
bilkul completely
bilkul! exactly!
bilkul nahī of course not; definitely not
bilkul sahī quite correct
bilkul Thīk absolutely, I agree
billī cat
binā without
binā lAd kā petrōl unleaded petrol, unleaded gas
binā mahsūl kā (sāmān) duty-free (goods)
binā mahsūl kī dukān duty-

free shop
bindiyā dot on the forehead
birlā rare, uncommon
bistarā bed
bībī wife
bīch centre, middle
 bīch me between; in the middle
 bīch vālā the middle one
 bīch kā central; medium
 bīch kā chātā beach umbrella
 bīch ke māp kā medium-sized
bīmā insurance
bīmār ill, (US) sick
bīmārī illness; disease
bīṝī sigreṬ manāhī vālā Ḍibbā nonsmoking compartment
bīs twenty
blāwz blouse
bōjh, bōjhā weight; burden; load
bōlnā to speak
bōtal bottle
bōtal khōlne kī chābī bottle-opener
brek brake
brihaspat vār (H) Thursday
briṬen Britain, UK
brīf kes briefcase
buddhū idiot
budhvār Wednesday
buk karānā to book
buKhār temperature, fever
bulānā to call
burā bad, offensive
burī tarah (se) badly
burush brush
but (U) statue

buzurg senior citizen
būṝhā/buṝhiyā old
būth kiosk
būṬ boot (footwear)

ch

chacherā bhāi cousin (male)
chacherī bahan cousin (female)
chale jāō! go away!
chaliye let's go
chalnā to walk; to move
chalō chale! let's go!
chalte banō get lost
chalū karnā to switch on
chammach spoon
chamṝā leather
chamṝī skin
chapṬā flat (adj)
charbī fat
charbī vālā khānā rich (food)
chaṝhnā to get on (to train etc); climbing
chashmā glasses, spectacles; fountain (for drinking)
chaṬāi mat
chaṬṬān rock
chavālīs forty-four
chavvan fifty-four
chawbīs twenty-four
chawdā fourteen
chawhattar seventy-four
chawk square (in town)
chawrāhā crossroads, intersection
chawrānve ninety-four
chawrāsī eighty-four

chawRā wide
chawRī saRak avenue
chawsaTh sixty-four
chawthāi hissā quarter
chawtīs thirty-four
chābī key; bottle opener
chābī kā chhallā keyring
chāchā uncle (father's younger brother)
chāchī aunt (paternal)
chād moon
chādar sheet
chāhe ... even if ...
chāhiye wanted
  āpkō kyā chāhiye? what do you want?
  mujhe ... chāhiye I want ...; I need ...
chāhnā to want
  vō ... chāhtā hA he wants to ...
  mA ... nahī chāhtā/chāhtī I don't want to ... (said by man/woman)
chākū knife
chālīs forty
chāndī silver
chāppal sandals
chār four
chāval rice
chāy kī chammach teaspoon
chāy kī dukān tea house
chāy-pānī kī dukān café
chAk cheque, (US) check
chArī cherry
chehrā face
chhabbīs twenty-six
chhajjā balcony
chhappan fifty-six

chhat ceiling; roof
chhattīs thirty-six
chhavRī basket
chhāh shade
  chhāh me in the shade
chhātā umbrella
chhātī chest; breast
chhāyā (H) sunshade
chhA six
chhed hole
chhiālīs forty-six
chhiānve ninety-six
chhiāsaTh sixty-six
chhiāsī eighty-six
chhihattar seventy-six
chhipānā to hide (something)
chhipkalī lizard
chhipnā to hide (oneself)
chhīk sneeze
chhōRnā to leave (leave behind)
chhōTā small; short
chhōTā aspatāl clinic
chhōTā chākū penknife
chhōTā rāstā shortcut
chhōTā tawliyā facecloth
chhōTī mātā chickenpox
chhōTī mōTar sāikil moped
chhurī-kāTe cutlery
chhuTe sāmān kā daftar left luggage (office), baggage check room
chhuTTī holiday, vacation
chhūT gayī missed (bus)
chhūTnā to leave (depart)
chillānā to shout
chimTī pliers; tweezers
chiRiyā bird
chiRiyāghar zoo
chitr (H) picture, painting

chitrshālā (H) art gallery
chiTTe bālō vālā/vālī blond (adj)
chiTThī letter
chiTThī kā kāgaz writing paper
chīn China
chīnī Chinese; sugar
chīnī ke bartan crockery
chīnī miTTī ke bartan china
chīTī ant
chīyars! cheers! (toast)
chīz thing
chōgā dressing gown
chōlī bra; blouse
chōr thief
chōrī burglary
chōT bruise; injury
chōT lagnā to hurt, to injure
chummā kiss
chunanā to choose
chungī Customs
chup! shut up!
chup rahō! quiet!
churānā to steal
churuT cigar
chūhā mouse; rat
chūlhā cooker
chūmnā to kiss
chūnā mortar; lime
chūnā lagā diyā rip-off (prices)
chūredār sābun soap powder
chūRiyā bangles
chūtaR bottom (of person)

d

dab gayā jammed
daftar office
dakshin (H) south
dakshin afrīkā (H) South Africa
dakshin afrikā kā (H) South African
dakshinī (H) southern
dakshin-pashchim (H) southwest
dakshin-pūrv (H) southeast
daK distance
dal (H) group
damā asthma
damkal fire brigade
danD fine
dangā riot
dar exchange rate
darāz drawer
dard ache; pain; sore
dard miTāne kī davā painkillers
dardnāk painful
dargāh shrine
dariyā sea; river
darī carpet
darjī tailor
darj karānā to check in
darmiyānā medium
darpan (H) mirror
darrā pass (in mountains)
darvān doorman, porter
darvāzā door
darzan dozen
das ten
das lākh million

dastak knock on the door
dastāne gloves
dastāvez document
dastkārī kī dukān craft shop
dastKhat (U) signature
dastūr custom
davā drug; medicine
davā kī dukān/davāKhānā pharmacy, chemist's
dawr course (main course etc)
dawrā fit, attack
dawR race (for runners, cars)
dawRnā to run
dayālu kind
dādā grandfather
dādī grandmother
dāg stain
dāKhilā admission charge
dām price
dāmād son-in-law
dāru alcoholic drink
dāRhī beard
dāt tooth
dāt me bharne kā masālā filling (in tooth)
dāt me dard toothache
dātōõ kā DākTar dentist
dāt sāf karne kā brash toothbrush
dāt sāf karne kā reshā dental floss
dāvat invitation; party (celebration)
dāvat denā to invite
dāyā right (not left)
dāyī taraf muRe turn right
dāyī taraf on the right
dāyrā circle
de denā to deliver

dehāt country, countryside
dekhbhāl karnā to look after
dekhnā to see; to check
dekhne jānā to visit (place)
dekhte rahnā! look out!
denā to give
der delay; late
desh (H) country
devī goddess
devtā god
dhadhaktī āg fire
dhadhā profession; business
dhakka shock
dhakkā denā to push
dhanvān rich
dhanyvād (H) thank you
dharm (H) religion
dhaR bust
dhat tere kī! damn!
dhāgā thread
dhārā stream
dhātu metal
dhīmā slow
dhīre dhīre (H) gradually; slowly
dhōbī washerman
dhōbī ghāT laundry (place)
dhōkhā to swindle
dhōnā to wash
dhōtī cloth worn around the waist
dhuā smoke
dhudhlā cloudy, dull
dhulāi ghar laundry (place)
dhulāi ke kapRe laundry (clothes)
dhulāi kī dukān launderette
dhundh fog
dhurī axle

149

dhūl dust
dhūl bharā dusty
dhūp sunshine
  dhūp me in the sun
  dhūp niklī hA it's sunny
dhūp kā chashmā sunglasses; goggles
dhūp me jhulasnā sunburn
dhūp me jhulsā sunburnt
dhūp se bachne kī krīm sunblock
dhūp seknā to sunbathe
dhyān rakhe! be careful!
dikhāiye show me
dikkat trouble
dil heart
dilchasp interesting
dilchaspī interest
  merī ... me dilchaspī hA I'm interested in ...
dil kā dawrā heart attack
dillī Delhi
dilpasand favourite
din day
  dō din bād in two days from now
din bhar kī sAr day trip
disambar December
diyāsalāyi matches
dījiye give me
  ek awr dījiye may I have another one?
dīvār wall
dō two
  dō ... a couple of ...
  dō bār twice
  dō bistarō vālā kamrā twin room
  dō hafte fortnight, two weeks
dōnō both
dōnō me se ek either of them
dōnō me se kōī nahī neither (one) of them
dōpahar afternoon; noon, midday; at midday
  dōpahar me in the afternoon
  dōpahar kō at noon
  dōpahar kā khānā lunch
  dōpahar ke bād pm
dōst friend
dōstānā friendly
dubhāshiyā interpreter
dublā skinny
dudhūvālā milkman
dukān shop
dukhnā to feel pain
  dukh rahā hA? is it painful?
dulhan bride
duniyā world
durg fort
durghaTnā (H) accident
durghaTnā vibhāg (H) casualty department
dushman enemy
dūr far
dūr darshan (H) television
dūrī distance
dūr kī telīphōn kāl long-distance call
dūshit (H) polluted
dūsrā another; second (adj); other; the other one
dūsrā nām surname
dūsrā rāstā diversion, detour
dūtāvās (H) embassy

dh

D

Dabal double
Dabal bistar double bed
Dabal kamrā double room
Dabal rōTī kī dukān bakery
DakAtī robbery
Dallī lump
DanDa truncheon, nightstick
Dāk mail, post
Dākā raid
Dāk baks letterbox, mailbox
Dāk gāRī express (train)
Dāk kā kōD postcode, zip code
Dāk-Khānā post office
Dāk-Khāne me jamā chiTThiyā poste restante, general delivery
Dāk me Dālnā to post, to mail
Dāk se bhejnā to post, to mail
DākTar/DākTarnī doctor (man/woman)
Dākū robber, bandit
DāT cork; plug (in sink)
DāT rebuke
Dāyal karnā to dial
Dāyal karne kā kōD dialling code
Dāyrī diary
DAk deck (on ship)
DAk kursī deckchair
Degchī saucepan
Derā Dālnā to camp
Dhakkan cap (of bottle)
Dhaknā lid
Dhalvā steep (hill)
Dhābā roadside café

Dhāchā pattern
Dhibrī nut (for bolt)
Dhīlā loose (handle etc)
DhūDhnā to look for
Dibbā carton; can, tin; coach, carriage, compartment
Dōngī dinghy; canoe
Drāivar driver
Drāmā play (in theatre)
Dūbjānā to drown
DyawDhī foyer

e

eDs bīmārī AIDS
ehsānmand grateful
ek a, an; one
ekānt secluded
ek bār once
ekdam at once, immediately
ek hazār thousand
ek lākh hundred thousand
ek sāth together
ekspres express (train)
ek vakt kā khānā half board
erī heel (of foot)
erī lagāne kā kāwnTar shoe repairer's
eyar kanDīshan air-conditioned
eyar kanDīshan kamrā air-conditioned room
eyar kanDīshan karnā air-conditioning

f

fan (U) art
fankār (U) artist
fark difference
farsh floor (of room)
farvarī February
fasT eD first aid
fasT eD kā baksā first-aid kit
fawran immediately, at once,
  straight away
fāram form, document
fAks kar denā to send a fax
fAshan me nahī unfashionable
fAshan parast fashionable
fAslā decision
fehrisht me dī gayī flāit
  scheduled flight
fikRõ kī kitāb phrasebook
film film, movie
film dhōnā film processing
filmī sitārā film star
fī sadī per cent
fisalne vālā slippery
flAT flat, apartment
frānsīsī French
friz fridge
fuT foot (measurement)
fuTbāl football
fuvvārā fountain
fūl flower

g

gaddā mattress
gaddī cushion; saddle (for
  bike)

gadhā donkey; stupid
gahrā deep, dark (colour)
gahrā nīlā navy blue
gaj yard
galat wrong
galatfahmī misunderstanding
galā throat; neck
gale kā hār necklace
galiyārā corridor
galiyāre kī sīT aisle seat
galī street; lane
galīchā carpet
galtī error, mistake; fault
gambhīr (H) serious
gandagī dirt
gandā filthy, dirty
ganjā bald
garaj kaRak kā tūfān
  thunderstorm
garam warm; hot
garbh nirōdhak gōlī (H)
  contraceptive pill
garbhvatī (H) pregnant
gardan neck
garīb poor (not rich)
garmī heat; summer
  garmiyō me in (the) summer
gaRbaRī disorder; breakdown
  (of machine)
  kyā gaRbaRī hA? what's
  wrong?
gavāh witness
gazab unexpected;
  unbelievable; extraordinary
gāiD ke sāth sAr guided tour
gāl cheek
gāli swearing
gānā music; song; sing
gāne vālā/vālī musician;

singer (man/woman)
gānjā marijuana
gāṛī train
  gāṛī se by rail
  gāṛī khaṛī karnā to park
gāv village
gāy cow
gāyab missing
gāyab hōnā to disappear
gArkānunī unlawful
ged ball
ghanTā hour
ghar home; house
  kyā vō ghar par hA? is he in?,
  is he at home?
gharelū uRān domestic flight
ghaRiyāl crocodile
ghaRī clock; wristwatch
ghaTiyā poor quality
ghaTiyā māl rubbish, garbage
ghās grass
ghās kā mAdān lawn
ghāT jetty
ghāTī valley
ghāyal injured
ghinōnā revolting
ghōRā horse
ghōRā gāRī horse-drawn
  carriage
ghōslā nest
ghughrālā curly
ghuR savāRī horse riding
ghuTnā knee
giārā eleven
gilās glass (for drinking)
gintī number, figure
girjā church
girnā to fall
gīlā wet; damp

gōd lap
  parbat kī gōd foothill; valley
gōlā circle
gōl-dāyrā circle (in theatre)
gōlī pill; bullet
gōrā fair (adj)
gōsht meat
gufā cave; tunnel
gulāb rose
gulābī pink
guldastā bouquet
gum missing
gumTā bruise; lump (on body)
gun (H) quality
gurdā kidney
gurdvārā temple (Sikh)
guruvār Thursday
guRiyā doll
gusal (U) bath
gusalKhānā bathroom
gussā karnā to be angry
gustāKh rude
gustaKhi māf! forgive the
  rudeness!

h

had se zyādā sāmān excess
  baggage
haDDī bone
haDDī kā TūTnā to fracture
haftā week
halkā light (not heavy); weak
  (drink)
halkā bhūrā beige, light
  brown
halkā khānā snack
halkā nīlā light blue

hallāgullā uproar; street fighting

halō hello (answer on phone)

halvāi shop selling sweets and savoury snacks

ham we

  ham hA we are

  ham the we were

hame us

hameshā always

hamlā attack

harā green

harārat feverishness

har chīz everything

har ek everyone; each, every

hargiz nahī not in the least

har kahī everywhere

harkārā courier

har rōz every day; per day

hasnā to laugh

hastākshar (H) signature

hatthā handle (on door)

haTānā to move; to remove

havā breeze; air

havādār draughty

havāi aDDā airport

havāi aDDe kī bas airport bus

havāi Dāk se by airmail

havāi jahāz plane, airplane

  havāi jahāz se by air, by plane

havāi jahāz se jānā to fly

havāi lifāfā airmail envelope

havāi patr (H) airmail letter

havālāt custody; lock-up

havāldār police constable

havelī big mansion

hā yes

hādasā (U) accident

hādase ka mahakmā (U) casualty department

hāl: kyā hāl hA? how are you?

hālāki although

hālenD Netherlands

hāl hī me recently, the other day

hāmārā our; ours

hāmilā (U) pregnant

hāth hand

hāthī elephant

hāth kā sāmān hand luggage

hāth kī gharī wristwatch

hāTh kā pankhā fan

hāy re! oh no!

hA is; are

  ham hA we are

  āp hA you are

hAnD bAg handbag, (US) purse

hAratangez (U) amazing

hijaRā eunuch

himālay pahāR the Himalayas

hindī Hindi

hind mahāsāgar Indian Ocean

hindustānī Indian; Hindi

hindū Hindu

hissā piece, part

hīrā diamond

hōgayā: kyā hōgayā? what has happened?

hōkar through, via

hōlī Festival of Colours

hōnā to be; to have; to happen

hōshiyār clever, intelligent; careful

  hōshiyār rahe! be careful!

hōsh me sober (not drunk)
hōsh me hA conscious
hōTal hotel
hōTal kā kamrā hotel room
huā: kyā huā? what
  happened?
hū am

i

idhar over here
  idhar hĀ it's this way
ijāzat permission
ikattīs thirty-one
ikaTThā karnā to collect
ikhattar seventy-one
ikkis twenty-one
iksaTh sixty-one
iktālīs forty-one
ikyānave ninety-one
ikyāsī eighty-one
ikyāvan fifty-one
ilāj karnā to cure
ilākā area, region
ilāke kā kōD area code
imām (U) priest
imārat building
imtahān exam
in these
inhe them (nearby)
injan engine
inkā their; theirs (nearby)
inkō them (nearby)
intzār karnā to wait; to look
  forward to
is this
ishthār poster;
  advertisement; leaflet

iskā his; her; hers (nearby)
isrār (U) insist
istakbāl (U) reception
is taraf over here
istarī iron (for ironing)
istemāl karnā to use
itar perfume
itnā as much as this
  itnā burā nahī not so bad
  itnā hī acchhā as good as
  itnā zyādā nahī not so much
itvār Sunday
izāzat denā to let, to allow
izzat honour
īmāndār honest
  īmāndārī se fairly
īshvar (H) God

j

jab when
jabRā jaw
jab se since
jab tak until; while
jagah place
jahāz ship
  jahāz se by ship
jahrīlā poisonous
jalan jealousy
jalānā to switch on; to light
jaldī quick; soon; early
jaldī karnā to hurry
jaldī karō! hurry up!
jaldī se quickly
jale kā dāh burn
jal gayā it's burnt
jalnā to burn
jamā deposit (as part payment)

jamā huā frozen
jamāne: gujre jamāne me in the past
janāb (U) Mr
janānā ladies' room
janāzā (U) funeral
jangal forest, woods
janmdin (H) birthday
janūb (U) south
 janūb me (U) in the south
janūb afrīkā (U) South Africa
janūb afrīkā kā (U) South African
janūbī (U) southern
janūb-magrib (U) southwest
janūb-mashrik (U) southeast
janvarī January
jaRāū pin brooch
javāhirāt jewellery
javān young
jawharī jeweller's
jāchpaRtāl karnā to check
jāganā to stay awake
jāgate rahō! beware!
jāgh thigh
jāghiyā shorts; (under)pants
jāl net
jālī fake, forgery
jānā to go
jān bachāne kī jākeT life jacket
jān bachāne kī peTī lifebelt
jān būjh kar deliberately
jāne dījiye! never mind!
jāne kī jagah destination
jānkārī information
jānkārī kā daftar information office
jānkārī kī jagah information

desk
jānvar animal
jāō! go away!
jāRā winter
 jāRe me in (the) winter
jāz sangīt jazz
jAn dharm Jainism
jeb pocket
jeb katrā/katrī pickpocket (man/woman)
jel prison
jhagRā quarrel
jhanDā flag
jhaT quickly
jhaTkā jerk; shock
jhaTpaT quickly
jhāRū broom, brush
jhilmilī shutter (on window)
jhilmilī pardā blinds
jhīl lake
jhōlā bag
jhūThā false
jhūTh bōlnā to tell a lie
jigar liver (in body)
jins (U) sex
jism (U) body
jitnī jaldī hōsake as soon as possible
jī expression of respect
jī hā yes, please
 jī nahī no; no, thanks; sorry
jībh tongue
jīn jeans
jīvan (H) life
jōKhim bharā risky
jōr with extra strength; with exertion
jōRā/jōRī couple; pair
judā separate

julāb laxative
jumme rāt (U) Thursday
jurmānā fine
jute kī eRī heel (of shoe)
jūā gambling
jūlus procession; demonstration
jūtā shoe
jūte kī pālish shoe polish
jyādā: mujhe ... jyādā pasand hA I prefer ...

k

kab? when?
kabhī ever
kabhī kabhī sometimes
kabhī nahī never
kabr grave
kabristān cemetery
kabutar pigeon
kabz constipation
kafnī upper unsewn garment
kahā? where?
  āp kahā se hA? where are you from?
  ye kahā hA? where is it?
  kyā kahā? sorry?, pardon me?
kahī somewhere
kahnā to say
kahte hA: ise ... kahte hA he is called ...
  is kō kyā kahte hA? what's it called?
kaī several
kal tomorrow; yesterday
kal rāt last night

kalam pen
kalā (H) art
kalāī wrist
kalākār (H) artist
kal se ek hafte bād a week (from) tomorrow
kal subah tomorrow morning; yesterday morning
kam less; low (prices)
  kam mahangā inexpensive
kamar waist
kamāl kā brilliant
kamānī lever
kambal blanket
kamīz shirt
kampanī company, business
kamrā room; flat, apartment
kam se kam at least
kamzōr weak (person)
kandhā shoulder
kangan bracelet
kanghī comb
kapRā cloth, material
kapRe clothes
kapRe ājmāne kā kamrā fitting room
kapRe badalnā to get changed
kapRe dhōnā washing, laundry
kapRe dhōne kā pāuDar washing powder
kapRe pahannā to get dressed
kapRe phAlāne kī rassī clothes line
kapRe Tāgne kī chimTī clothes peg

kare:

āp ... kare you should ...

āp ... mat kare you
shouldn't ...

karnā to do

mA kyā karū? what should I
do?

kaRā hard

kaRhāi pan

kaRvā bitter

kasāi kī dukān butcher's

kasrat kī jagah gym

kaTawtī discount

kaThin (H) difficult

kaThināyī (H) difficulty

kawā crow

kawn? who?

kawnsā? which one?

kawnse? which ones?

kā of

... kā banDal a pack of ...

... kā jōRā a pair of ...

kāch glass (material)

kāfī quite; very; enough;
coffee

kāfī ... plenty of ...

kāfī baRā a lot bigger

kāfī sārā quite a lot

kāgaz paper

kāgaz ke rumāl tissues,
Kleenex®

kāgpech corkscrew

kālar collar

kālā black; dark (hair)

kālā bāzār black market

kālej college

kām job; work

kām kā useful

kām me lage hue busy

kān ear

kānūn law

kār car

kār se by car

kār chalānā to drive

kār chalāne kā lāisens driver's
licence

kārīgar mechanic

kārkhānā factory

kārōbār business

kāryakram (H) programme

kāsā bronze

kāTā fork

kāTnā to cut; to bite

kāunTar counter

kAmp kī jagah campsite

kAmp lagānā to camp

kAmre kī dukān camera shop

kAmre kī flAsh flash (for camera)

kAnchī scissors

kAse how

āp kAse hA? how are you?
(to man)

kAsh kāunTar cash desk,
cashier

kAsī how

āp kAsī hA? how are you? (to
woman)

ke of

ke alāvā apart from

ke andar into; inside

ke bād after; next, after that

ke bāhar outside

ke bāre me about

ke bīch me among

ke dawrān during

ke jAsā similar

ke Khilāf against

ke liye for

kendra (H) centre
kendrīya (H) central
ke nīche under
ke pare beyond
ke pār across
ke pās near; next to; at
... ke pās beside the ...
ke rāste via
ke sāth with
ke sivā except
keval (H) only
ke zariye through, by means of
khabar dār! watch out!
khabbā left-handed
khanDhar ruins
kharāb bad
kharch karnā to spend
kharōch scratch
khasrā measles; German measles
khaTārā old banger
khaTiyā cot
khaTTa sour
khādī handwoven cotton cloth
khādī kī Tōpī white cap
khākā drawing
khālā (U) aunt
khā lō! eat up!
khānā food; meal; dish; to eat
khāne kā kamrā dining room
khāne-pīne kā Dibbā buffet car
khāRī bay
khās girjā cathedral
khāsī cough
khāsī kī davā cough medicine

khāta bank account
khel sport; game
khel kā mAdān playground
khelkūd athletics
khelnā to play
khelne ke jūte trainers (shoes)
khet farm
khilawnā toy
khiRkī window
khiRkī ke pās by the window
khiRkī vālī sīT window seat
khīchnā to pull
khōjnā to search
khōl crown (on tooth)
khōlnā to unlock; to open; to unpack
khōnā to lose
khōye sāmān kā daftar lost property office
khudā hāfiz (U) good night
khujīli itch
khulā open
khulāsā brief
khulā TikaT open ticket
khulī saRak motorway, freeway, highway
khullā change (smaller notes)
khulnā to open (of shop etc)
khulne kā vaKt opening times
khushbū scent, fragrance
khūb pakā well-done (meat)
khūbsūrat attractive
kinārā shore
kirāyā rent; fare
kirāye kī kar car rental; rented car
kirāye par for hire, for rent
kirāye par lenā to hire, to

kī

ki

rent
kishtī boat; ferry
kiskā? whose?
kism sort, type
  kis kism kā ...? what sort
  of ...?
kismat luck
kitāb book
kitābō kī dukān bookshop,
  bookstore
kitnā? how much?; how
  many?; what?
kitnā vaKt lagegā? how long
  does it take?
kitne? how much?; how
  many?; what?
  kitne pAse lagege? how
  much is it?
  kitne baje hA? what's the
  time?
kī of
kī bazāy instead
kīchaR mud
kījiye please; please do
  ye mat kījiye! don't do that!
kīl nail (metal)
kīmat price; cost; charge;
  value
  is kī kīmat kyā hA? how
  much is it?
kīmat lagnā to cost
kīmtī valuable
kī nisbat than
kīRā insect; worm
kīRā kāTnā insect bite
kīRe mārne kī davā antiseptic;
  disinfectant; insect repellent
kī sagāi hō chukī engaged (to
  be married)

kī taraf towards
kō to; at; with regard to
kō dekhnā to look at
kōD nambar dialling code
kōhnī elbow
kōī somebody, someone;
  anybody
kōī bāt nahī you're welcome,
  don't mention it; it doesn't
  matter
kōī dikkat nahī! no problem!
kōī nahī nobody, no-one
kō jānnā to know (a person)
kōnā corner
  kōne me in the corner
  kōne par on the corner
kōT coat
kōTharī cabin
kōThī mansion
kōT rakhne kā kamrā
  cloakroom
kōT Tāngne kī khūTī
  coathanger
kōyal cuckoo
kripayā (H) please, kindly
krismas se pahlā din
  Christmas Eve
kritagya (H) grateful
kshamā (H) apology
kuchh anything; something
kuchh had tak to some
  extent
kuchh nahī nothing
kudratī natural
kuhrā mist; fog
kukar cooker
kul total
kulī coolie, railway porter;
  labourer

kul milākar altogether
kumārī (H) Miss
kunbā (U) family
kursī chair
kurtā typical Indian upper garment
kuttā dog
kutubnumā compass
kuvārā bachelor
kūchī brush (artist's)
kūdnā to jump
kūlhā bottom (of person); hip
kūRā karkaT rubbish, trash
kūRedān dustbin, bin, trashcan
kyā? what?
　kyā ye ... hA? is this ...?
　kyā ... hA? is it ...?; do you ...?
　kyā bāt hA? what's the matter?
　kyā hāl hA? how are you?
　kyā kahā? sorry?, what did you say?
kyō? why?
　kyō nahī? why not?
kyōki because

K

Kabūl karnā to accept
Kad height
Karīb-Karīb almost
Katār queue
Kawmiat (U) nationality
Kawmī (U) national
KāT bite
Khabar news

Kharāb bad; disgusting; bad state
　ye zyādā Kharāb hA it's worse
Khargōsh rabbit
Kharīdārī rakhne kā ThAlā carrier bag
Kharīdnā to buy
Khatarnāk dangerous
Khatm end
Khatm hōnā/Khatm karnā to finish
Khatrā danger
Khatre kī hālat emergency
Khatre kī hālat me bāhar jāne kā rāstā emergency exit
Khayal idea
Khākā map (city plan)
Khālis straight (whisky etc)
Khālī empty
Khālī nahī engaged, busy; engaged, occupied
Khāmōsh! (U) quiet!
Khāmōshī silence
Khārish rash (on skin)
Khās (H) main; special
Khāsiyat quality
Khāskar especially
KhāTūn (U) lady
Khāvind (U) husband
Khizã (U) autumn, (US) fall
Khud by myself
Khudā āpkā bhalā kare! (U) bless you!
Khudā hāfiz (U) goodbye, bye; good night
Khud-bakhud lenā self-service
Khumār hangover
KhunKharābā bloody fighting

Khurāk diet
Khush happy, glad
  āp se milkar baRī Khushī huī pleased to meet you
Khush kismatī se fortunately
Khūbsurat beautiful; pretty
Khūn blood
KhūTī tent peg
Kilā castle

I
■

lachīlā elastic
lachīlā fītā elastic band
lafz (U) word
lagbhag (H) nearly; approximately
lahar wave; current
lahū blood
lakīr line
lakRī wood (material)
lambā long; tall
lapeTne kā kāgaz wrapping paper
laRāi fight
laRkā boy
laRkī girl
lawnDebāz gay
lāgat charge, fee; cost
lāgat kā kārD charge card
lāl red
lālchī greedy
lānā to get, to fetch; to bring
lārī lorry
lAns lens (of camera)
le ānā to fetch
le jānā to take; to lead; to carry

lekin but
lenā to take, to accept; to have; to collect
leTnā to lie down
lifāfā envelope
lifT lift, elevator
likhnā to write
  ... ne likhā written by ...
likhne kā kāgaz writing paper
ling (H) sex (gender)
lījiye: ye lījiye here you are
lōg people
lōkal stopping train
lōk nritya folk dancing
lōkpriy (H) popular
lōk sangīt folk music
lugat (U) dictionary
lūngi wraparound cloth from waist down
lūT liyā robbed

m
■

macchhar mosquito
macchhardānī mosquito net
macchhar mārne ki davā mosquito repellent
machhī, machhlī fish
machhlī vālā fishmonger's
madad help
madad gār helpful
madad karnā to help
madāri roadside performer; magician
madhyāntar (H) interval
maflar scarf (for neck)
magar macchh crocodile
magrib (U) west

magrib me in the west
magribī (U) western
mahafil party
mahak scent, fragrance
mahakmā department
mahal palace
mahangā expensive
mahbūbā girlfriend
mahilā (H) lady
mahilā shawchālay (H) ladies'
  toilets, ladies' room
mahīnā month
mahsūs karnā to feel
makān building; house
makān ke andar indoors
makkhi fly
makkhi chūs miser
makRī spider
maKbarā tomb
mandir temple
mangalvār Tuesday
mangetar fiancé; fiancée
man-māne dām rip-off prices
mantra charm
manzil floor, storey
marammat karnā to mend, to
  repair
marā huā dead
mardānā (pākhānā) (U) gents'
  toilet, men's room
mardāne kapRe menswear
marham ointment, cream
marham-paTTī dressing (for
  cut)
marī huī dead
marnā to die
martbān jar
mashhūr famous
mashīn machine

mashrik (U) east
  mashrik me in the east
mashrikī (U) eastern
masjid mosque
maslā problem
masta carefree; happy
mastak head
mastī happiness; intoxication
masūRā gum (in mouth)
mat no
  mat! don't!
matā (H) mother
matbab meaning
matlab hōnā to mean
matlī nausea
mawsam weather
mawsamī bukhār hayfever
mawt death
mayī May
mazāk joke
mazākiyā funny, amusing
mazā lenā to enjoy oneself
mazbūt strong
mazedār delicious; enjoyable;
  exciting
mazhab (U) religion
mā mum
mābāp parents
māchis matches
māchis kā Dibbā matchbox
māfī apology
māf kījiye sorry; excuse me
māf kījiye, galat nambar sorry,
  wrong number
māgnā to borrow; to ask for
māhvārī period,
  menstruation
mākūl (U) appropriate,
  suitable

mā

163

māl goods
mālik/mālkin owner (man/woman)
mālis massage
mālūm: mujhe mālūm nahī I don't know
āpkō pakkā mālūm hA? are you sure?
māmā uncle (mother's brother)
māmūlī ordinary, average
mānnā to agree
mA māntā/māntī hū I agree (said by man/woman)
māp size
mārg road
mārnā to kill; to hit
māsik dharm (H) period, menstruation
māsī aunt (maternal)
māsTar/masTarānī jī teacher (man/woman)
māsūm simple
māthā forehead
māyūs disappointed; despondent
mA I
mA hū I am
mAch match (football etc)
mAdān park; open field; ground
mAl dirt
mAlā filthy (room etc); polluted
mAnezarānī manageress
me in; into; at; among
meharbān kind, generous
meharbānī karke please, kindly
mehmān guest
mehmāndārī hospitality

mek make (brand name)
mel connection; fast train
melā carnival, fair
merā/mere/merī my; mine
merā apnā ... my own ...
merī duā! good luck!
mez table
mez kursī vagArā furniture
mezpōsh tablecloth
miāh form of address used when speaking to a Muslim (literally: Muslim gentleman)
milānā to introduce
milānevālī flāit connecting flight
milnā to meet; to find
milne jānā to visit (person)
milne kī jagah meeting place
minaT minute
ek minaT me in a minute
ek minaT rukō! just a minute!
mirch masāle vālā spicy
misāl example
misāl ke tawr par for example
misTrī mechanic
mīThāī sweet, pudding; sweets, candies
mīTTī ke bartan pottery
mīl mile
mīThā sweet (taste)
mōchī shoe repairer's
mōmbattī candle
mōr peacock
mōR bend, turning (in road)
mōtī pearl
mōTar car
mōTā thick; fat

mā

mōtī akl kā thick, stupid
mōzā stockings; socks
mubārakbād best wishes
  mubārakbād!
  congratulations!
muddat period (of time)
muft free (no charge)
muft savārī karnā to hitch-
  hike
muh mouth
muhallā suburb
muhtarmā (U) Mrs; Miss
mujhe me
  mujhe bhī me too
mukāmī (U) local
mukhy (H) main
mukhtalif (U) different
mulākāt appointment;
  meeting
mulāyam soft
mulk country, nation; state
mumbAī Bombay
mumkin possible
munhasir hA (U) it depends
  ... munhasir kartā hA (U) it
  depends on ...
murdā dead
musalmān Muslim
musāfir passenger
mushkil hard, difficult
mushkilāt difficulty
musībat disaster
muskarānā to smile
mustakbil (U) future
mūchh moustache
mūrkh stupid
mūrti (H) statue

n

na ... na ... neither ... nor ...
nadī river
nafrat karnā to hate
nahar canal
nahāne kā tawliyā bath towel
nahāne kā Tab bathtub
nahī no; not; didn't
  nahī! don't!
  mA bhī nahī nor do I
naklī fake, imitation
naklī dāt dentures
nakshā map
naKdī cash
naKdī kā kāunTar cash desk
naKdī kī mashīn cash
  dispenser, ATM
naKdī me badalnā to cash
nalsāz plumber
namaste (H) hello; goodbye
nambar number
namī dene vālā moisturizer
namī vālā humid
nashe me chūr drunk
nashīlī davā drugs (narcotics)
naT nut (for bolt)
navambar November
navāb king
navāsī eighty-nine
navve ninety
naw nine
nawjavān teenager
nawkā yacht
nawkrānī maid
nayā new
nayā sāl New Year
nayā sāl mubārak! Happy

New Year!

naye Dhang kā up-to-date

naye fAshan kā trendy

naye sāl se pahle kī rāt New Year's Eve

nazar rakhnā to keep an eye on

nazārā view; scenery; sights

nazdīk near

nāch dance

nāchnā to dance

nāg (H) cobra

nā-gavār shocking

nāi (kī dukān) barber's

nāk nose

nākābandi roadblock

nākhūn fingernail

nākhūn kī pālish nail varnish

nākhūn sāf karne kā burush nailbrush

nāli drain; pipe

nām name

āpkā nām kyā hA? what's your name?

nāmumkin impossible

nāmunāsib not suitable

nāpne kā fītā tape measure

nārangī orange (colour)

nārāz angry

nārve Norway

nārvejian Norwegian

nāsamajh silly

nāshtā breakfast

nāsūr ulcer

nāTak play (in theatre)

nāv (H) boat

nApāl Nepal

nApālī Nepali

nApī nappy, diaper

netā politician; leader

nichlī manzil ground floor, (US) first floor

nijī private

nijī gusalkhānā private bathroom

nijī sTīriō personal stereo

nikar pants, panties

nikās (H) exit

nīlām auction

nimantran (H) invitation

nimantran denā (H) to invite

ninyānave ninety-nine

nirāsh (H) disappointed

nirāshājanak disappointing

nirbhar: ye nirbhar hA (H) it depends

... par nirbhar kartā hA (H) it depends on ...

nirdesh karnā to point out

nirdesh pushtikā handbook

nirdōsh (H) innocent

nirnay (H) decision

nirōdh condom

nishān kā takhtā signpost

nīchā low

nīche under, below; down

nīche jānā to go down (the stairs etc)

nīche kī ōr downstairs; downwards

nīlam sapphire

nīlā blue

nōT banknote, (US) bill

nōTbuk notebook

nōval novel

nritya (H) dance

nuksān loss

nuks vālā faulty

numāish exhibition

nusKhā prescription

ō

ōTh lips

p

pachānve ninety-five

pachās fifty

pachāsī eighty-five

pachchīs twenty-five

pachpan fifty-five

paglā mad; idiot

pagRī turban

pahan kar dekhnā to try on

pahāR mountain

pahāRī hill; hillman

pahāR kī chaRhāī karnā mountaineering

pahchānnā to recognize

pahiyā wheel

pahiyōvālī kursī wheelchair

pahlā first

pahle before; ago; at first
   ek ghanTe pahle an hour ago
   ek hafte pahle a week ago

pahle āp after you

pahle darje first class (travel etc)

pahle se hī already

pahlī bār first time

pahlī manzil first floor, (US) second floor

pahuch arrival

pahuchnā to arrive, to get in

pakaRnā to hold; to catch

pakā ripe (fruit)

pakānā to cook

pakkā karnā to confirm; to fix, to arrange

palastar plaster, Bandaid®

pandit priest; brahmin; wise man

pandrā fifteen

pankti (H) queue

pannā piece of paper; leaflet; page; emerald

pansārī grocer's

par on; at

parchhāi shadow

parde curtains

pardesh abroad

pardeshī foreign; foreigner

pareshān worried

pareshānī bharā annoying

pareshān karnā to disturb

parichay karānā (H) to introduce

parichārikā (H) stewardess

parivār family

parīkshā (H) exam

parsō the day after tomorrow; the day before yesterday

parvatārōhan (H) mountaineering

paRāv stopover

paRhnā to read

paryaTan kāryālaya (H) tourist information office

pasand: mujhe ye (bahut) pasand hA I like it (a lot)

pasand karnā to like

pashchim (H) west
pashchim me in the west
pashchimī (H) western
paslī rib
patā address
patā karnā to find out
pate kī kitāb address book
path way; road
pati (H) husband
patīlā pan
patjhaR (H) autumn, (US) fall
patlā thin
patlūn trousers, (US) pants
patr (H) letter
patrakār journalist
patrikā (H) magazine
pattā leaf
patthar stone; rock
paTrī pavement, sidewalk; track
paTTā strap
paTTī bandage
pawdhā plant
pawnD pAsā pound (money)
pawnD vazan pound (weight)
pawp gānā gānevālā/gānevālī pop singer (man/woman)
pawp sangīt pop music
pāch five
pāgal idiot; mad, crazy
pākhānā (U) toilet, rest room
pāl sail
pālā frost
pālish polish
pānā to find
pānī water
pānī kā jahāz boat
pānī ke jahāz kī sAr cruise
pās near; beside

kyā āpke pās ... hA? do you have any ...?
pās me nearby
pāTh (H) lesson
pāyjāmā pyjamas
pAdal on foot
pAdal chalne kā dāyrā pedestrian precinct
pAdal ghumnā phirnā trekking
pAdal pār karne kā rāstā pedestrian crossing
pAdal safar trek
pAdā huā born
pAgām (U) message
pAr foot (of person)
pAr kā angūThā toe
pAsaTh sixty-five
pAsā money
pAse denā to pay
pAse kī vāpsī refund
pAse lagnā to charge; to cost
pAsevālā rich
pAtālīs forty-five
pAtīs thirty-five
pechish diarrhoea; dysentery
penshan pāne vālā/vālī pensioner (man/woman)
peR tree
peshā profession
peshāb ghar urinals
peshgī in advance
peT stomach
peT dard stomach ache
peTī belt
peT me gaRbaRī upset stomach
peTrōl petrol, (US) gas
peTrōl kā kanasTar petrol/gas

can
peTrōl sTashan petrol station, gas station
pey (H) drink
phal fruit
phaniyar sāp cobra
phasā stuck
phaTā nal burst pipe
phāTak gate
phAlne vālā infectious
phAlne vālī bīmārī infection
phek denā to throw away
pheknā to throw
phephRe lungs
phir again
phir kahiye? pardon (me)?
phir kahnā to repeat
phir milege see you later
phōn karnā to call, to phone
phōn kā AksTAnshan telephone extension
phōn kā karD cardphone
phōn kī lāin phone line
phuTkar small change
phūl flower
phūldān vase
phūl vālā florist's
pichhattar seventy-five
pichhlā last; previous
pichhlā hissā back (part)
pichhle hafte last week
  pichhle hafte se since last week
pichhlī bār last time
pissū flea
pitā (H) father
piTThā rucksack
pīchhe behind
pīchhe ānā to follow

pīlā yellow; pale
pīnā to drink
pīne kā pānī drinking water
pīr (U) Monday
pītal brass
pīTh back (of body)
pīTh dard backache
plāsTik kā thAlā plastic bag
pletfāram platform, (US) track
pōshāk dress; costume
pōsTar poster
pōsTkarD postcard
pōtā grandson
pōtī granddaughter
prabhāv shālī (H) impressive
prabhu God
pradarshanī (H) exhibition
pradhān (H) head, chief person
pradhān mantrī (H) prime minister
prasann (H) glad
prasādhan grih (H) toilet, restroom
prashn (H) question
prasthān (H) departure
prathā (H) custom
prati din (kā) (H) daily
pratishat percent
pravesh (H) entrance
pravesh shulk (H) admission charge
prākritik (H) natural
prāthmiktā (H) priority
prem (H) love
prishTh (H) page
pul bridge
pulis police
pulis kā sipāhī policeman

pu

pulis kī mahilā sipāhī (H)
policewoman
pur-aman (U) peaceful
purānā second-hand; old
purāne Dharre kā old-
fashioned
purāne tawr tarīke kā
traditional
purāne zamāne kī chīze
antique
purōhit (H) priest
purush (H) man; gents' toilet,
men's room
purush shawchālay (H) gents'
toilet, men's room
pustakālay (H) library
pustikā (H) brochure
pūchhnā to ask
pūchh tāchh kī DāyrecTarī
directory enquiries
pūnam night of full moon
pūrab (H) east
  pūrab me in the east
pūrabī (H) eastern
pūrā full
pūrī tarah se completely
pūrnimā night of full moon
pyālā cup; mug; dish, bowl
pyār love
pyār karnā to love
pyās: mujhe pyās lagī hA I'm
thirsty

r

rabaR rubber
radd karnā to cancel
raftār speed

rahā: kyā hō rahā hA? what's
happening?, what's going
on?
rahnā to live
  āp kahā rahte/rahtī hA?
where do you live? (to a
man/woman)
rajisTrī Dāk se by registered
mail
rakhnā to put; to keep
  āp ise rakh lījiye please keep
it
rakhvālā/rakhvālī caretaker
(man/woman)
raKam amount (money)
rang colour
rangīn film colour film
rasīd receipt
rasōī kitchen
rasōī kā tawliyā tea towel
rassā rope
rassī string
ravāngī departure
ravāngī kā ārām ghar
departure lounge
ravivār Sunday
razāī duvet
rāh dekhnā to expect
rājā king
rāj marg main road
rākhdānī ashtray
rāk sangīt rock music
rāshī (H) amount
rāshtrīy (H) national
rāshTrapati (H) president (of
country)
rāshTrīyatā (H) nationality
rāstā path; route; gate (at
airport)

rāt night
 ek rāt kā per night
 rāt kō at night
rāt bhar kā safar overnight
rāt kā darbān night porter
rāt kī pōshāk nightdress
rāt kī rihāish awr nāshtā bed and breakfast
rekhā (H) line
rekhā chitr (H) drawing
relgāRī train
 relgāRī se by train
rel kā āKhirī sTeshan rail terminus
rel me sōne kā Dibbā sleeping car
relve railway
resham silk
restōrā restaurant
restōrā kā Dibbā restaurant car
ret sand
rezgārī small change
risālā (U) magazine; brochure
rishtedār relative
rishvat bribe
ritu season
rīTāyar: mA rīTāyar hōgayā/hōgayī I'm retired (said by man/woman)
rivars chārj kawl collect call
rizarv karnā to reserve
rōbdār impressive
rōgan paint
rōknā to stop
rōnā to cry
rōshnī light
rōzānā daily (adverb)
 rōzānā kā daily

ruī cotton wool, absorbent cotton
ruknā to stop
rumāl handkerchief; napkin
rūbī ruby
rūm sarvis room service
rūs Russia
rūsī Russian
rūThnā to be angry; to be displeased

s

sab all; all of them
sabaK lesson
sab khāne full board
sab se acchhā best
sabse baRā main
sabse Kharāb worst
sabse ūpar at the top
sabse ūpar kī manzil top floor
sabzī vālā greengrocer's
sabziyā vegetables
sach true
 sach! sure!
sachmuch! really?
sadar (U) president
safar journey
safar salāmat rahe! (U) have a good trip!
safed white
sahelī female friend
sahī valid; accurate
sahī salāmat safe
saktā: mA nahī ... saktā/saktī I can't ... (said by man/woman); I couldn't ... (said by man/woman)

kyā mA ... le saktā/saktī hū? can I have ...? (said by man/woman)

sakte: kyā āp ... sakte/saktī hA? can you ...? (to man/woman);

sakht hard

salām (U) hello

salīkedār (U) polite

samandar sea

 samandar kā kinārā coast; beach

 samandar ke kināre by the sea

 samandar ke kināre par on the beach

samandar pār karnā crossing (by sea)

samasyā (H) problem

samay (H) time

samāchār (H) news

sambhav (H) possible

samjhā: mA (nahī) samjhā/samjhī I (don't) understand (said by man/woman)

 āp samjhe? do you understand?

sammelan (H) conference

sampark karnā to contact

samudra taT (H) coast; beach

sandesā (H) message

sandūk box

sanDās toilet, rest room

sangam where two rivers merge

sangīn (U) serious

sangīt music

sangīt kār (H) musician

sangīt sammelan concert

sankhyā (H) number

sapnā dream

sardi-jhukām flu

sardiyō winter

 sardiyō me in (the) winter

sarhad border (of country)

sarkār government

sarkārī chhuTTī public holiday

sarvis chārj service charge

sarvis kī jagah service station

saRak road, street

 saRak par on the street

 saRak par durghaTnā (H) road accident

saRkō kā nakshā road map; streetmap; network map (for buses etc)

saRsaTh sixty-seven

sastā cheap, inexpensive

sastī klās economy class

sasur father-in-law

sasurāl vāle in-laws

satāsī eighty-seven

sathattar seventy-seven

satrā seventeen

sattar seventy

sattā-īs twenty-seven

sattānve ninety-seven

sattāvan fifty-seven

savāl question

saw hundred

sawpanā to hand over

sābun soap

sādā mild; plain; informal

sādhāran (H) general; normal; ordinary

sādhu holy man

sāf clean; clear
sāfā scarf (for head)
sāhab! sir!
sāikil bike, bicycle
sāikil chalānā cycling
sāikil kī dukān cycle shop
sāikil pamp bicycle pump
sāikil rikshā cycle rickshaw
sāikil vālā/vālī cyclist
  (man/woman)
sāl year
sālā brother-in-law
sāl girah birthday
sāl girah mubārak! happy
  birthday!
sālī sister-in-law (wife's sister)
sāmān luggage, baggage;
  equipment
sāmān bādhnā to pack
sāmān khōlnā to unpack
sāmān kī māg baggage claim
sāmān le jāne vālī Trālī
  luggage trolley
sāmne in front; opposite
  bilkul sāmne at the front
  sāmne kā opposite, facing
  sāmne kī taraf the opposite
    direction; in front
sānt saint
sāp snake
sārā kā sārā the whole lot
sāre whole
sāRi sari
sās mother-in-law
sās lenā to breathe
sās sasur parents-in-law
sāt seven
sāthī companion; friend
sāth kī chhōTī galī side street

sāth lenā to share; to
  accompany
sāth me lage dō bistar twin
  beds
sāTh sixty
sāvdhān (H) careful
sāvdhān! be careful!
sāvlā rang tan
sāyā (U) sunshade
sAlāb (U) flood
sAlānī tourist
sAr sightseeing tour; trip
sAr-sapāTā picnic
sAR karnā to travel
sAtālīs forty-seven
sAtīs thirty-seven
se by; from; than
  ... se hō kar jānā to go
    through ...
sefTī pin safety pin
sehat bakhsh (U) healthy
se kam under (less than)
sekanD second (of time)
sekanD klās second class
  (travel etc)
shabd (H) word
shabdkōsh (H) dictionary
shahar town; city
  shahar me in town
shahar kā bīch city centre,
  town centre
shakkī suspicious
shakhs (U) person
shanivār awr itvār weekend
  shani awr itvār kō at the
    weekend
shanīchar Saturday
sharāb drink; alcohol
sharāb-Khānā bar

sharif honest; honourable
sharīr (H) body
sharmīlā shy
shaTar shutter (on camera)
shatranj chess
shaukīn fan (sports)
shawchālay (H) toilet, rest room
shawk hobby
shābāsh! well done!
shādī wedding
shādī kī angūThī wedding ring
shādī kī sālgirah wedding anniversary
shādī se pahle kā nām maiden name
shādīshudā married
 āp shādīshudā hA? are you married?
 mA shādīshudā hū I'm married
shāgird disciple
shākāhārī vegetarian
shām evening
 shām kō in the evening
shāmil include
shām kā khānā supper, dinner, evening meal
shāndār posh
shānt (H) peaceful; silence
shāririk bodily
shāvar shower (in bathroom)
shāvar ke sāth with shower
shāvar krīm shower gel
shāyad probably; I might; perhaps, maybe
shāyad hī hardly
shāyad hī kabhī hardly ever

shāyad nahī I might not; perhaps not, maybe not
shāyikā (H) couchette
shAmpū shampoo
shikār hunt
shikārā Kashmiri canoe
shikāyat complaint
shikāyat karnā to complain
shōr noise
shrī (H) Mr
shrīmatī (H) Mrs
shubh janmdin! (H) happy birthday!
shubh kāmnāye (H) best wishes
shukriyā thanks, thank you
shukrvār (H) Friday
shulk fee
shumāl (U) north
 shumāl me in the north
 shumāl kī taraf to the north
shumālī (U) northern
shumālī āyarlAnD (U) Northern Ireland
shumāl magribī (U) northwest
shumāl mashrīkī (U) northeast
shuruāt start, beginning
 shuru me at the beginning
shuru hōnā/shuru karnā to start, to begin
shuru kā nām first name
shūny (H) zero
sifar zero
sifārat Khānā (U) consulate; embassy
sifārish recommendation
sigreT cigarette
 āp sigreT pīte hA? do you smoke?

sikā huā grilled
sikh Sikh
sikhāhā to teach
sikkā coin
sikke badalne kā daftar bureau de change
sikke badalne kī dar exchange rate
sikke lene vālā phōn payphone
sinemā cinema, movie theater
singal: ... ke liye singal a single to ...
singal bistar single bed
singal kamrā single room
singal Tikat single ticket, one-way ticket
sir head
sir dard headache
sirf (U) only, just
  sirf ek only one
sitambar September
sīdhā direct
sīkhnā to learn
sīkhne vālā/vālī learner, beginner (man/woman)
sīlā humid
sīmā (H) border
sīnā to sew
sīRhiyā stairs
  sīRhī par on the steps
sīT seat
sīT par lagī peTī seat belt
skarT skirt
skāTlAnD Scotland
skāTlAnD kā Scottish
skin Dāiving skin-diving
skūl school

skūTar scooter
slīpar sleeper, sleeping car
slīping bAg sleeping bag
smārak (H) monument
snān (H) bath
sōchnā to think
sōfā sofa, couch
sō jānā to go to bed
sōlā sixteen
sōlā āne sach absolute truth
sōmvār (H) Monday
sōnā gold; to sleep
sōne kā kamrā bedroom
spashT (H) clear, obvious
spen Spain
spenī Spanish
spin-Drāyar spin-dryer
spōk spoke (in wheel)
sthānīy (H) local
strī (H) woman
sTārTar starter (of car)
sTeshan station; train station
subah morning
  subah kō in the morning
  subah sāt baje at seven am
suhāgrāt honeymoon
suhāvnā pleasant; mild (weather)
suī needle
sukhāna-savārnā to blow-dry
sundar lovely, beautiful
suniye! excuse me!
sunnā to listen; to hear
supar mārkeT supermarket
supārī betel nut
surāhī jug
sust lazy
suvidhā janak (H) convenient

sūchnā (H) information
sūjan swelling, inflammation
sūjā huā swollen
sūkhā dry
sūraj sun
sūraj Dūbne kā vakt sunset
sūryāsT (H) sunset
sūt cotton
sūT suit
svasTh (H) healthy (person)
svatantra (H) free
svād (H) flavour, taste
svādishT (H) delicious
svāgat (H) reception (for guests)
svāsThyaprad (H) healthy (food, climate)
svīkār karnā to accept
syfar zero

t

tab then (at that time)
tajrabā kār experienced
tak by; up to, until
takiyā pillow
takiye kā gilāf pillow case
taKhtā bunk
taKlīfdeh annoying
taKrīban (U) nearly; roughly
talāKshudā divorced
talāsh karnā to look for
talī sole (of shoe, of foot)
tambākū tobacco
tambū tent
tandurast (U) healthy
tang tight (clothes etc); narrow (street)

taraf side; direction
is taraf over here
tarjīh (U) priority
tarzumā (U) translation
tarzumā karnā (U) to translate
tarzumān (U) translator
tashtarī plate; saucer
tasme shoelaces
tasvīr painting, picture; portrait
tasvīr khānā (U) art gallery
tatAyā wasp
tawliyā towel
tay karnā to decide
tayyār ready
āp tayyār hA? are you ready?
tādād amount
tāgā horse-drawn carriage
tājjub kā incredible, amazing
tāk shelf
tālā lock
tālā khōlnā to unlock
tālevālī almārī locker (for luggage etc)
tālī clapping
tār telegram
tārā star
tār par chalne vālī gāRī cable car
tāsh playing cards
tāyā uncle (father's older brother)
tāzā fresh
tArnā to swim
tArne kā jāghiyā (swimming) trunks
tArne kā tālāb (swimming) pool
tArne kī pōskāk swimming costume

176

tAtālīs forty-three

teis twenty-three

tel oil

terā thirteen

tetīs thirty-three

tez intelligent; sharp; hot; fast; bright

tez bukhār high fever

tez havā strong wind

thakā tired

thakā huā exhausted

thānedār sāhab officer (said to policeman)

tharmas bōtal Thermos® flask

tharmāmīTar thermometer

thā was

　ye thā it was

thāilAnD Thailand

thāilAnD kā Thai

thālī plate (metal)

thānā police station

the were

　āp the you were

　ham the we were

thī was

　ye thī it was

thōRā little; short (time, journey); a few, some

　thōRā baRā a big bit

　thōRā sā ... a bit of ...

　thōRe din a few days

thōRe vaKt ke liye denā to lend

tihattar seventy-three

tilchaTTā cockroach

tirānve ninety-three

tirāsī eighty-three

tīn three

tīs thirty

tōd belly

tōhfā present, gift

tōhfe ke chīzō kī dukān gift shop

trepan fifty-three

tresaTh sixty-three

tukRā splinter

tum you

　tum hō you are

tumhārā your; yours

turant (H) immediately

tūfān storm

tūth pest toothpaste

tyōhār festival

T
■

Takhnā ankle

Takkar crash, (road) accident

Takrā jānā to knock over

Tarm term (at university, school)

TaTTi toilet (slang, used in remote areas, not polite)

TaTTū pony

Tāg leg

Tāim Tebal timetable, (US) schedule

Tāī tie, necktie

TāiTs tights, pantyhose

Tāpū island

Tāyar tyre

Tāyar kī Tyūb inner tube

TāyleT pepar toilet paper

Taksī aDDā taxi rank

Taksī Drāivar taxi-driver

Talkam pāuDar talcum powder

TAmpān tampons
TAnis tennis
TAnis kā ballā tennis racket
TAnis kā ged tennis ball
TAnis kā mAdān tennis court
Tebal TAnis table tennis
Tek crutches
Teliphōn būTh phone box
Teliphōn karnā to phone
Telivizan television
Telīphōn (tele)phone
Telīphōn kārD phonecard
Telīphōn kī kitāb phone book
Temprechar temperature
Tep tape
Tep RikārDar tape recorder
Thaharnā to stay
Thaharne kī jagah guesthouse;
  accommodation
ThanDā cool; cold; soft drink
Tharre vālā fizzy
ThAlā bag
ThiyeTar theatre
Thīk OK, all right; right,
  correct
  āp Thīk hA? are you OK?
  Thīk! right!
  Thīk nahī not well
  Thīk tarah se properly
  (repaired, locked etc)
  Thīk-Thāk nahī out of order;
  unwell
ThōDī chin
Thōknā to knock
TikaT stamp; ticket
TikaT ghar ticket office; box
  office
Tin tin, can
Tin khōlne kī chābī tin-

opener, can-opener
Tīkā vaccination
Tīlā hill
Tīm team
Tī sharT T-shirt
Tōkrī basket
Tōlī party, group
Tōp hat
Tōpī cap, hat
TōTī tap, faucet
Trālī trolley
Trām tram
TrAfik traffic
TrAfik kī rukāvat traffic jam
TrAfik lāiT traffic lights
TrAk sūT tracksuit
TrAval ejAnT travel agent's
TrAvlar chAk traveller's
  cheque
Tre tray
TukRā piece
Tūr chalāne vālā tour
  operator
TūrisT jānkārī kā daftar tourist
  information office
Tūr ka gāiD tour guide
TūTī broken (leg etc)
TūTī huī broken
TūTī-phūTī damaged
TūT jānā to break

u

ubālnā to boil
ublā pānī boiled water
udāharan (H) example
udās sad
udhar over there

udhar hA it's that way
udhār denā to lend (money)
udhār lenā to borrow (money)
ullū owl; stupid
ullū kā paThhā idiot
ultā pultā upside down
ulTī ānā to vomit
umar age
  āpkī umar kyā hA? how old
  are you?
ummīd hope
ummīd hA hopefully
ummīd karnā to expect, to
  hope
un those
unanchās forty-nine
unattīs twenty-nine
unāsī seventy-nine
unglī finger
unhattar sixty-nine
unkā their (further away); theirs
  (further away)
unkō unhe them (further away)
unnīs nineteen
unsaTh fifty-nine
untālīs thirty-nine
upanyās (H) novel
up-dūtāvās (H) consulate
uRān flight
uRān kā nambar flight
  number
uRān ke vakt hāzir standby
  (flight)
us that
use him; her; to him; to her
  (further away)
ushā kāl (H) dawn
uskā his; her; hers (further
  away)

uske bād then, after that
uske liye for her; for him
uske sāTh with her; with
  him
uskī his; hers (further away)
uskō him; her; to him; to her
  (further away)
us taraf over there
ustarā razor
ustare kā bleD razor blades
utarnā to get off
uthlā shallow (water)
uttar (H) north
uttarī āyarlAnD (H) Northern
  Ireland
uttarī (H) northern
uttar kī taraf to the north
uttar me in the north
uttar pashchim (H) northwest
uttar pūrvī (H) northeast
uThnā to get up (in the morning)
ūbāne vālā boring
ūbgayā bored
ūchā high; tall (building); loud
ūchāi height (mountain)
ūche kism kā upmarket
ūchī chaTTān cliff
ūn wool
ūpar up; above; up there
  ... ke ūpar on top of ...
ūpar jānā to go up (the stairs
  etc)
ūpar kī manzil me upstairs

V

vagArā et cetera
vah great, terrific

vahā there; over there
  vahā ūpar up there
  vahī right there
vahī the same
vakīl lawyer
vaKt time
  is vaKt this time
  kyā vaKt hA? what time is it?
varnā otherwise
vasant (H) spring (season)
vayask (H) adult
vazan weight
vazīre-āzam (U) prime minister
vādy manDalī (H) orchestra
vākaī really
vālā: ye vālā this one
vālid (U) father
vālidā (U) mother
vāpas ānā to get back (return); to come back
vāpas denā to give back
vāpas jānā to go back (return)
vāpas phōn karnā to ring back
vāpsī: ... ke liye ek vāpsī a return to ...
vāpsī TikaT return ticket, round trip ticket
vārD ward (in hospital)
vāshar washer (for bolt etc)
vāskaT waistcoat
vātar skī waterski
vātānukūlit (H) air-conditioned
vātāyan small window
vāTarprūf waterproof
vakum klīnar vacuum cleaner
vAn van

vAsā hī the same as this
ve they (further away); those
  ve hA they are
  ve the they were
vels Wales
velsh Welsh
vest inDīz kā West Indian
vibhāg (H) department
vichār (H) idea
videsh abroad
vilāyatī kājal eyeliner
vinamr (H) polite
vinD sarfing windsurfing
vinD skrīn windscreen
vinD skrīn vāipar windscreen wiper
viruddhh (H) against
vishvās karnā (H) to believe
vivran (H) description
vīzā visa
vō he; she; it; they (far); that
  vō thā he was
  vō thī she was
  vō vālā that one
vōltej voltage
vyakti (H) person
vyast (H) busy
vyākaran (H) grammar
vyāpār (H) business
vyāyām shālā (H) gym

y

yadyapi (H) although
yahā here
  sunil ke yahā at Sunil's
  yahā par down here
  kyā vō yahā hA? is he in?, is

he here?
yahūdī Jewish
yakīn karnā to believe
yā or
  ... yā ... (either) ... or ...
yād: āpkō yād hA? do you
  remember?
  mujhe yād nahī I don't
  remember
  muhje yād hA I remember
yādgār monument
yādgār nishānī souvenir
yātāyāt (H) traffic
yātrā (H) journey
yātrā sukhad rahe! have a
  good trip!
yātrī (H) passenger
ye he; she; it; they (nearby);
  this; these
  ye thā/ye thī it was
yōg yoga
yū As e USA
yūnān Greece
yūnānī Greek
yūnivarsiTī university
yūrōp Europe
yūrōpian European

Z

zabān (U) language
zamānat deposit (as security)
zamīn ground; land
zamīn ke andar kī rel
  underground (railway), (US)
  subway
zamīn par on the ground
zanānā women's

zanānā Dibbā ladies'
  compartment
zanānā gusal Khānā ladies'
  toilets, ladies' room
zarā mahangā a bit expensive
zarā thōRā a little bit
zarūr certainly, definitely
zarūrī important, urgent;
  vital; necessary, essential
zāhir (U) clear, obvious
zāyaz reasonable (prices etc)
zāykā (U) taste, flavour
zikr karnā to mention
zilā district
zindagī life
zindā alive
zip zip, zipper
zīn saddle (for horse)
zōrdār strong
zukām cold
zummā (U) Friday
zyādā more; most, most of
  all
  zyāda vakt most of the time
  zyādā nahī not much, not a
  lot
  itnā zyādā nahī not so much
zyādātar mostly

Hindi

→

English
Signs and
Notices

Contents

General Signs

आर्ट गैलरी	ārT gAlarī	art gallery
बस स्टैंड	bas sTAnd	bus stop
बाल उद्यान	bāl udyān	children's playground
सिनेमा हाल	sinemā hāl	cinema, movie theater
विदेशी दूतावास	videshī dūtāvās	embassy
फायर स्टेशन	fire sTeshan	fire station
बाग	bāg	garden
राजकीय पर्यटक कार्यालय	rājkīya paryaTan kāryālay	government tourist office
संग्रहालय	sangrahālay	museum
पुलिस स्टेशन	pulis sTeshan	police station
संरक्षित इमारत	samrakshit imārat	protected monuments
राज्य हस्तकला एम्पोरियम	rājy hast-kalā empōriyam	state handicraft emporium
राज्य पर्यटक कार्यालय	rājy paryaTak kāryālay	state tourism office
टेलीफोन एक्सचेंज	Teliphōn exchange	telephone exchange
रंगमंच	rangmanch	theatre
यात्रा एवं पर्यटन संचालक	yātrā evam paryaTan sanchālak	travel and tour operator

Airport, Planes

देशीय विमानपत्तन	deshīya vimānpattan	domestic airport
अन्तर्राष्ट्रीय विमानपत्तन	antarrāshTrīya vimānpattan	international airport
देशीय टर्मिनल	deshīya Tarminal	domestic terminal
अन्तर्राष्ट्रीय टर्मिनल	antarrāshTrīya tarminal	international terminal
उड़ान सूचना प्रदर्शन पट्ट	uRān sūchanā pradarshan paTTa	flight information
उड़ान सूचना	uRān sūchanā	flight information
आगमन	āgaman	arrival
प्रस्थान	prasthān	departure
चैक इन काउंटर	check-in kāunTar	check-in desk
आरक्षण खिड़की	ārakshan khiRākī	reservations counter
पूछताछ	pūchhtāchh	enquiries

सुरक्षा जांच खिड़की / काउंटर	surakshā jāch khiRkī/ kāunTar	security check
प्रवेश	pravesh	way in, entrance
निर्गम	nirgam	way out, exit
एयरपोर्ट मैनेजर	airport manager	airport manager
शिशु लॉबी	shishū lawbī	baby area
सामान की ट्राली	sāmān kī trawlī	baggage trolley, baggage cart
बैंक काउंटर	bAnk kāunTar	bank, exchange
किराये पर कार सेवा	kirāye par kār sevā	car rental service
दवाई की दुकान	davāī kī dukān	drugstore and shopping plaza
कैमिस्ट तथा दुकानें	kemist tathā dukāne	drugstore and shopping plaza
निशुल्क दुकानें	nishulk dukāne	duty free shop
प्राथमिक चिकित्सा	prāthmik chikitsa	first aid
होटल आरक्षण खिड़की	hōTal ārakshan khiRkī	hotel reservations desk
इमीग्रेशन	immigration	immigration
आवश्यक सूचना	āvashyak sūchanā	important notice
फोटो खींचना वर्जित है	phōtō khīchanā varjit hA	photography prohibited
डाक सेवायें	dāk sevāe	postal services
पूर्वदत्त टैक्सी सेवा	pūrvadatta tAksī sevā	prepaid taxi service
सार्वजनिक टेलीफोन (एस टी डी / आइ एस डी)	sārvajanik Teliphōn (STD/ISD)	public telephone (STD/ISD)
भोजनालय	bhōjanālaya	restaurant
विश्राम कक्ष	vishrām kaksh	resting rooms
सीमित / प्रतिबद्ध क्षेत्र	sīmit/pratibaddh kshetra	restricted area
कृपया अपना टिकट एवं पासपोर्ट दिखायें	kripayā apnā TikaT evam pāspōrT dikhāye	show your ticket and passport
पारगमन यात्रियों के लिये शयनशाला स्थल	pārgaman yātriyō ke liye shayanshālā sthal	sleeping accommodation for passengers in transit
अल्पाहार स्थल	alpāhār sthal	snack bar

केवल विमान परिचालकों के लिये	keval vimān chālakō ke liye	crew only
आपातकालीन निर्गम	āpātkālīn nirgam	emergency exit
ख़तरा	Khatrā	danger

Banks, Money

बैंक ड्राफ्ट / हुण्डी	bAnk draft/hunDī	bank drafts
नकदी भुगतान	nakdī bhugatān	cash payment
नकदी पावती	nakdī pāvati	cash receipt
कैडिट कार्ड्स	kreDit kārDz	credit card
विदेशी मुद्रा काउंटर	videshī mudrā kāunTar	foreign exchange counter
आज की विदेशी मुद्रा दरें	āj kī videshī mudrā dare	exchange rate
मैनेजर	mAnejar	manager
प्रबन्धक	prabandhak	manager
मुख्य प्रबन्धक	mukhya prabandhak	senior manager
ट्रैवलर्स चैकों का भुगतान	TrAvalarz chAkō kā bhugatān	traveller's cheques cashed

Bus Travel

बस स्टॉप	bas sTop	bus stop
पूछताळ कार्यालय	pūchhtāchh kāryālaya	enquiries desk
अन्तर्राजकीय बस अड्डा	antarrājkīya bas aDDā	interstate bus terminal
स्थानीय बस अड्डा	sthānīya bas aDDā	local bus stop
पूर्वदत्त टैक्सी	pūrvadatta tAksī	prepaid taxi
पूर्वदत्त स्कूटर रिक्शा	pūrvadatta skūTar rikshā	prepaid auto-rickshaw
टिकट खिड़की	TikaT khiRkī	ticket desk

Days

सोमवार	sōmvār	Monday
मंगलवार	mangalvār	Tuesday
बुधवार	budhvār	Wednesday

बृहस्पतिवार, गुरुवार	brihaspat vār, guruvār	Thursday
शुक्रवार	shukrvār	Friday
शनिवार	shanivār, shanīchar	Saturday
इतवार, रविवार	itvār, ravivār	Sunday

Health

अस्पताल	aspatāl	hospital
कैज्युल्टी	kAzhualTī	casualty
दंत	dant	dental
डाक्टर	DākTar	doctor
औषधालय	awshadhālaya	pharmacy
ई एन टी	ī-en-Tī	ear nose and throat
आपात्कालीन	āpātkālīn	emergency
आई सी यू	āī sī yū	intensive care unit
चौबीस घण्टे खुला है	chawbīs ghanTe khulā hA	open 24 hours
बाह्य रोगी विभाग	bāhy rōgī vibhāg	outpatients' department
चिकित्सक	chikitsak	physician
वार्ड संख्या	vārD sankhyā	ward number
ऐक्स रे	Aks-re	X-ray

Hiring, Renting

वातानुकूलित लाग्ज़री कोच	vātānukūlit lagzarī kōch	air-conditioned luxury coaches
किराये के लिए मकान	kirāye ke liye makān	furnished apartment for rent
स्कूटर रिक्शा के किराये भाड़े का चार्ट	skūTar riksha ke kirāye/ bhāRe kā chārT	auto-rickshaw fare chart
किराये के लिये कारें	kirāye ke liye kāre	car rental
चार्टर्ड बस	chartered bus	chartered bus
टैक्सी भाड़े की सारणी	tAksī bhāRe ki sāranī	taxi fare chart
किराये के लिये खाली ह	kirāye ke liye khālī hA	to let

Hotels

होटल	hōTal	hotel
अतिथि-गृह	atithi-grih	guesthouse
स्वागत कक्ष	svāgat kaksh	reception
प्रतीक्षा कक्ष	pratīksha kaksh	lobby
स्वागत	svāgat	welcome
दो व्यक्तियों के लिये	dō vyaktiyō ke liye	double room
एक व्यक्ति के लिये	ek vyakti ke liye	single room
वातानुकूलित कमरा	vātānukūlit kamarā	air-conditioned room
लिफ़्ट	lifT	lift, elevator
तल, मंज़िल	tal, manjil	floor
निर्गम	nirgam	exit
मदिरा कक्ष	madira kaksh	bar
नाई	nāī	barber's shop
व्यापार-केन्द्र	vyāpār kendra	business centre
कॉफ़ी-कक्ष	kāfi kaksh	coffee shop
सम्मेलन-कक्ष	sammelan kaksh	conference room
भोजन-कक्ष	bhōjan kaksh	dining room
डाइनिंग हॉल	Dāining hāl	dining room
डिस्कोथेक	Diskōthek	discotheque
शौचालय-पुरुष	shawchālay-purush	gents' toilet, men's room
शौचालय-स्त्री	shawchālay-strī	ladies' toilet, ladies' room
धुलाई घर	dhulāī gar	laundry
लॉन्ड्री	lawnDrī	laundry
वाहन खड़ा न करें	vāhan khaRā na kare	no parking
भोजनालय	bhōjanālay	restaurant
दुकानें	dukāne	shops
पर्यटन यात्रा	paryaTan yātrā	sightseeing tours
नाश्ता एवं भोजन	nāshtā evam bhōjan	snacks and meals
तरण ताल	taran tāl	swimming pool
टैक्सी	TAksī	taxi
पर्यटन सूचना	paryaTan sūchanā	tourist information
सेवक, स्टीवर्ड	sevak, 'steward'	waiter; steward

Lifts, Elevators

लिफ्ट	lifT	lift, elevator
ऊपर	ūpar	up
नीचे	nīche	down
तल, मंजिल	tal, manjil	floor
केवल सम संख्या अंक वाले तलों के लिये	keval sam sankhyā ank vāle talõ ke liye	for floors with even numbers
केवल विषम संख्या अंक वाले तलों के लिये	keval visham sankhyā ank vāle talõ ke liye	for floors with odd numbers
अत्यधिक भार ... व्यक्ति	atyadhik bhār ... vyakti	maximum load ... persons
धूम्रपान निषेध	dhūmrapān nishedh	no smoking
खेद है लिफ्ट की मुरम्मत हो रही है	khed hA lifT kī marammat hō rahī hA	sorry, lift/elevator under repair

Medicines

दवाई की दुकान	davāī ki dukān	drugstore, pharmacy
पट्टी	paTTī	bandage
सोने से पहले	sōne se pahle	before going to bed
कैप्सूल	kApsūl	capsules
औषध विकेता	awshadh vikretā	chemist, pharmacist
इंजैक्शन	injekshan	injection
प्रयोग की विधि	prayōg kī vidhī	instructions for use
मरहम	marham	ointment
कैंची	kAchī	scissors
पीने की दवा	pīne kī davā	syrup
गोलियाँ	gōliyā̃	tablets
... गोलियाँ प्रतिदिन	... gōliyā̃ pratidin	... tablets per day
चम्मच	chammach	teaspoon
दिन में ... बार	din me ... bār	... times per day
चेतावनी-निर्धारित मात्रा से अधिक लेना खतरनाक है	chetāvanī: nirdhārit mātrā se adhik davā lenā khatarnāk	warning: it is dangerous to exceed the stated dose

Months

जनवरी	janvarī	January
फ़रवरी	farvarī	February
मार्च	mārch	March
अप्रैल	aprAl	April
मई	mayī	May
जून	jūn	June
जुलाई	julâi	July
अगस्त	agast	August
सितम्बर	sitambar	September
अक्तूबर	akTūbar	October
नवम्बर	navambar	November
दिसम्बर	disambar	December

Notices on Doors

खींचिए	khīchiye	pull
धकेलिए	dhakeliye	push
प्रवेश	pravesh	entry
निर्गम	nirgam	exit
प्रवेश निषेध	pravesh nishedh	no admission, no entry
केवल प्राधिकृत व्यक्तियों के लिए	keval prādhikrit vyaktiyõ ke liye	authorized personnel only
खुला है	khulā hA	open
बन्द है	band hA	closed
बाहर	bāhar	out
लंच के लिए बंद है	lanch ke liye band hA	closed for lunch
घन्टी	ghanTī	bell
स्वागत	svāgat	reception
कुत्ते से सावधान	kutte se sāvadhān	beware of the dog
गेट के सामने वाहन खड़ा न करें	geT ke sāmane vāhan khaRā na kare	no parking in front of the gate
कृपया जूते उतारिये	kripayā jūte utāriye	please remove your shoes

Numbers

सिफर, शून्य	sifar, shūny (H)	0
एक	ek	1
दो	dō	2
तीन	tīn	3
चार	chār	4
पाँच	pāch	5
छ:	chhA	6
सात	sāt	7
आठ	āTh	8
नौ	naw	9
दस	das	10
ग्यारह	giārā	11
बारह	bārā	12
तेरह	terā	13
चौदह	chawdā	14
पंदरह	pandrā	15
सोलह	sōlā	16
सतारह	satrā	17
अठारह	aTThārā	18
उन्नीस	unnīs	19
बीस	bīs	20
इक्कीस	ikkis	21
बाईस	bā-īs	22
तेईस	teis	23
चौबीस	chawbīs	24
पच्चीस	pachchīs	25
छब्बीस	chhabbīs	26
सत्ताईस	sattā-īs	27
अठाईस	aTThā-īs	28
उन्तीस	unattīs	29
तीस	tīs	30
इकतीस	ikattīs	31
बत्तीस	battīs	32
तैंतीस	tetīs	33
चौंतीस	chawtīs	34
पैंतीस	pAtīs	35
छत्तीस	chhattīs	36

192

सैंतीस	sAtīs	37
अड़तीस	aRtīs	38
उन्तालीस	untālīs	39
चालीस	chālīs	40
इकतालीस	iktālīs	41
बयालीस	bayālīs	42
तैंतालीस	tAtālīs	43
चौवालीस	chavālīs	44
पैंतालीस	pAtālīs	45
छियालीस	chhiālīs	46
सैंतालीस	sAtālīs	47
अड़तालीस	aRtālīs	48
उन्चास	unanchās	49
पच्चास	pachās	50
एकावन	ikyāvan	51
बावन	bāvan	52
त्रेपन	trepan	53
चौव्वन	chavvan	54
पचप्पन	pachpan	55
छप्पन	chhappan	56
सतावन	sattāvan	57
अठावन	aTThāvan	58
उन्सठ	unsaTh	59
साठ	sāTh	60
इकसठ	iksaTh	61
बासठ	bāsaTh	62
त्रेसठ	tresaTh	63
चौसठ	chawsaTh	64
पैंसठ	pAsaTh	65
छिआसठ	chhiāsaTh	66
सड़सठ	saRsaTh	67
अड़सठ	aRsaTh	68
उन्हतर	unhattar	69
सत्तर	sattar	70
एक्हतर	ikhattar	71
बहतर	bahattar	72
तिहतर	tihattar	73
चौहतर	chawhattar	74
पंचहतर	pichhattar	75

छिहत्तर	chhihattar	76
सत्तहत्तर	sathattar	77
अठहत्तर	aThattar	78
उन्नासी	unāsī	79
अस्सी	assī	80
एकासी	ikyāsī	81
बयाहसी	bayāsī	82
तिरासी	tirāsī	83
चौरासी	chawrāsī	84
पच्चासी	pachāsī	85
छिहासी	chhiāsī	86
सत्तासी	satāsī	87
अठासी	aTThāsī	88
नवासी	navāsī	89
नब्बे	navve	90
एकान्नवें	ikyānave	91
बानवें	bānve	92
त्रियानवे	tirānve	93
चौरानवे	chawrānve	94
पच्चानवे	pachānve	95
छियानवे	chhiānve	96
सत्तानवे	sattānve	97
अठानवे	aTThānve	98
निन्यान्वे	ninyānave	99
सौ	saw	100
दो सौ	dō saw	200
तीन सौ	tīn saw (etc)	300
एक हज़ार	ek hazār	1,000
दो हज़ार	dō hazār (etc)	2,000
एक लाख	ek lākh	100,000
दो लाख	dō lākh (etc)	200,000
दस लाख	das lākh	1,000,000

Place Names

आगरा	āgrā	Agra
अमृतसर	amritsar	Amritsar
बैंगलौर	banglōr	Bangalore
कलकत्ता	kalkattā	Calcutta

चण्डीगढ़	chanDIgaRh	Chandigarh
चेन्नाई (मद्रास)	chennāī (madrās)	Chenai (Madras)
दार्जिलिंग	dārjiling	Darjeeling
गंगटोक	gangtōk	Gangtok
गोआ	gōā	Goa
हैदराबाद	hAdarābād	Hyderabad
जयपुर	jApur	Jaipur
कन्याकुमारी	kanyākumārī	Kanniyakumari
काश्मीर	kāshmīr	Kashmir
खजुराहो	khajurāhō	Khajuraho
लखनऊ	lakhnawu	Lucknow
मुम्बई (बम्बई)	mumbAī (bambAi)	Mumbai (Bombay)
नई दिल्ली	nayī dillī	New Delhi
पुरी (उड़ीसा)	purī (ōrīsā)	Puri (in Orissa)
शिमला	shimlā	Simla
उदयपुर	udaypur	Udaipur
वाराणसी	vārānasī	Varanasi (Benares)

Post Office

डाकघर	Dāk ghar	post office
मुख्य डाकघर	mukhy Dak ghar	General Post Office
पत्र पेटिका	patra peTikā	letter box, mailbox
हवाई डाक	havāī Dāk	airmail
कूरियर	kuriyar	courier
स्पीड डाक	spīD pōsT	express mail
पार्सल	pārsal	parcels
दूरभाष	dūrbhāsh	phone
पिन कोड	pin kōD	post code, zip code
मेल बाक्स संख्या	mel baks sankhyā	P.O. Box number
डाक टिकटें	Dāk tikaTe	postage stamps
पोस्ट मास्टर	pōsT māsTar	post master
रजिस्टर्ड डाक	rajisTard Dāk	registered mail
टेलीग्राम	telīgrām	telegrams

Public Buildings

हवाई अड्डा	havāī aDDā	airport
बैंक	bAnk	bank
कालेज	kawlej	college
क्रिकेट का मैदान	krikeT kā mAdān	cricket ground
जिला न्यायालय	zilā nyāyālay	District Court
दूतावास	dūtāvās	embassy
उच्च न्यायालय	uchcha nyāyālay	High Court
अस्पताल	aspatāl	hospital
इंडोर स्टेडियम	inDōōr sTeDium	indoor stadium
बाज़ार	bāzār	market
संसद भवन	sansad bhawan	Parliament House
राष्ट्रपति निवास	rāshTrapatdi nivās	President's house
प्रधानमंत्री निवास	pradhān mantrī nivās	Prime Minister's house
खेल का मैदान	khel kā mAdān	stadium
विश्व विद्यालय	vishwa vidyālaya	university

Public Holidays

क्रिसमस	krismas	Christmas
दिवाली	dīvālī	Divali, Festival of Lights
दशहरा	dashaharā	Dussehra (Hindu festival marking the triumph of good over evil)
ईद-उल-फ़ितर	īdulfitar	end of Ramadan
गुरुनानक जन्मदिवस	gurūnānak janmdivas	Guru Nanak's birthday
होली	hōlī	Holi, Festival of Colours
ईद-ए-मिलाद	īdmilād	Id-e-Milad (Muslim festival)
स्वतंत्रता दिवस	svatantratā divas	Independence Day
जन्माष्टमी	janmāshTamī	Krishna's birthday
गांधी जयन्ती	gāndhī jayantī	Mahatma Gandhi's birthday
रक्षा बन्धन	rakshā bandhan	Raksha Bandhan (Hindu festival)
गणतंत्र दिवस	ganatantra divas	Republic Day

Rail Travel

रेलवे स्टेशन	relve sTeshan	railway station, train station
आगमन	āgaman	arrival
प्रस्थान	prasthān	departure
प्रवेश	pravesh	entrance
निर्गम	nirgam	exit
आरक्षण सारणी	ārakshan sāranī	reservations chart
आरक्षण काउंटर	ārakshan kāunTar	reservations desk
प्लेटफार्म	pleTfārm	platform, track
प्लेटफार्म टिकट	pleTfārm TikaT	platform/track ticket
प्रथम श्रेणी	pratham shrenī	first class
द्वितीय श्रेणी	dvitīya shrenī	second class
वातानुकूलित कुर्सी यान	vātānukūlit kursī yān	air-conditioned carriage
आरक्षित कोच	ārakshit kōch	reserved coach
राजधानी ऐक्सप्रेस	rājdhānī ekspres	Rajdhani Express
शताब्दी ऐक्सप्रेस	shatābdī ekspres	Shatabadi Express
रसोई-भण्डार	rasōī-bhanDār	pantry, buffet car
कंडक्टर	kanDakTar	conductor
संवाहक	samvāhak	conductor
टिकट निरीक्षक	TikaT nirīkshak	ticket inspector
कुली	kuli	coolie, railway porter
स्टेशन मास्टर	sTeshan māsTar	station master
रेलवे पुलिस	relve pulis	railway police
अमानती सामानघर	amānatī sāmānghar	cloakroom
विश्राम-कक्ष	vishrām kaksh	resting rooms
शौचालय	shawchālaya	toilets, rest rooms
प्रसाधन	prasādhan	toilets, rest rooms
शौचालय-स्त्री	shawchālaya-mahilā	ladies' toilet, ladies' room
पेय जल	peya jal	drinking water
ख़तरा	Khatrā	danger

Restaurants, Bars

| भोजनालय | bhōjanālaya | restaurant |
| ओपन एयर रैस्टोरंट | ōpan eyar resTōrenT | open-air restaurant |

197

मदिरा कक्ष	madirā kaksh	bar
कॉफ़ी शाप	kāfī shawp	coffee shop
आईसक्रीम पार्लर	āiskrīm pārlar	ice-cream parlour
वातानुकूलित	vātānukūlit	air-conditioned
चौबीस घण्टे परिवेषण	chawbīs ghanTe pariveshan	24-hour service
नाश्ता	nāshtā	breakfast
सायंकालीन भोजन	sāyam kālīn bhōjan	evening meal
लंच (दोपहर का भोजन)	lanch (dōpahar kā bhōjan)	lunch
चाईनीज़ भोजन	chāinīz bhōjan	Chinese food
यूरोपिय	yūrōpīya	Western European
फास्ट फूड	fāsT fūD	fast food
व्यंजन सूची	vyanjan sūchī	menu
मुगलाई	mugalāī	Mughlai cuisine
विभिन्न प्रकार के भोजन	vibhinna prakār ke bhōjan	Indian, Chinese, European etc cuisine
दक्षिण भारतीय भोजन	dakshin bhārtīya bhōjan	Southern Indian cuisine
पानी	pānī	water
आरक्षित	ārakshit	reserved table
कैशियर	kAshiyar	cashier

Road Signs

दुर्घटना संभावित क्षेत्र	durgaTanā sambhāvit kshetra	accident blackspot
चेतावनी-लोग काम पर हैं	chetāvanī-lōg kām par hA	caution, men at work
चैक प्वांइट	chAk pōinT	checkpoint
जांच के लिए रुकें	jāch ke liye ruke	checkpoint
साईकिल-पथ	sāikal path	cycle path
वाहन धीरे चलायें	vāhan dhīre chalāye	drive slowly
अपनी लेन में चलें	apnī len me chale	keep in lane
बायीं ओर चलें	bāī ōr chale	keep left
दायीं ओर चलें	dāī ōr chale	keep right
वाहन खड़ा न करें	vāhan khaRā na kare	no parking

यू टर्न निषेध	yū tarn nishedh	no U-turns
पैदल यात्री	pAdal yātrī	pedestrian
हार्न निषेध क्षेत्र	hārn nishedh kshetra	do not sound horn in this area
आगे स्कूल है	āge skūl hA	school ahead
आगे नुकीला मोड़ है	āge nukīlā mōR hA	sharp bend ahead
आगे गति अवरोधक है	āge gati avarōdhak hA	speed bump ahead
गति सीमा ६० किलोमीटर	gati sīmā sāTh kilōmīTar	speed limit 60 kph
रुकें	ruke	stop
भूमिगत पार-पथ	bhūmigat pār-path	subway, underground passage
यू टर्न अनुमत	yū tarn anumat	U-turns allowed

Sport, Trekking

फ़िशिंग	fishing	fishing
कायाकिंग	kayaking	kayaking
रैफ्टिंग	rAfting	rafting
राक क्लाइम्बिंग	rock climbing	rock climbing
ट्रैकिंग	TrAking	trekking

Urdu

English
Signs and Notices

Contents

General Signs

آرٹ گیلری	ārt galarī	art gallery
بس سٹینڈ	basistand	bus stop
چلڈرن پارک	children pārk	children's playground
سینما ہال	sinemāhāl	cinema, movie theater
سفارت خانہ	safārat khanā	embassy
فائر سٹیشن	fire sTeshan	fire station
باغ	bāg	garden
گورنمنٹ ٹورسٹ آفس	government tourist office	government tourist office
میوزیم	museum	museum
پولیس سٹیشن	pulis sTeshan	police station
یادگار عمارتیں	yādgār imarte	protected monuments
سٹیٹ ہینڈی کرافٹس ایمپوریم	istate handicraft emporium	state handicraft emporium
سٹیٹ ٹورازم آفس	istate tūrism õffis	state tourism office
ٹیلیفون ایکسچینج	Teliphōn exchange	telephone exchange
تھیٹر	ThiyeTar	theatre
ٹریول اینڈ ٹور آپریٹر	travel and tour operator	travel and tour operator

Airport, Planes

قومی ہوائی اڈہ	kavmi havāi aDDā	domestic airport
بین الاقوامی ہوائی اڈہ	bAnul agvāmī havāi aDDā	international airport
ڈومیسٹک ٹرمینل	domestic tarminal	domestic terminal
انٹرنیشنل ٹرمینل	international tarminal	international terminal
پروازوں کے بارے میں معلومات	parvazōnke bare me mālumāt	flight information

پروازوں کے بارے میں بتانے والی تختی	parvazke bare me batanevalī takhTī	flight information
آمد	āmad	arrival
روانگی	ravāngī	departure
چیک ان کاؤنٹر	check in kāunTar	check-in desk
ریزرویشن کاؤنٹر	reservation kāunTar	reservations counter
پوچھ تاچھ	puch tāch	enquiries
سیکیورٹی چیک کاؤنٹر	security check kāunTar	security check
اندر جانے کا راستہ	underjāne kā rāsTa	way in, entrance
باہر جانے کا راستہ	bāhar jane ka rāsTa	way out, exit
ایرپورٹ مینجر	airport manager	airport manager
انفنٹ لابی	infant lōbbī	baby area
سامان کے لیے ٹھیلا	sāmān ke liye thela	baggage trolley, baggage cart
بینک کاؤنٹر (زر مبادلہ)	bAnk kāuntar (zare mabadala)	bank, exchange
کار رینٹل سروس	car rental service	car rental service
دواخانہ اور بازار	dawakhanā awr bazār	drugstore and shopping plaza
ڈیوٹی فری شاپ	duty-free shop	duty-free shop
فوری طبی امداد	fawri tibbi imdād	first aid
ہوٹل ریزرویشن کاؤنٹر	hōTel reservation kāunTer	hotel reservations counter
امیگریشن	immigration	immigration
ضروری اطلاع	zaruri iTTalā	important notice
فوٹو کھینچنا منع ہے	fōtu khAnchna mana hA	photography prohibited
ڈاکخانہ	dāk khānā	postal services
پری پیڈ ٹیکسی سروس	pirī peid taxi service	prepaid taxi service
پبلک ٹیلیفون (ایس ٹی ڈی آر آئی ایس ڈی)	(STD/ISD) public telephone	public telephone (STD/ISD)
ریستوران	restōrā	restaurant

آرام گاہ مسافِروں کے	ārāmgāh musāfirōn ke	resting rooms
محدود علاقہ	mehdud elakā	restricted area
اپنا ٹکٹ اور پاسپورٹ دکھائیے	apna TikeT awr pāsspōrT dikhāyn	show your ticket and passport
مسافِروں کے ٹھہرنے کی جگہ	theharne kī jagah	sleeping accommodation for passengers in transit
اسنیکس بار	isnaks	snack bar
صرف عملے کے لئے	sirf amle ke lie	crew only
ناگہانی ضرورت کے وقت استعمال ہونے والا دروازہ	nāgahani zarurat ke vakt istamāl hōnevala darvāza	emergency exit
خطرہ	khaTra	danger

Banks, Money

بینک ڈرافٹ	bAnk draft	bank drafts
نقد ادائیگی	tadad adāygi	cash payment
نقد کی رسید	nakad kī rasīd	cash receipt
کریڈٹ کارڈ	credit card	credit card
غیر ملکی زرِ مبادلہ کاؤنٹر	gArmulki zaremabadla kāunTar	foreign exchange counter
شرحِ زرِ مبادلہ	sharah zaremabadla	exchange rate
منیجر	manager	manager
چیف منیجر	chief manager	senior manager
سفری چیک بھنائے جاتے ہیں	safricheck bhunāy jāte hA	travellers' cheques cashed

Bus Travel

بس اڈھ	basistand	bus stop
پوچھ تاچھ کی کھڑکی	puch tāch kī khirki	enquiries desk
انٹرسٹیٹ بس ٹرمینل	interisTate bas tarminal	interstate bus terminal
لوکل بس سٹینڈ	local basisTand	local bus stop
پری پیڈ ٹیکسی/ر آٹورکشا	pirīpayed taxi/ awTō rikshā	prepaid taxi/ auto-rickshaw
ٹکٹ کی کھڑکی	TikaT kī khirkī	ticket desk

Days

پیر	pīr	Monday
منگل	mangalvār	Tuesday
بدھ	budhvār	Wednesday
جمعرات	jumme vāt	Thursday
جمعہ	zummā	Friday
ہفتہ (سنیچر)	hafta, shanīchar	Saturday
اتوار	itvār	Sunday

Health

ہسپتال	aspatāl	hospital
کازوالٹی	kazvalTī	casualty
دندانی (ڈینٹل)	dandānce (dental)	dental
ڈاکٹر	DawkTar	doctor
دواخانہ	davākhānā	drugstore, pharmacy
کان، ناک اور گلا (ای۔این۔ٹی)	kān nāk awr galā (ENT)	ear nose and throat
ایمرجنسی	emergency	emergency
انٹینسو کیئریونٹ (آئی۔سی۔یو)	intensive care unit (ICU)	intensive care unit
چوبیس گھنٹے کھلا ہے	chawbīs ganTe khulā hA	open 24 hours

شعبہ برائے غیر رہائشی مریض (او۔پی۔ڈی)	(shōbā barāy gAr) rihāyshī mariz	outpatient's department
ماہر طبیب	māhirtabīb	physician
وارڈ نمبر	ward number	ward number
ایکس رے	xray	X-ray

Hiring, Renting

طویل مسافت والی ایر کنڈیشنڈ تفریحی بسیں	tavīl masāfat vāli air-conditioned tafrihi base	air-conditioned luxury coaches
آراستہ کمرے کرائے پر ملتے ہیں	ārāstā kamre kirāye par milte hA	furnished apartment for rent
آٹو رکشا کے کرائے کا چارٹ	awTō rakshā ke kirāye kā chārT	auto-rickshaw fare chart
کار کرائے پر ملتی ہے	kār kirāye par miltī hA	car rental
چارٹرڈ بس	chartered bus	chartered bus
ٹیکسی کے کرائے کا چارٹ	taxi ke kirāye kā chārT	taxi fare chart
کرائے پر دینے کے لیے	kirāye par dene ke liye	to let

Hotels

ہوٹل	hōTel	hotel
مہمان خانہ	mehmān khānā	guesthouse
استقبالیہ (ریسیپشن)	istaKbāliā (reception)	reception
لابی	lābī	lobby
خوش آمدید	khushāmded	welcome
دو افراد کے لئے کمرہ (ڈبل روم)	dō afrād ke liye kamrā	double room
ایک فرد کے لئے کمرہ (سنگل روم)	ek fard ke liye kamrā	single room

دو افراد کے لئے ایر کنڈیشنڈ ڈبل کمرہ	air-conditioned double kamrā	air-conditioned double room
لفٹ (ایلیویٹر)	lifT	lift, elevator
منزل	manzil	floor
باہر جانے کا راستہ	bāhar jāne kā rāstā	exit
میخانہ (بار)	mAKhānā	bar
حجام کی دکان	hajjām kī dukān	barber's shop
تجارتی مرکز	tijārtī markaz	business centre
کافی خانہ	kāfīKhānā	coffee shop
کانفرنس ہال	kānfrens hāl	conference room
طعام خانہ	tāmKhānā	dining room
رقص گاہ (ڈسکوتھک)	raksgāh	discotheque
بیت الخلا ۔ مردانہ	bAtul khala mardānā	gents' toilet, men's room
بیت الخلا ۔ زنانہ	bAtul khala zanānā	ladies' toilet, ladies' room
لانڈری	laundry	laundry
گاڑی کھڑی کرنا منع ہے	gārī kharī karnā manā hA	no parking
ریسٹوران	restōrā	restaurant
دکانیں	dukāne	shops
قابل دید مقامات کی سیر کے لئے سفر	gābile dīd makāmāt ki sAr ke liye safar	sightseeing tours
ہلکا پھلکا کھانا اور کھانا	halkā phulkā khānā awr khānā	snacks and meals
اسٹیوارڈ	sTuarD	steward
سوئمنگ پول	swimming pool	swimming pool
ٹیکسی	taxi	taxi
معلومات برائے سیاح	mālōmat barāye sayyah	tourist information
ویٹر	veTer	waiter

Lifts, Elevators

لفٹ	lifT	lift, elevator
اوپر	ūpar	up
نیچے	nīche	down
منزل	manzil	floor
طاق اعداد والی منزلوں پر جانے کے لئے	juft ādvāli manzilōn par jāne ke liye	for floors with even numbers
جفت اعداد والی منزلوں پر جانے کے لئے	tāk ādvāli manzilōn par jāne ke liye	for floors with odd numbers
زیادہ سے زیادہ اشخاص کا بار	ziyada se ziyade ... ashkhash kā bhā	maximum load ... persons
سگریٹ نوشی منع ہے	sigreTnōshī mana hA	no smoking
معاف کیجئے، لفٹ کی مرمت ہو رہی ہے	māf kījiye, lifT kī marammat hō rahī hA	sorry, lift/ elevator under repair

Medicines

دواخانہ	dawakhānā	drugstore, pharmacy
پٹی	paTTī	bandage
سونے سے پہلے	sōne se pahle	before going to bed
کپسول	kApsūl	capsules
دوافروش	davāfarōsh	chemist, pharmacist
ٹیکہ (انجیکشن)	Tīkā	injection
ہدایات برائے استعمال	hidāyat barāyl istamāl	instructions for use
مرہم	marham	ointment

قینچی	kAnchī	scissors
شربت	sharbat	syrup
گولیاں	gōliyā	tablets
دن میں ۔۔۔۔ گولیاں	din me ... gōliyā	... tablets per day
چائے کا چمچہ بھر	chāy kā chamchā bhar	teaspoon
دن میں ۔۔۔۔ بار	din me ... bār	... times per day
احتیاط ۔۔۔۔ بتائی گئی خوراک زیادہ استعمال مضر ہے	ehtiyat batāi gayī khōrāk zyādā istamāl muzir hA	warning: it is dangerous to exceed the stated dose

Months

جنوری	janvarī	January
فروری	farvarī	February
مارچ	mārch	March
اپریل	aprAl	April
مئی	mayī	May
جون	jūn	June
جولائی	julāi	July
اگست	agast	August
ستمبر	sitambar	September
اکتوبر	akTūbar	October
نومبر	navambar	November
دسمبر	disambar	December

Notices on Doors

کھینچیے	khenchiye	pull
دھکیلیے	dhakeliye	push
داخل ہونے کا راستہ	dākhil hōne kā rāstā	entry
باہر جانے کا راستہ	bāhar jāne kā rāstā	exit
داخلہ منع ہے	dākhlā manā hA	no admission, no entry

صرف بااختیار کارکنان کے لئے	sirf bā akhtiār karkunan ke liye	authorized personnel only
کھلا ہے	khulā hA	open
بند ہے	band hA	closed
باہر	bāhar	out
دوپہر کے کھانے کے لئے بند	dōphar ke khāne ke liye band	closed for lunch
گھنٹی	ganTi	bell
استقبالیہ (ریسیپشن)	istaKbāliā (reception)	reception
کتے سے ہوشیار	kutte se hōshyār	beware of the dog
دروازے کے سامنے گاڑی کھڑی کرنا منع ہے	darvāze ke sāmne gāRī khaRā karnā manā hA	no parking in front of the gate
برائے کرم اپنے جوتے اتار دیجئے	barāy karam apne jūte utārdijiye	please remove your shoes

Numbers

٠	sifar, shūny (H)	0
١	ek	1
٢	dō	2
٣	tīn	3
۴	chār	4
۵	pāch	5
٦	chhA	6
۷	sāt	7
٨	āTh	8
٩	naw	9
١٠	das	10
١١	giārā	11
١٢	bārā	12
١٣	terā	13
١۴	chawdā	14
١۵	pandrā	15

۱۶	sōlā	16
۱۷	satrā	17
۱۸	aTThārā	18
۱۹	unnīs	19
۲۰	bīs	20
۲۱	ikkis	21
۲۲	bā-īs	22
۲۳	teis	23
۲۴	chawbīs	24
۲۵	pachchīs	25
۲۶	chhabbīs	26
۲۷	sattā-īs	27
۲۸	aTThā-īs	28
۲۹	unattīs	29
۳۰	tīs	30
۳۱	ikattīs	31
۳۲	battīs	32
۳۳	tetīs	33
۳۴	chawtīs	34
۳۵	pAtīs	35
۳۶	chhattīs	36
۳۷	sAtīs	37
۳۸	aRtīs	38
۳۹	untālīs	39
۴۰	chālīs	40
۴۱	iktālīs	41
۴۲	bayālīs	42
۴۳	tAtālīs	43
۴۴	chavālīs	44
۴۵	pAtālīs	45
۴۶	chhiālīs	46
۴۷	sAtālīs	47
۴۸	aRtālīs	48
۴۹	unanchās	49
۵۰	pachās	50

۵۱	ikyāvan	51
۵۲	bāvan	52
۵۳	trepan	53
۵۴	chavvan	54
۵۵	pachpan	55
۵۶	chhappan	56
۵۷	sattāvan	57
۵۸	aTThāvan	58
۵۹	unsaTh	59
۶۰	sāTh	60
۶۱	iksaTh	61
۶۲	bāsaTh	62
۶۳	tresaTh	63
۶۴	chawsaTh	64
۶۵	pAsaTh	65
۶۶	chhiāsaTh	66
۶۷	saRsaTh	67
۶۸	aRsaTh	68
۶۹	unhattar	69
۷۰	sattar	70
۷۱	ikhattar	71
۷۲	bahattar	72
۷۳	tihattar	73
۷۴	chawhattar	74
۷۵	pichhattar	75
۷۶	chhihattar	76
۷۷	sathattar	77
۷۸	aThattar	78
۷۹	unāsī	79
۸۰	assī	80
۸۱	ikyāsī	81
۸۲	bayāsī	82
۸۳	tirāsī	83
۸۴	chawrāsī	84
۸۵	pachāsī	85

۸٦	chhiāsī	86
۸۷	satāsī	87
۸۸	aTThāsī	88
۸۹	navāsī	89
۹۰	navve	90
۹۱	ikyānave	91
۹۲	bānve	92
۹۳	tirānve	93
۹۴	chawrānve	94
۹۵	pachānve	95
۹٦	chhiānve	96
۹۷	sattānve	97
۹۸	aTThānve	98
۹۹	ninyānave	99
۱۰۰	saw	100
۲۰۰	dō saw	200
۳۰۰	tīn saw	300
۱۰۰۰	ek hazār	1,000
۲۰۰۰	dō hazār	2,000
۱۰۰۰۰۰	ek lākh	100,000
۲۰۰۰۰۰	dō lākh	200,000
۱۰۰۰۰۰۰	das lākh	1,000,000

Place Names

آگرہ	āgrā	Agra
امرتسر	amritsar	Amritsar
بنگلور	banglōr	Bangalore
کلکتہ	kalkaTTā	Calcutta
چندی گڑھ	chanDīgarh	Chandigarh
چنائی (مدراس)	chenāī (madrās)	Chenai (Madras)
دارجلنگ	dārjiling	Darjeeling
گنگٹوک	gangtōkī	Gangtok
گوآ	gōā	Goa
حیدرآباد	hAdarābād	Hyderabad

214

	jApur	Jaipur
جے پور	kanyākumārī	Kanniyakumari
کنیاکماری	kāshmīr	Kashmir
کشمیر	khajurāhō	Khajuraho
کھاجراہو	lakhnawu	Lucknow
لکھنو	mumbaī (bambAi)	Mumbai (Bombay)
ممبئ (بمبئ)	nayī dillī	New Delhi
نئ دلی	purī (ōrīsā)	Puri (in Orissa)
پوری (اڑیسہ)	simlā	Simla
شملہ	udaypur	Udaipur
اودے پور	vārānasī	Varanasi (Benares)
واراناسی		

Post Office

ڈاک خانہ	Dāk khānā	post office
بڑاڈاکخانہ	baRa Dāk khānā	General Post Office
لیٹر باکس	letter box	letter box, mailbox
ہوائی ڈاک	havāi Dāk	airmail
پیغام رساں (کور ئیر)	pAgām rasōn courier	courier
سپیڈ پوسٹ	ispīd post	express mail
پارسل	parsal	parcels
ٹیلیفون	Telīphōn	phone
پن کوڈ	pin code	post code, zip code
میل باکس نمبر	mail box number	P.O. Box number
ڈاک ٹکٹ	Dāk TikaT	postage stamps
پوسٹ ماسٹر	post masTar	postmaster
رجسٹرڈ ڈاک	registered Dāk	registered mail
تار	tār	telegrams

Public Buildings

ہوائی اڈہ	havāi aDDā	airport
بنک	bAnk	bank
کالج	kālej	college
کرکٹ سٹیڈیم	krikeT isteDiam	cricket ground
ضلع عدالت (ڈسٹرکٹ کورٹ)	zilāadālat (district court)	District Court
سفارت خانہ	sifārat khānā	embassy
عدالت عالیہ (ہائی کورٹ)	adālate āliā (high court)	High Court
ہسپتال	aspatāl	hospital
انڈور سٹیڈیم	indoor isteDiam	indoor stadium
بازار	bāzār	market
پارلیمنٹ ہاؤس	parliament house	Parliament House
صدر کی رہائش گاہ	sadar kī rihAshgāh	President's house
وزیرِ اعظم کی رہائش گاہ	vazīre āzam kī rihāishgāh	Prime Minister's house
سٹیڈیم	isteDiam	stadium
جامعہ (یونیورسٹی)	jāmiā (university)	university

Public Holidays

کرسمس	krismas	Christmas
دیوالی	dīvālī	Divali, Festival of Lights
دسہرا	dasehrā	Dussehra (Hindu festival marking the triumph of good over evil)
عیدالفطر	īdulfitar	end of Ramadan
گورو نانک کا یومِ پیدائش	gurū nānak kā yōme pAdāish	Guru Nanak's birthday

216

ہولی	hōlī	Holi, Festival of Colours
عید میلاد	īdmilād	Id-e-Milad (Muslim festival)
یوم آزادی	yōme āzādi	Independence Day
جنم اشٹمی	jan māshTamī	Krishna's birthday
گاندھی جینتی	gāndhī jayentī	Mahatma Gandhi's birthday
رکشا بندھن	rakshā bandhan	Raksha Bandhan (Hindu festival)
یوم جمہوریہ	yōme jamhūria	Republic Day

Rail Travel

ریلوے اسٹیشن	relve sTeshan	railway station, train station
آمد	āmad	arrival
روانگی	ravāngī	departure
داخلہ	dākhlā	entrance
باہر جانے کا راستہ	bāhar jāne kā rāstā	exit
ریزرویشن چارٹ	reservation chart	reservations chart
ریزرویشن کاؤنٹر	reservation kāunTar	reservations desk
پلیٹ فارم	pletfārum	platform, track
پلیٹ فارم ٹکٹ	pletfārum TikaT	platform/ track ticket
درجہ اول (فرسٹ کلاس)	darjā avval (first class)	first class
درجہ دوم (سیکنڈ کلاس)	darjā dōyam (second class)	second class
اے۔سی چٹر کار	AC chArkar	air-conditioned carriage
ریزرو ڈ کوچ	reserved coach	reserved coach

217

راجدھانی ایکسپریس	rājdhānī express	Rajdhani Express
شتابدی ایکسپریس	shatābdi express	Shatabadi Express
نعمت خانہ (پینٹری)	nemat khānā (pantry)	pantry, buffet car
کنڈکٹر	kanDakTar	conductor
ٹکٹ چیکر	TikaT chAkar	ticket inspector
قلی	kulī	coolie, railway porter
سٹیشن ماسٹر	sTeshan master	station master
ریلوے پولیس	relve pulis	railway police
سامان گاہ (کلوک روم)	sāmāngāh (cloakroom)	cloakroom
آرام گاہ	ārāmgāh	resting rooms
بیت الخلا	bAtul khalā	toilet, rest rooms
بیت الخلا برائے خواتین	bAtul khalā barāy khavātīn	ladies' toilet, ladies' room
پینے کا پانی	pīne kā pānī	drinking water
خطرہ	khaTrā	danger

Restaurants, Bars

ریستوران	restōrā	restaurant
کھلا ریستوران	khulā restōrā	open-air restaurant
مَیخانہ (بار)	mAkhānā (bar)	bar
کافی شاپ	coffee shop	coffee shop
آئس کریم پارلر	ice-cream parlour	ice-cream parlour
ایئر کنڈیشنڈ	air-conditioned	air-conditioned
۲۴ گھنٹے کھلا ہے	24 ganTe khula	24-hour service
ناشتہ	hA nāshtā	breakfast
عشائیہ (شام کا کھانا)	eshAya (shām kā khānā)	evening meal
ظہرانہ (دوپہر کا کھانا)	zahrana (dōphar kā khānā)	lunch

چینی خوراک (چائنیز فوڈ)	chīnī khurāk (Chinese food)	Chinese food
کانٹی نینٹل	continental	Western European
فاسٹ فوڈ	fast food	fast food
مینیو	menyū	menu
مغلائی	muglai	Mughlai cuisine
قسم قسم کے کھانے	kism kism ke khāne	Indian, Chinese, European etc cuisine
ساؤتھ انڈین کھانے	South Indian khāne	Southern Indian cuisine
پانی	pānī	water
مخصوص میز (ریزروڈ ٹیبل)	makhsūs meze (reserved table)	reserved table
کیشیئر	cashier	cashier

Road Signs

وہ علاقہ جہاں حادثے کا خطرہ ہے	vō ilakā jaha hādse kā khatrā hA	accident blackspot
خبردار! عملہ کام کر رہا ہے	khabardār amlā kām kar rahā hA	caution, men at work
چیک پوائنٹ	checkpoint	checkpoint
سائیکل چلانے کا راستہ	sāikil chalāne kā rāstā	cycle path
گاڑی آہستہ چلائیے	gāRi āhista chalāiye	drive slowly
اپنی قطار میں گاڑی چلائیے	apnī katār me gāRi chalāiye	keep in lane
بائیں طرف چلیے	bāyī taraf chaliye	keep left
دائیں طرف چلیے	dāyī taraf chaliye	keep right
گاڑی کھڑی کرنا منع ہے	gāRī khaRī karnā manā hA	no parking
مڑنا منع ہے	muRna manā hA	no U-turns

219

پیدل چلنے والے	pAdal chalne vale	pedestrian
وہ علاقہ جہاں شور کرنا منع ہے	vō ilakā jaha shōr karnā manā hA	noise prohibited in this area
آگے سکول ہے	āge iskūl hA	school ahead
آگے تیکھا موڑے	āge tīkhā mōRe hA	sharp bend ahead
آگے اسپیڈ بریکر ہے	āge ispīD brekar hA	speed bump ahead
معینہ رفتار 60 کلو میٹر	muāyna raftār 60 kilōmeTer	speed limit 60 kph
ٹھہریے	Thahriye	stop
زیریں راستہ	zerin rāstā	subway, underground passage
مڑنے کی اجازت ہے	muRne kī ijāzat hA	U-turns allowed

Sport, Trekking

مچھلی کا شکار (فشنگ)	machhlī kā shikār (fishing)	fishing
کایاکنگ	kayaking	kayaking
ریفٹنگ	rafting	rafting
راک کلائمبنگ	rock climbing	rock climbing
ٹریکنگ	Traking	trekking

Menu Reader:
Food

Essential Terms

bread Dabal rōTī
butter makkhan
cup pyālā
dessert miThāi
fish machhlī
fork kāTā
glass gilās
knife chākū
main course Khās khānā
meat gōsht, mās (H)
menu menyū
pepper kālī mirch
plate plet
  (metal) Thālī
salad salād
salt namak
set menu fiks menyū
soup shōrbā
spoon chammach
starter pahlā dawr
table mez

excuse me! suniye!
I'd like ... mujhe ... chāhiye
another ..., please ek awr ... dījiye
could I have the bill? bil lāiye?

Basic Words

āTā flour
chaTnī sauce; ketchup; chutney
chīnī sugar
dahī yoghurt
dūdh milk
ghī clarified butter
jaggery unrefined sugar
makkhan butter
murabbā jam
panīr cheese
rāī mustard
sarsō mustard
sattū flour (Bihar)
shahad honey
shōrbā soup; gravy
sirkā vinegar
vanaspati makkhan margarine

Beef and Beef Dishes

dam gōsht beef baked with yoghurt and black pepper
gāy kā gōsht beef
Hydrabadi masālā beef Hyderabad spicy beef
kāshmīrī dam gōsht Kashmiri beef steamed in a casserole

Biryanis

bhunā murg biryanī tandoori chicken biryani

chanā biryanī chickpea/ garbanzo biryani (Pakistan)
jhīngā biryanī prawn biryani
jhīngā maTar biryanī prawn biryani with peas
kāshmīrī biryanī Kashmiri biryani
kīma biryanī minced meat biryani
maTar, anDe biryanī peas and egg biryani
meat biryanī lamb biryani
mugal meat biryanī lamb biryani in a sauce made with yoghurt
mugal murg biryanī chicken biryani in a sauce made with yoghurt
murg biryanī chicken biryani
murg tikkā biryanī biryani with boneless pieces of chicken
sabej biryanī vegetable biryani
tikkā meat biryanī biryani with boneless pieces of lamb

Bread, Pancakes

appam rice pancake, speckled with holes, soft in the middle (Southern India)
ālū gōbhī parāThā paratha stuffed with potatoes and cauliflower
ālū parāThā paratha stuffed with potatoes

baTūrā soft deep-fried bread made from white flour (Delhi)

bhājī deep-fried cakes of vegetables in chick-pea flour batter

bhel pūrī small vegetable-stuffed puri with tamarind sauce (Bombay)

bhūrī Dabal rōTī brown bread

chapātī unleavened bread made of wholewheat flour and baked on a griddle

chōkar vālī Dabal rōTī wholemeal bread

dōsā deep-fried pancakes made from rice flour and pulses (Southern India)

Dabal rōTī bread; loaf

gujrātī pūrī puri made with pulses and peas

idli steamed bread made from rice flour and lentils (Southern India)

idli sambar lentil and vegetable sauce with steamed bread made from rice flour and lentils (Southern India)

kachōRī small thick cakes of salty deep-fried bread

kāshmīrī nān nan made with dried fruit and nuts

kathi rolls kebabs rolled into griddle-fried bread (Calcutta)

katlam paratha stuffed with minced meat

kīma nān nan stuffed with minced meat

kīma parāThā paratha stuffed with minced meat

loochi delicate puri often mixed with white flour (Bengal)

makki kī roTī fried corn bread

masālā dōsā potato and vegetable curry wrapped in a crispy rice pancake (Southern India)

mughlai parāThā spicy fried bread with egg

nān white leavened bread cooked in a clay oven

panī pūrī small vegetable-stuffed puris dunked in peppery and spicy sauce

panīr nān cheese nan

parāThā layered wholewheat bread made with butter or oil, rolled thin and fried on a griddle; sometimes stuffed with meat or vegetables

peshāwari nān nan made with butter and nuts

pūrī soft deep-fried bread

rōTī unleavened bread made of wholewheat flour and baked on a griddle

rumali rot 'handkerchief' bread (Northern India, Muslim)

sabzī vālī nān nan stuffed with vegetables

safed Dabal rōTī white bread

sāg pūrī spinach puri

tandūrī parāThā paratha cooked in a clay oven

tandūrī rōTī flat bread cooked in a clay oven

TamāTar lahsan nān garlic
and tomato nan
uttapam thick rice pancake
often cooked with onions
(Southern India)

Chicken and
Chicken Dishes

ālū murgī chicken cooked
with potatoes
kāshmīrī murg Kashmiri
chicken
madrās murg chicken
Madras – chicken pieces
with spices, onions, garlic
and ginger (Southern India)
masāledar murgī chicken in a
red (bell) pepper sauce
methī murgī chicken cooked
with fenugreek leaves
murg dāl chicken cooked
with pulses
murgī chicken
murgī rasedār chicken curry
with gravy
**murg makkhanī, makkhanī
murgī** chicken in a rich
butter sauce
murg musallam whole
chicken baked in the oven
(Mughlai)
murg sāg chicken cooked
with spinach
nāriyal murgī chicken cooked
with coconut cream
(Southern India)
pasanda murg chicken with

yoghurt and ground
almond sauce (Pakistan)
sāg vālī murgī chicken
cooked with spinach
shahjahāni murgī chicken
cooked with almonds and
sultanas
shakūthi chicken with
roasted coconut (Goa)

Chutneys,
Pickles,
Condiments

ām kā achār mango pickle
ām kī chaTnī mango chutney
ām kī mīThī khaTTī chaTnī
sweet and sour mango
chutney
chaTnī chutney
hare dhaniye kī chaTnī fresh
coriander chutney
harī mirch chaTnī green chilli
chutney
kālī mirch black pepper
khūbāni chaTnī apricot
chutney
mirch pepper
mīThā khaTTā āchār sweet
and sour pickle
namak salt
nimbū kā āchār lime pickle
pudīnā chaTnī mint chutney
sabzī kā āchār mixed
vegetable pickle
**seb, āRū awr khūbānī kī
chaTnī** apple, peach and
apricot chutney

sōnth sweet and sour sauce made from tamarind

subje white coconut chutney

Cooking Methods, Types of Dish

bhājī curry; vegetables

bhunā (huā) roasted; grilled

biryanī rice cooked with meat, chicken or vegetables and served with a sauce; the cooked rice is layered over the meat or vegetables

chaTpaTā spicy

dam steamed

garam hot

halka mild, moderately hot

jalfrezi with tomatoes and green chilli; medium-hot

jhal very hot and spicy

kaRāhī method of cooking meat with dry masala; indicates dishes of medium strength

kaRva bitter

khaTmīThā sweet and sour

khaTTā sour

kōrmā meat braised in a mild yoghurt sauce

mīThāī sweet

molee hot curry (usually fish) with coconut (Kerala)

mughlai mild, creamy Mughlai recipe

namkīn salty; savoury

pathia hot thickened curry with lemon juice

talā huā fried

tandūrī traditionally tandoori dishes were cooked in a clay oven, but nowadays are generally cooked in any oven

tez strong; hot and spicy

tikkā pieces of boneless meat (usually chicken breast) marinated in yoghurt, herbs and spices and traditionally cooked in a clay oven

tikkā masālā tikka in a medium-strength sauce

Desserts, Sweets/Candies, Biscuits, Cakes

āiskrīm ice cream

barfī fudge made from milk which has been boiled down and condensed

besan laDDū sweet chickpea/ garbanzo flour balls

bhāng kulfi hashish ice cream

chhenā sweet/candy made from thick curdled milk

dudh peRā barfi balls

gājar kā halvā halva made from carrots and cream

gulab jamun deep-fried sponge ball soaked in syrup

halvā type of sweet/candy made from semolina, fruit

or vegetables, ghee and sugar

jalebī curly-shaped deep-fried sweet/candy made from flour and soaked in syrup

khōyā milk thickened by boiling, used in making sweets/candies

kulfī Indian ice cream

laDDū sweet/candy made from semolina, chickpea/garbanzo flour, raisins and sugar

malāi kulfī cardamom ice cream

miThāī dessert, pudding; sweets, candies

peRā type of sweet/candy (Bengal)

rasgullā balls of soft cream cheese soaked in syrup (Bengal)

ras malāi balls of cream cheese flavoured with rosewater and soaked in cream (Northern India)

sandesh type of sweet/candy made from cream cheese, nuts and sugar (Bengal)

Eggs and Egg Dishes

anDā egg

anDe kī bhājī hard-boiled eggs in a curry

anDe vindalū hard-boiled eggs in a very hot curry

ekūri spicy scrambled eggs (Bombay)

Khūb ublā anDā hard-boiled egg

malāidar anDe hard-boiled eggs in a spicy cream sauce

ublā anDā boiled egg

Fish and Fish Dishes

bōmbay duck dried bummelo fish

dahī macchī mild fish curry with yoghurt, ginger and turmeric (Bengal)

hare masāle vālī macchī grilled fish with lemon and fresh coriander

jhīngā prawns

kekRā crab

khaT mīThi macchī sweet and sour fish

macchī, machhlī fish

masāledār macchī fried spicy fish

mācher jhōl mild fish stew (Bengal)

pōmfret type of flatfish

tali macchī fried fish with spices

TamāTar macchī fish in spicy tomato sauce

Fruit and Nuts

akhrōT walnut
amrūd guava
anānās pineapple
angūr grapes
anjīr figs
ām mango
āRū peach
bādām almond
chakōtrā grapefruit
chiku type of fruit; resembles a kiwi in appearance and tastes a bit like a pear
girīdār mevā nuts
kāgzī nībū lime
kājū cashew
kelā banana; plantain
khajūr dates
khūbānī apricot
Kharbūzā melon
mūngphalī peanuts
nāriyal coconut
nāshpātī pear
nībū lemon; lime
pahāRī bādām hazelnuts
pān chopped or shredded betel nut wrapped in a leaf, used as an aid to digestion
pān masālā mix of betel nut, fennel seeds, sweets/candies and flavourings
phal fruit
pistā pistachio
rasbharī raspberry
santarā orange
seb apple
sTrābarī strawberry
supārī betel nut

tarbūz water melon

Lamb and Lamb Dishes

ālū meat lamb and potato curry (Delhi)
bheR kā gōsht lamb
dō piazā lamb curry with onions
gōsht meat, usually mutton
kāshmīrī kōfte Kashmiri meatballs
kāshmīrī rōgan jōsh Kashmiri red lamb curry
kāshmīrī yakhni Kashmiri lamb curry
kīmā meat; minced lamb
kīmā kōfta meatball curry
kīmā maTar minced lamb with peas
kōfte meatballs
malāi kōfta meat balls cooked in creamy sauce
pudine vālā kīma fried minced lamb with mint
rān masāledar whole leg of lamb in a spicy yoghurt sauce
rōgan jōsh red lamb curry in a sauce made from spices, onions, garlic, ginger and ground almonds
sāg vālā meat lamb curry with spinach
shabdeg lamb with turnips (Mughlai)
shāhi kōrma 'royal' lamb in a rich creamy almond sauce

Meat

bheR kā gōsht lamb
chawp minced meat or
vegetables surrounded by
breaded mashed potatoes
cutlet minced meat or
vegetable burgers
dam meat steamed meat
gāy kā gōsht beef
gōsht meat, usually mutton
kīmā meat; minced lamb
mangsho meat curry (Bengal)
mās meat
momo meat dumpling
(Tibetan and Bhotian)
murgī chicken
sūar kā gōsht pork

Pork and Pork
Dishes

ālū vālā gōsht pork and
potato curry
chane vālā gōsht pork chops
with chickpeas/garbanzos
sūar kā gōsht pork
vindalū pōrk very hot and
sour pork curry (Goa)

Preserves

ām kā lacchā green mango
preserve
ām kā murabbā mango
preserve
gājar kā murabbā carrot
preserve

karōnda murabbā gooseberry
preserve
murabbā fruit preserve

Pulses

batak vālī dāl duck cooked
with pulses
chanā chickpeas, garbanzos
chanā dāl split
chickpeas/garbanzos
chanā masālā spicy
chickpeas/garbanzos
chanā sabut whole
chickpeas/garbanzos
dāl pulses
dāl awr anDe vāle kōfte deep-
fried egg and lentil balls in
batter
dāl gōsht meat cooked in
lentils
dāl tarka pulses with lots of
fried onions, garlic and
ginger
dhansak medium-hot meat
and lentil curry (Parsi)
gōsht dāl beef with pulses
(Pakistan)
jhīngā vālī dāl prawns with
pulses
kīma dāl minced meat with
pulses (Pakistan)
lōbhiā black-eyed beans
lōbhiā awr khumbī black-eyed
beans with mushrooms
mah sabut dāl split black
peas
masūr dāl split red lentils
meat dāl lamb with pulses

(Pakistan)
murg dāl chicken with pulses
(Pakistan)
mūng dāl whole green lentils
ravan black-eyed beans
rājmā red kidney beans
sabjī vālī dāl vegetables and
pulses cooked together
sāmbar wet lentil and
vegetable curry with
asafoetida and tamarind
(Southern India)
taRkā dāl lentils with a
dressing of fried garlic,
onions and spices
vaDā doughnut-shaped
deep-fried lentil cake

Rice

anDe pulāv rice with eggs
and fried onions
bhāt boiled rice
chanā dāl khichrī rice with
yellow split peas
chanā pulāv rice with
chickpeas/garbanzos
chāval rice
Hyderabad pulāv Hyderabad
rice
jhīngā pulāv rice with
prawns
kāshmīrī pulāv rice with
spices
kesar chāval saffron rice
khumbī pulāv rice with
mushrooms
kīma pulāv rice with minced
meat

macchī pulāv rice with fish
masāledar bāsmatī chāval
Basmati rice with spices
maTar pulāv rice with peas
meat pulāv rice with lamb
mītha pulāv rice with
almonds, sultanas and sugar
murgī pulāv rice with
chicken
pīle chāval saffron rice with
spices
pulāv rice gently spiced and
fried
pyāj pulāv rice with onions
sabjī pulāv rice with
vegetables
sāde chāval plain rice
uble chāval boiled rice

Salads

gājar awr piyaz kā salād
carrot and onion salad
gujarāti gājar kā salād carrot
salad (Gujarat)
kachumbar tomato, onion,
cucumber and fresh
coriander relish
pyāj kā lachchā onion relish
sem kā salād bean salad

Snacks

ālū tikkī potato patties
chanā chūRā dry spicy snack
mix similar to Bombay mix
chevRā dry spicy snack mix
similar to Bombay mix

gāthia similar to seviya but
made in pasta-like shapes

gōl gappe very thin crispy
wafers

kachōrī stuffed savoury
fritters

kīma samōse minced meat
samosas

maTThī deep-fried crunchy
savoury biscuits

ōniōn bhājī onions deep-
fried in batter made from
chickpea/garbanzo flour

pakōRe chopped vegetables
dipped in chickpea/
garbanzo flour batter and
deep-fried

panīr pakōRe Indian cheese
pakoras

pāpRi small savoury fried
disc-shaped snacks, made
from wheat flour batter

pāpRi chāT spicy papris

phal kī chāT spicy fruit salad

samōse meat or vegetables
in a pastry triangle, fried

seviya deep-fried crunchy
chickpea/garbanzo noodles

Spices, Herbs

adrak ginger

dālchīnī cinnamon

dhaniyā coriander

garam masālā combination
of black pepper and other
spices

haldī turmeric

harā dhaniyā fresh coriander

harī mirch green chilli

ilāychī cardamom

imlī tamarind

jīra cumin

kālī mirch black pepper

lāl mirch red chilli

lawng cloves

masālā mix of spices; spice

methī fenugreek leaves

mirch chilli

mīTha masālā mix of sweet
spices

pudīnā mint

Starters, Soups

achār pickles

ālū maTar samōsā pea and
potato samosa

ālū pakōRā potato pakora

ālū samōsā potato samosa

bhunā murgi large pieces of
chicken cooked in the oven
with yoghurt and spices

kāshmīrī kabāb minced meat
and chicken, barbecued

meat kā samōsā minced
meat or chicken samosa

mulligatawny curried
vegetable soup

murg pakōRā chicken pakora

nargis kabāb minced meat
kebab

pakōRe onion pakora –
onions in chickpea/
garbanzo flour batter,deep-
fried

pāpaR poppadum – plain or spiced thin crisp cracker made from chickpea/ garbanzo flour

reshmi kabāb minced meat and spices

sabji pakōRā vegetables deep fried in batter

shami kabāb small minced lamb cutlets, cooked in the oven

sīkh kabāb, shīk kabāb minced lamb grilled on a skewer

thukpa meat soup (Tibetan and Bhotian)

Tandoori Dishes

lahsun vālī tandūrī murg tandoori garlic chicken

masāledār tandūrī jhīngā king prawns in a spicy sauce

masāledār tandūrī lamb chawp lamb chop cooked in the oven in a spicy sauce

masāledār tandūrī macchī fish cooked in the oven in a spicy sauce

masāledār tandūrī tikkā murg boneless pieces of chicken breast cooked in the oven in a spicy sauce

pūrī tandūrī murgī whole tandoori chicken

shīsh kabāb shish kebab, small pieces of meat and vegetables on skewers

special tikkā murgī chicken tikka special

tandūrī traditionally tandoori dishes were baked in a clay oven, but nowadays are generally baked in any oven

tandūrī chicken chicken marinated in yoghurt, herbs and spices and cooked in the oven

tandūrī jhīngā tandoori king prawns

tandūrī macchī tandoori fish

tandūrī masālā murg tandoori chicken in a spicy sauce

tandūrī murg(ī) tandoori chicken

tandūrī special tikkā tandoori lamb tikka special

tandūrī tikkā meat boneless pieces of lamb marinated in yoghurt, herbs and spices and cooked in the oven

tandūrī tikkā murg boneless pieces of chicken, marinated in yohurt, herbs and spices and cooked in the oven

tikkā pieces of boneless meat (usually chicken breast) marinated in yoghurt, herbs and spices and traditionally cooked in a clay oven

tikkā meat lamb marinated in yoghurt and cooked in oven with spices

tikkā murg chicken breast marinated in yoghurt and

cooked in the oven with spices

Vegetable Dishes

These mostly originate from Northern India, but may also be found in other parts of India and Pakistan.

ālū bAgan potato and aubergine/eggplant curry

ālū bAgan kī bhājī aubergine/ eggplant cooked with potatoes

ālū bhājī potatoes in tomato sauce

ālū maTar (kī bhājī) potatoes cooked with peas, tomatoes, spices, onion and garlic

ālū methī potatoes with fenugreek leaves

ālū panīr potatoes cooked with Indian cheese

ālū sāg potatoes with spinach

bagari phūl gōbhī cauliflower with fennel and mustard seeds (Gujarat)

band gōbhī awr maTar bhājī cabbage cooked with peas (Punjab)

bAgan achārī aubergine/eggplant cooked in pickling spices

bAgan bhartā whole oven-baked aubergine/eggplant mashed and cooked with onions, tomatoes and spices

(Punjab)

bAgan simlā-mirch TamāTar sabjī aubergine/eggplant, (bell) pepper and tomato curry

bhājī vegetables; curry

bhinDī bhājī okra/gumbo curry

bōmbay ālū potato curry

dam arbī yam curry

dam ālū whole potatoes steamed with spices, yoghurt and almonds

gājar, maTar awr gōbhī kī bhājī mixed vegetable curry (Bengal)

gōbhī ālū cauliflower and potatoes

gōbhī musallam whole cauliflower baked in the oven

kaddū kī bhājī green pumpkin curry

karelā bhājī bitter gourd curry

khumbī bhājī mushroom curry

kofta balls of minced vegetables in a curry

kundrū bhājī curry made with a green vegetable that looks like a large gooseberry

kutchhi bhinDī sweet and sour okra/gumbo

malāi kofta vegetable kebabs in a rich cream sauce, medium-mild

masāledār sem spicy green

beans
peTha yellow pumpkin curry
phūl gōbhī awr ālū kī bhājī cauliflower and potato curry
phūl gōbhī kī bhājī cauliflower curry with onion and tomato
rasedār khumbī ālū mushrooms and potatoes in tomato, garlic and ginger sauce
rasedār shalgam turnip in tomato sauce
sabji vegetable curry; vegetable
sambhara cabbage with carrots and spices (Gujarat)
sāg ālū spinach and potato curry
sāg panīr spinach with Indian cheese
shōrbedār TamāTar thin sauce made from stewed tomatoes
sūkhe shalgam grated turnip cooked with spices
talā huā bAgan fried aubergine/eggplant slices
tōri bhājī marrow/squash curry

Vegetables

ālū potatoes
ālū ke katle chips, French fries
baRī sem broad beans

bAgan aubergine, eggplant
bhinDi okra, gumbo
brinjal aubergine, eggplant
chhōTī sem French beans
gājar carrot
gōbhī cauliflower
kaddū green pumpkin
karela bitter gourd
kāhū lettuce
khīrā cucumber
khumbī mushrooms
kundrū green vegetable that looks like a large gooseberry
lahsan garlic
lasoon garlic
maTar peas
mūlī mooli, white radish
palak spinach
pattā gōbhī cabbage
pAtha yellow pumpkin
pyāj onion
sabji vegetable; vegetable curry
sabziyā vegetables
sāg spinach; greens
sarson kā sāg mustard-leaf greens (Punjab, Northern India)
sem beans
sem phalī green beans
shalgam turnip
shimlā mirch (bell) pepper
tōri marrow, squash
TamāTar tomato

Yoghurt

akhrōT kā rāytā yoghurt with walnuts and fresh coriander

ālū rāytā yoghurt with potatoes

bAgan kā rāytā yoghurt with aubergine/eggplant

būndī kā rāytā yoghurt with small dumplings made of chickpea/garbanzo flour

dahī plain yoghurt

dahī vaRā yoghurt with lentil fritters

khīre kā rāytā yoghurt with cucumber

Menu Reader: Drink

Essential Terms

beer bīyar
bottle bōTal
coffee kahvā, kāfī
cup pyālā
fruit juice phal kā ras
glass gilās
milk dūdh
mineral water bōtal vālā pānī
soda (water) sōDa vāTar
soft drink ThanDā
sugar chīnī
tea chāy
tonic (water) Tānik vāTar
water pānī

another ..., please ek awr ... dījiye
a cup of ... ek pyālā ... de
a glass of ... ek gilās ...

Alcoholic Drinks

arak locally distilled spirit
bīyar beer
chang beer made from millet (Bhotian)
fene spirit distilled from coconut or cashew nuts (Goa)
lāgar bīyar lager
tadd date palm wine (Bengal)
toddy palm wine (Kerala)
tumba drink made from fermented millet and hot water (Bhotian)

Soft Drinks

barfīlī chāy iced tea
barf vālī chāy iced tea
bōTal vālā pānī bottled water
chakōtre kā ras grapefruit juice
chāy tea
dūdh milk
falūdā milk-shake with ice cream and nuts
gōlgappā pānī very spicy drink usually served with gōlgappas and pāpris
jīrā pānī appetizer made from tamarind and cumin seed
kahvā coffee
kāfī coffee
lassī yoghurt drink
masālā chāy spiced tea
nibū pānī lemon squash

pānī water
ras juice
santare kā ras orange juice
sharbat bādām almond sherbet
sharbat cold drink prepared from barks, flowers or resins, sugar and water
sharbat gulāb rose petal and rose water sherbet
sharbat sandal sandalwood-flavoured sherbet

Other Terms

barf ice
barf Dālkar with ice
bīnā barf kī without ice
bīnā chīnī kī without sugar
bīnā sharāb vālā non-alcoholic
chīnī sugar
dāru alcoholic drink
mādak alcoholic
sharāb drink; alcohol
sharāb vālā alcoholic
ThanDā cool; cold; soft drink